Farhad Malekian

Hypocrisy in International Criminal Justice

nova
science publishers
www.novapublishers.com

DOI: https://doi.org/10.52305/IJKE8577

Library of Congress Cataloging-in-Publication Data

Names: Malekian, Farhad, author.
Title: Hypocrisy in international criminal justice / Farhad Malekian.
Description: Hauppauge : Nova Science Publishers, 2025. | Series: Law, crime and law enforcement | Includes bibliographical references and index. |
Identifiers: LCCN 2024059282 (print) | LCCN 2024059283 (ebook) | ISBN 9798895302057 (hardcover) | ISBN 9798895303115 (adobe pdf)
Subjects: LCSH: International criminal law. | Criminal justice, Administration of--Philosophy. | International law and human rights.
Classification: LCC K5001 .M344 2025 (print) | LCC K5001 (ebook) | DDC 345--dc23/eng/20241230
LC record available at https://lccn.loc.gov/2024059282
LC ebook record available at https://lccn.loc.gov/2024059283

Published by Nova Science Publishers, Inc. † New York

Final Rulings

A child asked the American government what its purpose is:
To teach the norms of imperialist justice to every nation
Questioned the British government about the intention behind the gatherings of its parliament:
To promote a global justice of hypocrisy
Queried the French government, what is its task?
To defend the justice of colonialist hypocrites
Inquired to the Australian government, what is your duty?
To eliminate indigenous justice
What is your responsibility as the Canadian government?
To advance hypocritical injustice
The child approached the German, Dutch and Swedish governments:
To endorse the justice that serves our masters.
The child then sought answers from the United Nations, the European Union, and International Human Rights Organisations:
To secure the votes and vetoes for the injustice of hypocrites
Finally, the child directed a somewhat different question towards the prosecutor and judges at the International Criminal Court, asking what constitutes practical justice:
One by one, they seized their gavels of injustices and struck them against the child's head as they sat upon their benches.
The child collapsed and perished.
Subsequently, it was declared by the Court that he lacked the fortitude to comprehend or tolerate their hypocritical definitions of justice.
Ultimately, the child was laid to rest in the Lobbies of Governments.

Contents

Abstract

The quandary of physical justice is the most paradoxical aspect of the philosophy of justice. It has the power to eliminate true justice. Physical justice continuously claims victims and deems those who demand the establishment of their rights as barbaric oppressors. The concept of moral justice is consistently perceived as being guilty of committing crimes, even though its primary objective is to defend all men. The application of physical justice in this manner can cause the depreciation and deterioration of moral values within the system of justice and ultimately lead to the suppression of true sources. If the adoption of international conventions is pointless, then we should not even ratify them to begin with. This reflects our pursuit of moral justice which aims at uniting the moral attitudes of men alongside the brutal physical exploitation. The monopolised principles of physical justice within the structure of the systems of international human rights and criminal justice have promoted the imposition of immoral supremacy. Arguing about the autonomous systems of justice at the international level is insincere and promotes the supremacy of atrocities. We must then ask: how useful are these monopolised principles of physical justice to human civilisation? This is an indispensable argument wherein the domination of the law, human rights law, resolutions of the UN, and, particularly, moral justice rely on the arbitrary decisions of deep states, i.e., the hidden criminal intrigues of governments.

Introduction

Morality plays a key role in many of the most heated criminal justice debates. The entire system of international civilisation is or has to be based on practical reasons for the notion of morality. If the notion of morality did not guide civilisation and humanity, then civilisation would collapse and instead be guided by the self-interested principles of authoritarian powers. Although we do not reject that the international system of law and morality is more often based on who is better at colluding with others, as seen with the on-going genocide of the population of Palestine, the theory of civilisation is still based on the requirements of practical reasonableness.[1] The systems of international law, international human rights law, and international criminal justice should therefore be viewed as being vital to the development of all forms of modern jurisprudence, including the methods of identifying the theory of justice. This is particularly significant in the case of the theoretical description and analysis of the framework of justice. Due to this, within this work we presume that there are two primary forms of justice which guide international political and legal civilisation, i.e., physical justice and moral justice.

The system of physical justice is sometimes based on the rules of a constitution and other times on the rules of whoever is in power. However, we will see that there are essentially no differences between these two forms of justice based on the fact that the final decision-maker controls and enforces the words of the law. While physical justice appears to be good most of the time, however it has a very evil and brutal nature. This brutal nature of physical justice is sometimes found within the laws and principles in our international constitutions, statutes, and treaties. An example of this is the United Nations Charter, which is based on the monopolisation and control of moral justice in its final form. This reflects the autocracy of law over the rights of human beings and completes the appropriation of the philosophy of humanity. Another example of this is the North Atlantic Treaty Organisation,

[1] Study John J Mearsheimer and Stephen Walt, The Israel Lobby and U. S. Foreign Policy (New York: Farrar, Straus and Giroux. 2007).

also known as NATO or the Washington Treaty. This treaty created an alliance led by the American powertionist government and barbarically imposes the will of the power on the victims. An example of this can be seen with the Iraq War during which thousands of innocent people were killed in the name of controlling oil resources.[2]

Both of the aforementioned documents claim to promote what is good for human society and for the system of international justice as a whole. With this simple theory, they control moral justice. This indicates that both the United Nations and NATO have the intention of killing and monopolising any movements of moral justice and of controlling all governmental discourse through the imposition of the wills of physical justice. All these goals are ultimately decorated, interpreted, and argued by the theory of practical reasonableness for the sake of human civilisation. Thus, the controlling power of physical justice decides what counts as law, morality, justice, equality, and fairness. Therefore, there are no proper consolidated definitions of law and morality within the practical jurisprudence of law. This can clearly be seen through the examination of the history of the civilisation of mankind, which is simply a life of wars, or, simply put, physical justice. The intention is not to make a critical attack against the foundation of law or its methodological problems, but rather to underline that what we call law and morality is ultimately controlled by the brutality of war, which in turn is a clear manifestation of physical justice.

International human rights law and international criminal justice have been observed to develop under certain conditions and in accordance with certain military, political, and diplomatic strategies. In addition, from this diplomacy of political law, we have reached the present characterisation of the legal discipline, which is called international law. What could really define the nature of this law and who or what controls the power of the law can be easily seen in the practice of the Security Council and the power granted to certain members to punish others through the imposition of sanctions? This dynamic was present during the time of the League of Nations and continues to be seen in the United Nations today. We can therefore pose a number of questions concerning the legal nature of the law, and whether it really exists or if we are just dealing with the imposition of decisions by the powerful on the powerless and calling it law. To answer this and similar questions, we ought to examine if what is called law and justice includes moral justice or if it promotes the

---

[2] Farhad Malekian, *Powertionism in International Criminal Justice* (New York: Nova Science Publishers, 2022).

power of control over civilisations in the name of the law. This means the term "law" is simply a flower that is only beautiful as long as it is in the garden of the politics of the law and which seems to contain a moral sense of justice, even though it does not. Consequently, speaking about law has become a political institution.

The entire philosophy of law is business, and this is particularly evident regarding international human rights law and international criminal justice. Thus, all norms that speak about the existence of law disappear or are meaningless when it comes to the final decisions of the big authorities, or as I have called them: powertionist individuals, powertionist organisations, and powertionist governments.[3] All these groups and individuals are present within the inner structure of monopolisation of the law.[4] However, an important consequence follows. There is no accuracy in the system of justice when it comes to the argumentation of wills. Lies guide decisions, and the decision is a critique of what ought to be done without any particular consideration for the principles of moral justice. However, we should never let immoral or physical justice sleep in their juridical bedroom, and we should never believe that the notion of morality is sufficient to reverse the attitudes of physical justice on its own. However, this does not mean that the principles of moral justice should reduce their basic universal values concerning the rights of man and yield to the brutal conditions of the physical justice imposed by the permanent members of imperialist, authoritarian, totalitarian, dictatorial, oppressive, and powertionist governments.

The corrupted philosophies of law, justice, equality, and peace in the context of the provisions of Chapter VII seem to be pirated, and the rights of the children of victims have been usurped by those who are supposed to be the guardians of morality and physical justice. The masters of physical justice claim to be moralists, humanists, and democrats. They monopolize the law through the empty phrase of justice in order to mask their brutal massacres, the screams of children, the painful cries of the wounded, the chest-pounding grief, and the barbarity of their new Holocaust. That is how the system of physical justice kills the principles of moral justice and even accuses moral justice of the crimes that have been committed by the conspiracy of physical justice. However, it seems that no vindication of the brutality of justice or physical justice has ever been recorded in any documents of the United Nations. The corrupt use of the system of moral justice runs so deep and is so

---

[3] *Id.*
[4] *Id.*

intense that the entire system of international human rights has become an integral part of the injustice of physical justice. Although we assume that the system of international human rights, and even of international criminal justice, should be free from any kind of monopolisation and mistreatment of their principles, the practice of the United Nations shows that they are not.[5]

This standpoint is significant when we realize that the concepts of appropriate justice, norms, and equality are not based on the values of wisdom, supremacy of reasonableness, or on the ethical or philosophical understanding of the rights of victims, but rather on the interests of the authorities controlling physical justice. We are inevitably driven to such a desperate state that the notion of morality of most governments follows the wills of the masters of physical justice. Even more surprising is that the immoral and unjust decisions of physical justice most often occur outside of the criminal's territories. Thus, if we do not confess that the pure principles of justice have positive objectives concerning authenticity for the benefit of human civilisation, then we are also incapable of understanding the empirically monopolized politics of the powertionist governments and their physical justice. In reality, justice cannot progress without first acknowledging the reasonable requirements of moral justice. Although understanding the terms of justice is indeed a very difficult art, understanding the brutality of physical justice does not require an expert. The rights of all human beings must be held as sacred by the system of physical justice if it intends to restore moral justice and not be accused of brutality.

I must admit that the questions surrounding the antagonism of physical justice against moral justice are endless since the goal of physical justice is to overcome all forms of morality and impose a form of positive authoritarian law. However, at the same time, authorities of physical justice, which is a form of positive law that derives its legal validity from natural law, ignore this significant function of justice and present it as being in conformity with the reasonable requirements of natural law - even though this is generally not the case.[6] Nevertheless, any justification used in order to construct positive law based on the natural necessities of morality is, under all circumstances, vital and unavoidable in the system of jurisprudence. Any measure taken against

---

[5] Id. Consult also Farhad Malekian, *Imperative Philosophy of International Criminal Justice: Visible Power – Invisible Essence* (New York: Nova Science Publishers, 2022).

[6] Consult significant views of Spooner Lysander, Natural Law; or the Science of Justice: A Treatise on Natural Law, Natural Justice, Natural Rights, Natural Liberty, and Natural Society; showing that all Legislation whatsoever is an Absurdity, a Usurpation, and a Crime. Part First. [1882], available at http://oll.libertyfund.org/titles/spooner-natural-law-or-the-science-of-justice-1882 (Accessed: on 18 December 2017).

these necessary requirements of natural and moral law is essentially a violation, however they go unpunished. This is because those who identify violations and are supposed to apply punishments are the authorities themselves, and they control the law.

This work therefore offers a brief account of the conflicts between physical and moral justice into consideration. A simple argument presented in this work is that certain forms of conduct or omissions under the umbrella of physical justice should never occur. This includes the commission of international crimes and genocide against populations in occupied regions that are struggling for the right to self-determination. This means that we are searching for a justice that respects the characteristics and circumstances of the victims and essentially presenting righteousness. The significance lies not in whether the law is enshrined in human rights provisions, but in which power enforces the law. The argument here is simply that justice is not itself the entire notion of morality - however, it is an integral part of it. This indicates that there is a certain connection between physical justice and moral justice, which should be respected. Consequently, the notion of justice may not be notably benevolent for the parties, but it moves and goes beyond the basic truthfulness of the moral essence of judgments.[7]

Farhad Malekian
Uppsala, Sweden,
3rd March; 4th June
23rd June; 12th September 2023
f.malekian.in.crim.l@telia.com
f.malekian.in.crim.l@gmail.com.

[7] With full appreciation for the kind service of the librarians Felicia Kälvemark and Edward Winrow at the Dag Hammarskjöld Library in Uppsala, Sweden.

Chapter 1

Promoting the Aroma of Justice

1. Challenges to Justice

Justice is always a necessary substance in all societies. No human society can argue that it does not need an appropriate understanding of the notion of justice.[8] It is possible to assume that justice is a standard practice in all aspects of familial, clan, group, domestic, regional, and international relations. We refer to this as the automatic application of justice or humanity, which is not only indispensable, but also a standard expectation of living together. Our plan is not to kill justice, its norms, soil, soul, understanding, nor its natural positive aroma. What is the purpose of talking about humanity? Justice is a fundamental principle of humanity, and its concept and spirit cannot be sustained without kindness, charity, compassion, thoughtfulness, gentleness, and empathy. It also includes many other principles, including the appropriate understanding of human rights and nature.

Thus, when one talks about justice, one does not necessarily speak about the establishment or creation of rights by different constitutions or institutions, but rather about the feeling that human beings have the right to be satisfied for the duration of their lives. Even if this has not been proven or is impossible to prove, it should still be the standard expectation of humans. Ultimately, justice involves applying the good dreams for others such as nature, animals, and ourselves. In order to satisfy justice, justice has to contain true norms. Such norms are designed to contain truthfulness for all men without any discrimination based on their nature, race, or cultural norms.

What is the concept of real justice and its automatic application? Naturally, the concept of justice differs from case-to-case and from culture-to-culture. This is because there is no particular framework that establishes the shape of justice. Every culture and society has its own pattern of justice. Cultural attitudes may differ regarding certain social questions. For instance, sexual relations before marriage may be permitted in Europe. A couple may not ever need to get married and still be seen as the proper parents of any children they have. A real-world example of this can be seen with the

[8] Examine Farhad Malekian, *Judgments of Love in Criminal Justice* (Springer, 2017, 2018).

legislations of Scandinavian countries and their full recognition of non-married couples, and even same-sex couples

According to the old traditions of Europe, same-sex relations were not accepted and were condemned by most citizens of Europe as well as by social authorities. The idea that their relationship could be accepted as normal and that same-sex couples could officially be permitted to adopt children was impossible to imagine. Same-sex couples at the time found the societal conditions to be unjust and immoral, while for the vast majority of the European population, they were acting justly and in fact reflected the application of appropriate justice, and defended the basic principles of morality in Europe. Therefore, in order to improve the positions of the victims, European countries have evolved and adapted to new cultural situations. This has meant that social authorities and their citizens have had to move away from several centuries' worth of culture and traditions to adopt a new mentality.

However, the current situation is different in many other countries in Africa, Asia, and particularly the Middle East. Such countries hold the view that permitting same-sex couples to adopt children would be unjust and unreasonable for the children, even though it seems reasonable for European countries and is based on the provisions of domestic legislation in democratic countries. However, many may also discuss what democracy really is and what its content and practical essences are. Furthermore, many countries in Asia forbid both same-sex relations and marriages. The legislation of a considerable number of states may even call for the punishment of such couples. A clear example of this type of regulation can be found within the legislations of many African, Arab, and Middle Eastern states such as Iran, Iraq, Afghanistan, Egypt, and Pakistan. Both cultures may assert that their laws and interpretations, including their cultures, are right and therefore apply the concept of real justice and fulfil the necessary requirements of various definitions of justice.

This is how physical justice and moral justice may be interpreted in the implementation of the rules or principles that appear to be necessary for the prevention of violations of physical justice and moral justice. [9] However, we

---

[9] Farhad Malekian, *Trading Virginity of International Criminal Justice* (Nova Sciences Publishers, 2020); Mark J Osiel, Obeying orders: Atrocity, Military Discipline, and the Law of War (Transaction Publishers, 1999); Timothy L. H McCormack, *The Law of War Crimes: National and International Approaches* (Brill, 1997); Rene Provost, *International Human Rights and Humanitarian Law* (2002); William A. Schabas, *War Crimes and Human Rights: Essays on the Death Penalty, Justice and Accountability* (Cameron May,

should not forget the fact that both notions of justice do not conflict as much when it comes to certain matters relating to national regulations or the exercise of customs. This is based on the fact that certain practices and norms of legal disciplines are not as connected to certain international political matters that are key elements in political victories and political lies.[10] That is why the physical justice has several facets which work in different ways for different reasons and different interests. Physical justice may even use the aforementioned matters as tools to escape from its constitutional responsibilities and get closer to reaching its final goals.[11] In other words, the main problem facing physical justice is monopolisation. Furthermore, the main goal of physical justice is to control the interpretation of the systems of international human rights and international criminal justice and squash any counter-arguments.[12]

2. Fixing Justice

Consequently, the concept of real justice may vary between nations and cultures. Thus, one definition of real justice may exist within the norms of another culture. This is because the concept of real justice is not determined by the cultural norms of one nation or another, even though both sides may strongly assert that their understanding of the concept of real justice is fair concerning certain matters. In other words, cultural norms may or may not fulfil the requirements for understanding justice. However, we should not put aside the fact that this understanding of justice is personal and cannot be permanent because of the need to regulate all matters into the notion of the realisation of justice.

What is the concept of real justice then? The answer to this question is both difficult and sensitive. The reason for this is very simple: we are looking

---

2008); Steven R. Ratner, Jason S. Abrams, and James L. Bischoff, *Accountability for Human Rights Atrocities in International Law: Beyond the Nuremberg Legacy*, (3rd ed., Oxford Press, 2009); Eric Stover, *My Neighbour, My Enemy: Justice and Community in the Aftermath of Mass Atrocity* (Cambridge University Press, 2004); Benjamin B. Ferencz, *New Legal Foundations for Global Survival: Security Through the Security Council* (Oceana Publications, 1994). See also Farhad Malekian, 'Judging International Criminal Justice in the Occupied Territories,' 12 International Criminal Law Review (2012), 827–869.

[10] *Id.*

[11] Farhad Malekian, *International Criminal Vacations: Tears of Justice* (New York: Nova Science Publishers, 2024).

[12] *Id.*

for a comprehensive definition of the concept of justice, which is particularly complicated in cases where the performance and application of justice are largely in the hands of the authorities. The fact is that the notion of justice has different forms, and although all deal with the concept of justice, they differ significantly. Sometimes, justice is in one's own possession; this is personal justice, as we judge one another and determine how to deal with that particular situation based on our own judgement. This justice arises in daily situations and includes our rapid judgments. This means we should make decisions based on the particular situation. The term "justice" was not used to describe our performance of justice at the time of our conduct. However, it may come back to us when we are no longer in that situation.

The most difficult part of this sense of justice is when we realize that our actions were not right and we should have taken another decision. However, regretfully, time has passed, and the situation has been resolved. The only matter that remains is that we remember that we could have made a different decision, even though we had other matters on our minds or did not take enough time to make the decision. Since decisions come and go, and since we exist under certain conditions, we ought to make decisions and move on. However, the consequences of our decisions remain and may haunt us psychologically. It may force us to question our decisions even after decades. I personally get tears in my heart, mind, and eyes when I think about deciding to get a Christmas tree - a decision made in haste.

Decades ago, I obtained the last Christmas trees from the seller with the intention of having a tree in each of our children's rooms. I was packing the trees into my old car alone. At that moment, a man on a bike with a young child appeared. The child was excited to be picking out a tree to bring home. While I was packing the trees into my car, the father asked me if the trees were mine and I said yes. I heard him then tell his daughter to not be upset and that they would find a tree somewhere else. They then left. I also started to leave but suddenly it occurred to me that I should give them one of the trees, as I had multiple. However, because it was winter in Sweden, it was too dark out to find them, especially because they had taken the bicycle paths.

I thought to myself, how can I go home and bring the trees into the house while singing the names of my four children? X, your Christmas is here, and so forth. I managed to do it for my children, albeit all while thinking about the sad face of the little girl. Although decades have since passed, at Christmastime, I still think about the decision I made and it breaks my heart. The situation caused her father to feel very upset due to his inability to remedy the situation. I still wish to see the child, express my deepest regrets, and fix my mistake. I violated moral justice out of infinite love for my family members. During Christmas, I was lost in the hallways of morality and felt like a dead tree with no roots. Despite taking care of children anonymously in different parts of my country every month for several decades, I still regret my actions that day.

3. Digging for Justice

The nature and philosophy of justice depend on each other from time-to-time, and our judgments or the theory of justice can decrease. The death of justice is therefore one of the most precarious situations that can arise following hasty judgments. It is uncommon for us to discuss this in our personal judgments. The theory of justice is far from being new as it has existed as long as civilisation itself. However, justice has presented itself under different philosophical or ethical theories and forced us to have different and more necessary or fundamental treatments. As a result, sometimes brutalities were called justice, barbarity was called fairness, and torture was called rehabilitation.[13]

There has therefore been an ongoing struggle between the vocabulary of justice and the legal authority, which in turn has led to different versions of justice that may be just at one time and unjust at another. This is one of the most conspicuous features in the history of the jurisprudence of the law and the abolition, modification, and renewal of the provisions of the law. With the expression of social and political justice, we refer to the protection against the autocracy of the political rulers with justice under their control. Therefore, even though justice may be personal, it is usually instrumental. This is one of the most challenging issues that has raised questions about the scope of justice and its codification.

This statement is valid regarding all laws and regulations. Although the notions of law and justice seem to be separate, the reality is different. The notion of justice and its definitions are plagued by a serious problem. We are forced to define justice under certain limitations that are both good and bad, have the virtue of both creation and destruction, and that are usually chained to various conditions and reasoning. That is why the definition of justice is

[13] Examine Michael Otterman, *American Torture: From the Cold War to Abu Ghraib and Beyond* (Pluto Press, 2007); Kristine Huskey with Aleigh Acerni, Justice at Guantanamo: One Woman's Odyssey and Her Crusade for Human Rights (2009).

sometimes complex and more often a noble and important subject of law that has hitherto been treated by various means with all the care it deserves, and yet is still not complete. This means that the greater part of human civilisation and its history of codification by various authoritarian powers, therefore only have an ambiguous, imperfect, and often false concept of what justice really is and what its elements are.

The fact is that a considerable number of writers and philosophers have spent a substantial amount of time trying to define justice; however, they have not been successful in convincing one another of their different interpretations. One of the main reasons for this is that the notion of justice and the elements of its interpretation are constantly changing. Although this is one of the advantages of the definition of justice and the development of its boundaries, it has also become a tool of monopolisation, whether by individuals, organisations, or states.[14] The situation has therefore been confusing, even for celebrated authors, almost exclusively narrowing the proper definition of the notion of justice and its possible understanding. As a result, certain maxims, elements, provisions, and terms that have been adopted by different societies and in their constitutions conflict with one another, and the philosophers who are involved in the definition of justice must take all this into consideration. However, they miss the general principles of justice because their understanding is sometimes tentative and vicarious.

As a result, the public or united consent required within the central definition of justice faces discrimination, whether deliberately or not, and it renders the definition of justice obligatory and confines the real definition and needs of the scope of justice within a restricted boundary. The definition of justice then becomes very exclusive in its own nature, in which the definition of justice and its principles for the whole human race are disconnected and follow a disjointed notion of justice that is not recommendable from a practical point of view. That is why we have had, and continue to have, a lot of problems and serious conflicts throughout the history of human civilisation. This represents a degradation of the definition of justice and its various essential principles, such as equality, humanity, respect, and love for the implementation of morality. This results in a misconception concerning the real origin of justice and how it should be dealt with for all men at the same level and degree.

---

[14] Examine Farhad Malekian, *Imperative Philosophy of International Criminal Justice: Visible Power – Invisible Essence* (New York: Nova Science Publishers, 2022); Farhad Malekian, *Powertionism in International Criminal Justice* (New York: Nova Science Publishers, 2022).

4. Platform of Injustice

One of the serious problems with the systems of justice, international criminal justice, and international human rights is that they lack the proper and equal delivery of the principle of justice, thereby causing us to arrive at a platform that is more beneficial for ourselves and our politics. We therefore put the principles of justice in a position where they are stuck, and these principles cannot develop the principles of equality and respect for all men. However, even knowing this, we continue to act as though the concepts of justice as interpreted by our society or government are not only correct, but also essential to the maintenance of peace and the prevention of conflicts. Indubitably, our understanding contains many principles of justice, albeit a version thereof that benefits us. In this way, we reduce the value of the principles of justice and the obligations of the universal law of man, which should be respected and binding in all situations.

Thus, we do not acquire an exact knowledge of that law that is necessary for the understanding of justice and its united development. We must be aware of the fact that it is not sufficient to simply know what the notion of justice is, as we must also understand how it is applied. It simply means that the notion of justice should not be based on personal privileges and the degradation of the rights of others. When we plunder the rights of others by different means and in the name of human rights, we cannot state that justice has been respected.[15] The imposition of our will and interests cannot be translated as the will of the opposite party and how they should understand and respect our principles of justice. The definition of justice must be crafted in a manner

---

[15] Examine international conventions such provisions of Declaration on Social Progress and Development, 1969, Universal Declaration on the Eradication of Hunger and Malnutrition, 1974, Declaration on the Elimination of All Forms of Intolerance and of Discrimination Based on Religion or Belief, 1981, Declaration on the Human Rights of Individuals Who are not Nationals of the Country in which They Live, 1985, Vienna Declaration and Program of Action: World Conference on Human Rights, 1993, Draft United Nations Declaration on the Rights of Indigenous Peoples, 1994, Cairo Declaration of Human Rights in Islam, 1990, American Convention on Human Rights, 1969, African Charter on Human and Peoples' Rights, 1981, Arab Charter on Human Rights, 2004, European Convention for the Protection of Human Rights and Fundamental Freedoms of 1950 as amended by Protocol No. 11 of 1998, Charter of Fundamental Rights of the European Union, 2000, Convention on the Reduction of Statelessness, 1961, Supplementary Convention on the Abolition of Slavery, the Slave Trade, and Institutions and Practices Similar to Slavery, 1956, Declaration on the Protection of Women and Children in Emergency and Armed Conflict, 1974, International Covenant on Civil and Political Rights, 1966, International Convention on the Protection of the Rights of All Migrant Workers and Members of Their Families, 1990.

agreeable to the nature of each subject of the system of justice in its practical form and must not hide in itself various lies and intrigues.

Hence, the notion of justice is a particular discipline consisting of a just and rational interpretation, with the nature of its principles and the requirements of its subjects on equal footing. All the treatises in which the notion of justice is blended and confounded with the typical notion of justice from only one nation are thus unacceptable. My reference here is to unequal treaties and the resort to the use of legal force by a party that claims they have implemented the provisions of an agreement, treaty, convention, protocol, resolution, constitution, or statute. A clear example of this is the United Nations Charter, which has been called an equal treaty even though it is actually the most unequal and miserable treaty of all time due to the provisions of Chapter VII, which in turn have created the modern form of global UN colonisation. Even though unequal treaties should be viewed as invalid, the United Nations Charter is not because of the simple reason that it is the private body of the five permanent members of the organisation.[16]

In general, conveying a distinct idea of the notion of justice or significant knowledge of the terms of justice and their role in the daily lives of a society and a nation promotes equality and prevent inequality. Thus, with the practical definition of justice, we should not cause the smearing of blood on the houses of the victims while strengthening the rights of the offenders by referring to the unequal and unfair definition of the term justice.[17] These issues frequently perplex us at both the national and international levels. The definition of justice must not violate the notion of morality, i.e., universal rules and principles must be respected at all times.[18]

The law or definition of justice is generally intended to ensure equal justice and not hinder rights or encourage injustice. In the traditional system, the overwhelming majority of writers meant all civilised nations when speaking about *jus gentium*, which was not only wrong but also, demonstrated the theory of discrimination and the priority of certain governments or nations over other nations. As a result, the definition of justice, or more accurately, the definition of natural justice was already monopolised by so-called civilised nations, and all other nations were labelled as uncivilized.

The problem was that the so-called civilised nation saw their own definition and understanding of the principle of justice as being above any

[16] James E. Hickey, *Challenges to Security Council Monopoly Power over the Use of Force in Enforcement Actions: The Case of Regional Organisations*, 10 Ius Gentium 75 (2004).
[17] *Id.*, pp. 81-83.
[18] *Id.*, 12-129.

other concept and therefore developed a definition that was desirable and profitable for themselves and not necessarily for other societies. Consequently, all other non-European nations do not get to enjoy the benefits of the *jus gentium,* or natural rights of man. African and most Asian nations are especially noteworthy in this regard. However, authoritarian powers forget the fact that if we speak about natural law and a law for all nations, we refer to human beings, and as should be a common understanding, there should not be any difference between humans.[19] In other words, we cannot derive a developed society that has been decorated by armed forces and weapons of destruction from a society that has no such weapons or an education system.[20] The former society we called civilised and the latter uncivilised, or animals, and chain them and put them in cages, e.g., in London. They also made distinctions between man and man, dog and dog, cat and cat, and cockroach and cockroach. This was based on the fact that the former grew up in the homelands of colonial power homes. The latter lived in their own homes without being cruel or slaughtering like the former.

5. Palpable Justice

The notion of justice does not mean education, and it does not require education either. There's never a need to start a war and therefore no need for weapons. Justice does not necessarily need courts or governmental departments in order to protect everyone. In other words, appropriate justice, authentic justice, equal justice, and a proper definition of the notion of justice, have nothing to do with the notion and criteria of civilized and uncivilized nations. Uncivilized nations are also referred to as the "Third World," developing states, or underdeveloped nations. If justice acts based on the understanding of those principles, then it is no longer promoting the definition of justice, but rather the will of imperialist nations or states.

We cannot call the killing of millions of civilians by the armed forces of the United States of America in Iraq, Afghanistan, Libya, Syria, and other parts of the world justice. How can such acts reflect a natural law of nations?

---

[19] Spooner Lysander, Natural Law; or the Science of Justice: A Treatise on Natural Law, Natural Justice, Natural Rights, Natural Liberty, and Natural Society; showing that all Legislation whatsoever is an Absurdity, a Usurpation, and a Crime. Part First. [1882], available at http://oll.libertyfund.org/titles/spooner-natural-law-or-the-science-of-justice-1882 (Accessed: on 18 December 2017).

[20] *Id.*

If humans are not recognized as equal and are victims of mass massacres by other nations, how can it be called equality? These criminal acts are neither part of civil law nor criminal law. They are not at all a presentation of international human rights provisions or international criminal justice. Therefore, they cannot bring peace into the hearts of victims, and their purpose is solely to kill and pirate the rights of the victims. The fact is that a new method or form of modern colonisation has emerged wherein stronger nations are colonizing the population and sovereignty of various nations across the globe.

Additionally, we are looking for the definition of justice in order to promote the recognition of the key essence of the term in all situations without any regard to nationality, language, religion, or any other attribute, including race or authority. In other words, those who refer to other nations as being part of the Third World not only lack an understanding of justice, they are also the main reason for the development of injustice and live in total ignorance of the needs of the *jus gentium*. This indicates that they need to work harder to fulfil the fundamental principles of humanity, which also involves respecting the essence of man.

The law of nature, or the universal law, outlines and adopts certain rules of rights for all human beings, whether they are able to talk or not, or capable of driving European vehicles or not, or whether they live in apartments or are homeless. Thus, any statement that binds man to the vocabulary of the Third World or civilized and uncivilized nations is not only wrong, but also an extreme violation of all provisions of international human rights that claim to be powerful and command respect. Almost all statements about the division of man based on his position and not reaching justice are grave violations of the law. A system of law or a system of regulation, whether national, regional, or international, that divides men based on their wealth is not only fighting against the basic foundation of *jus gentium,* but also against the universal origin of all men.

We are not arguing here about what rights are, what the source of justice is, and why justice is bound by the merit of *jus gentium*, or the law which is supposed to protect all men. What we mean by this is that the notion of justice must have a glimpse of the truth, and that truth cannot be argued separately from the needs of all men. It means that for every single presentation or reasoning we present, we must also effectively connect it to the rights of all men and not the desires of certain societies or nations. The task of extracting good rules of law from the crude ore or monopolized rules integrated into the discipline of the law is our duty as per *jus gentium*. We should, in fact, reduce the effect and spirit of justice into forms and procedural methods that can be applied in practice. However, we must say that true justice cannot be achieved by promoting one-eyed justice. Thus, preventing the imposition of one-eyed justice is the whole reason for speaking about the theory of justice, or equal *jus gentium* for all.

It is therefore not surprising to see a large number of conflicts created and described through the propaganda mechanism of the superpowers in the name of justice. This is what we observe all the time, digging into the definition of an appropriate understanding of the notion of justice. We have the immense variability of objects of justice and how they can be defined and delivered in rules that do not cause harm to any subject of the law in our minds. I am convinced that all subjects of the law, should also all be subjects of justice, and all subjects of justice must be integral parts of the same theory of implementation of its provisions. This implies the fact that all people are subject to the authority of the law of justice, and this law is essentially based on the principle of equality between the subjects of the law. This is what I call visible palpable justice. We cannot suppose that certain governments or nations of the world deceive the interpretation and presentation of the system of justice and, therefore, the authoritative function for the maintenance of justice. Such a situation brings the concept of injustice into existence, and its subjects can no longer trust justice. The lack of involvement of nations in the final presentation and imposition of justice rules is particularly evident.

6. Evacuating Justice with Injustice

We are not discussing the violations of rights, the disregard of the subjects of law, or giving one subject more rights than others here. Clearly, we are highlighting a system of justice that is morally correct and does not speak about the devaluation of the rights of its subjects.[21] The learned man may in fact acknowledge the reality that justice which is explained by certain subjects of the law that have authority under their control, may be an expression of

[21] On morality role in justice examine Fuller Lon Luvios, *The Morality of Law* (Virginia: Yale Law University, 2nd, ed., 1969); A. R. C. Duncan, *Practical Reason and Morality* (Nelson, 1957); M. J. Detmold, *The Unity of Law and Morality: A Refutation of Legal Positivism* (Canada: Law Book Co. of Australasia, 1984); Lea Brilmayer, *American Hegemony: Political Morality in a One Superpower World* (1994); Ahmad Haque Adil, *Law and Morality at War* (2017); Himma Kenneth and Brian Bix (eds), *Law and Morality* (2005); David Lyons, 'Moral Aspects of Legal Theory' in Kenneth Himma and Brian Bix (eds) *Law and Morality* (2005).

injustice. This indicates that justice is the will of the authorities in control of the meaning of the law. My explanations may be incorrect regarding certain authorities or nations, as their explanations are not correct for the vast majority of nations. The current development and movements of the principle of justice and its definition in Africa are particularly indicative of this. This situation demonstrates that there are significant differences between what the big political powers explain in the definition of justice, and what the victims of those powers say about the development of brutal provisions in the name of justice.

We have already observed that in order to create a correct and acceptable definition of justice and its applications, we need the rights of all nations to be respected - not only in the provisions of the law, but also in practice. African nations do not recognize the definition of justice that was imposed by the colonial powers and which has yet to be abolished from their politics and legal systems. This is regardless of the fact that we have established the United Nations and have also adopted the Declaration of Human Rights along with a considerable number of other international conventions on human rights that speak about human rights and justice. Although their messages are clear and present the reality of the provisions of justice and the rights of all nations under the system of *jus gentium*, the actual invisible mechanism of those provisions proves that colonialism has put on new clothes in the name of the declaration of human rights. A clear example of this is the juridical and colonial relations of certain African nations with the French government.

It is not sufficient to simply empower the law of the United Nations and the relevant conventions of human rights when the French government has maintained its colonial power in Africa and interfered in their economic, military, and political affairs. Additionally, every single movement of the French government concerning African nations implies the existence of a strong colonial power. Thus, justice cannot be reached with empty words. The very distinct notion of justice, or *jus gentium,* should only adopt appropriate methods and distance itself from maxims that have not been established by the common consent of African nations but through the imposition of military power. Even when the definition of justice and rights come up, they are often seen in a nexus of dependency and not with respect to freedom, insofar as they depend on the definition of justice presented by colonial or occupation power.

Certainly, in their transactions with the notion of justice, nations want to see justice as a principle of equality and not as a principle that is dictated by the new or old colonial power. In the observance of any rules of human rights law or justice, which must be the same, we do not need the maxims of authoritarian power, rather the maxims that connect the visible power of the institution of justice with the invisible, united essence of *jus gentium*. In other words, the natural rights of man must be respected at all times. The case concerning African nations is particularly revealing, as they have been treated with brutality as the cargo of our commercial trade. The most problematic fact is that the situation remains unchanged in various ways, and the justice of the superpower governments is still authoritative, dominant, and continues to control the natural rights of man - even ignoring them in the most severe cases.

In addition to being unfair, the notion that political or judicial systems in some countries must prioritize the principles of justice violates the conventions that have already been established and legitimized as the end of colonialism. Respect must be given to every subject of justice, and this must take shape in a reciprocal independence of the principles of justice. However, this notion is violated in practice. In our previous example, the French government permitted intervention in African nations due to the value of their resources. Would the French authorities sit silently and accept African nations sending their militaries to French territory? The answer is obvious. The political or legal bodies of all governments or nations do not have the right to colonize one another's resources; however, they do it anyway. In a manner suitable to the system of justice, we are legally and morally forced to respect the rights of other nations to their land and properties, even if they are not militarily strong. If military power reflects the spirit of justice and the reason for the presentation of justice, then we are not speaking about justice, but about the practice of military strength. This is something that has already been observed and will continue to be observed repeatedly.

7. The Science of Justice

The judicious author of justice, who is capable of understanding the reality of the law should eventually discover that the notion of justice contains a particular science, and this science is nothing more than equality which produces peace between nations if it is respected.

> The science of mine and thine - the science of justice - is the science of all human rights; of all a man's rights of person and property; of all his rights to life, liberty, and the pursuit of happiness. It is the science which alone can tell any man what he can, and cannot, do; what he can, and cannot, have; what he can, and cannot, say, without infringing the rights

> of any other person. It is the science of peace; and the only science of peace; since it is the science which alone can tell us on what conditions mankind can live in peace, or ought to live in peace, with each other. [22]

The notion of equality also reduces conflicts, such as those between the French government and the innocent, independent African states which are not independent in reality. The recent case of Niger reflects this along with the very strong colonial influence of France that can be seen in their legal, economic, political, and military affairs. Despite the abolition of colonisation following the establishment of the United Nations, French governments have continued to plunder African countries and interfere in their politics. However, they have denied this influence and interference. This indicates the domination and control of moral justice by physical justice.

The virtue of justice should come from that nature, which covers all individuals and nations. Nevertheless, we shall see in the course of these paragraphs that the notion of justice has been misinterpreted because of its independent nature. The idea that the notion of justice, and particularly human rights law, is not interfered with regarding its legal or moral characteristics is therefore invalid. We may state that the necessary change in that case is essential, but it is never completed. We may also conclude that the maxims of justice, as well as others considered to shape the international human rights law, are exactly the same; if not, then we are ignoring the provisions of the law. We therefore cannot treat the notion of justice and the reasoning of the system of human rights law separately.

We must get closer to the true idea of our system of justice, whether it is called civil law, criminal law, or human rights. All systems must fall under the notion of justice, or the undeniable rights of humankind. However, I acknowledge that not all notions of justice are the same, and there must be an essence to the notion of natural law of justice. In addition, if writers choose to call all notions of justice the same thing, they are unwittingly ignoring the essence of justice and only looking after their own personal interests. Nevertheless, the difference between the essence of man and the wrongful consent of humankind demonstrates our ignorance. The basic obligation which we are all bound to observe must be the same and cannot privilege the strong

[22] Spooner Lysander, *Natural Law; or the Science of Justice*: A Treatise on Natural Law, Natural Justice, Natural Rights, Natural Liberty, and Natural Society; showing that all Legislation whatsoever is an Absurdity, a Usurpation, and a Crime. Part First. [1882], available at http://oll.libertyfund.org/titles/spooner-natural-law-or-the-science-of-justice-1882 (Accessed: on 18 December 2017).

while hurting the weak. The principles and rules of all notions of justice must be the same as those of the system of human rights.

The only difference permitted can be in the mode of application from nation-to-nation, due to differences in cultural and procedural procedures. On the one hand, differences in modes of application do not change the basic role of justice and its interpretations. Justice may be served to different degrees on account of the differences. On the other hand, the notion of justice should not stray from its main intention and its invisible values. We are referring to the notion of justice that can encompass both visible and invisible norms. The visible norms are readable and imposable, whereas the invisible norms of justice form the foundation for the existence of its visible norms. The rules and decisions for the implementation of authentic justice are required to respect and follow the invisible rules of justice. These are the rules for which the visible norms of justice have been codified and entered into national and international legal systems.

We should clarify that the visible norms of justice cannot be purely applied to the subjects of justice if the main reason for their collection under the system of justice is not taken into consideration. This means that all interpretations or deductions made from the visible norms of justice must be identical to the essence of their existence, which is nothing other than the equal treatment and rights of all men under the same law. Indubitably, rules of justice must undergo some changes in order to accommodate the needs of the subjects with whom they are compatible.

It therefore appears that the mode of treating the notion of justice may be based on its relations to individuals, and these individuals have the same values, even though they may be temporary visitors under the sovereignty of certain given states. So far, at least as it is understood from the notion of universal or natural justice for all, justice requires more profound reflection and more extensive attention to the rights of the new subjects with the intention of protecting their rights under the sovereignty of another nation. It is through the basic principles of justice alone that the decisions of a court can deal with the equal application of the nature of the law. In the pursuit of the intentions of those very norms of justice, we look for their application to all men with equal interpretations. It is important that justice is aware of the rights of individuals i.e., its subjects. This also includes the system of international laws.

8. Regular Choice

We must remember that the duties of judges in a court and the rights of individuals are, in general, immutable due to their necessity for the proper execution of justice.[23] The concept of justice, or pure *jus gentium*, inherently belongs to the universal essence of humanity. Consequently, it should not be regarded as a mere choice made in a constitution. Due to its fundamental origin, the procedures of justice are essential. In other words, the actions of prosecutors, judges, and court participants must adhere to the common rights upheld by justice.[24] Those who work within the justice system are uniquely empowered to interpret norms that may be misunderstood. The nature and essence of the virtues of the norms of justice differ from those of the decisions of the authorities. The latter is based solely on political competition, whereas the former is based on the necessity of moral support. In many respects, the nature and essence of justice are not physical in reality. However, the reason for political and constitutional existence is essentially physical, and the power behind it is taken to be a political group, a political force, or military support. That is why the notion of justice comes into physical force in its natural form, i.e., pure applications of its intentions or biased applications for personal use. Thus, the issues concerning the definitions of justice and its legality may fall within the procedures of justice. Furthermore, attempting to understand improper justice may unintentionally lead to a fork-in-the-road deduction and corrupt the jurisdiction of justice.

There is therefore a significant difference between universal or natural justice and its physical form. *Accordingly, we should distinguish between physical justice, institutional justice, military justice, political justice, and natural justice. All these justices, with reservations for natural justice, are a form of establishment and gathering of individuals together to bring the roles of justice into reality in accordance with their own understandings*. Justice can be defined as either equal or unequal, and can also be autocratic and enforced through different names or sanctioned by new colonial powers. The modernisation of the colonial power rules in various names and presentations

[23] See Farhad Malekian, *Conscience of Judges in International Criminal Law, the Heart of Judgements* (New York: Nova Science Publishers, 2021).

[24] See Farhad Malekian, *Conscience of Judges in International Criminal Law, the Heart of Judgements* (New York: Nova Science Publishers, 2021); Farhad Malekian, *Conscience of Lawyers in International Criminal Law, the Burden of Doppelgängers* (New York: Nova Science Publishers, 2021); Farhad Malekian, *Conscience of Prosecutors in International Criminal Law, the Heart of the Matter* (New York: Nova Science Publishers, 2021).

is proof of this. Therefore, in the absence of specific norms of justice, we look for the reason why justice is not sufficient. Then we look to justice as a matter of dealing with certain situations that are visible.

However, the most essential reason for the norms of justice is still its invisible essence, which is not formulated and does not extend to how we or others interpret it. Since justice, our rights, and our duties towards the maintenance of those rights are perpetual and should not vary under different presentations of justice, this is what we call moral *justice.* Moral justice should not be modified by the rules of law or power politics and is consistent with the nature of its subjects, which can be humans, animals, nature, or the natural existence of the universe. As a result, no arbitrary rules can prevent its enforcement. It essentially prohibits exploitation of the roles and rules of justice.

The substance of moral justice is mandatory, and individuals, groups, or organisations are not permitted to treat it as optional or selectively enforce certain norms.[25] Moral justice is what it should be. However, physical justice changes all the time. As a result, one cannot find the consent of the subjects in all particular legal disputes. Thus, constitutional, civil, or human rights justice does not remain the same as universal justice, the law of nature, or *jus gentium.* The former regulates the actions of individuals from time-to-time, from politics-to-politics and from community-to-community.

Physical justice is often the result of political gains, while the moral justice presented in the essence of man is permanent. Therefore, moral justice

---

[25] "The theory of justice, as the drafters of international rules, obligations, and norms have supposed, does not normally function appropriately. The reason for this is that the international criminal system lacks a central international organisation aimed at solving its theoretical issues and conflicts, in contrast to the national criminal system.' The international conflicts are, therefore, sometimes very intensive and dangerous. The most common forms of these conflicts appear as war crimes, crimes against humanity, genocide, apartheid, torture, terrorism, aggression, and in most cases crimes against the humanitarian law of armed conflict. Due to this primary concept of international justice that can appear in international relations of states, justice is considered by some to be weak, inconvenient, and selective. It is this selection of justice or the violation of equality within the terms of international conventional norms or the international criminal social contract that creates conflict. 16 Examples of the selection of justice can be seen in the structure of the United Nations, which presents in its Security Council a clear example of monopolisation of international justice. Another clear instance is the IST and the selection of appropriate international criminal norms under the authority and supervision of the United States government." Farhad Malekian, 'Emasculating the Philosophy of International Criminal Justice in the Iraqi Special Tribunal,' Cornell International Law Journal, 58/5 (2005), pp. 676-677. Examine See *also* Robert Cryer, *Prosecuting International Crimes, Selectivity and the International Criminal Law Regime* (Cambridge University Press, Cambridge, 2005).

does not depend on physical justice, even though physical justice may contain moral justice. This is why the contents of physical justice may differ from state-to-state and even from nation-to-nation because different nations may have different understandings of cultural justice and therefore practice it differently. However, concerning moral justice, there should not be any differentiation between high and low justice. The entire justice system dictates what morality is and what it should be. Moreover, moral justice is not a written law, although it may be formulated into physical justice. The principle of moral justice reflects how we should act and compels us not to choose between provisions and interpretations. We must act without inflicting harm on others.

Chapter 2

Decorating Physical Justice

1. Manufacturing Justice

Physical justice dictates how to act, how to be, and how to respect the provisions of the given law, whether it is imperialist law, communist law, dictatorial law, Islamic law, Christian law, *Nazism law,* Stalinism law, or Zionism law. Physical justice may also have a moral law, but due to the circumstances and the value surrounding a situation, we may also face justice in the name of democracy, which may still not be pure justice and is instead mixed with different forms of injustice. These democratic societies do not see that their decisions are wrong and involve themselves in various criminal activities that seen as lawful and not criminal. For example, many European states are involved in weapons production and believe that it is not wrong since physical international justice permits it. Thus, there is a big difference between moral justice and physical justice, even though both systems may speak about justice and the maintenance of equal values.

This type of physical justice, or democratic justice, can be observed within both historical and modern British and French colonial laws. Both countries have their own legal systems with a large number of provisions regarding human rights law and justice. Both claim to have democratic laws despite both having some of the highest percentages of laws that violate the rights of other nations. Both speak about moral justice and the protection of international human rights law, while also being involved in the killing of the population of the world, directly or indirectly. These circumstances present obstacles that render the notion of moral justice obsolete and throw it in the face of authentic justice. Examples of this include when governments of both nations are involved in the manufacturing of weapons and their trade into the territories of other nations while being aware that those nations are not their allies and that their wars not only bring wealth for them, but also increase their access to resources.

We must make a choice between the description of justice and the description of the centuries of criminal conduct within the territories of other nations. This is why I will attempt to describe the value of moral justice and the issues with certain forms of physical justice throughout this work. I do not indulge in the assumption of physical justice in the system of our internal justice in general or in the system of international justice or global justice in particular.[26] I intend to say that justice is neither a mechanism of possession nor a mechanism of the values of man and his decisions. Rather, I will speak about moral justice as the body of our existence or as the necessary substance of our psychological protection. When justice does not care about the values of man or when justice has taken on different faces for the maintenance of its own criminal professional values under the authority of big criminals, then the value of justice has been murdered by physical justice. *This implies a funeral of moral justice. This funeral is under no circumstances curative, and victims of physical justice are forever the victims of serious international crimes under the power of the law.*

The different subjects of physical justice are consequently under serious attack, which is why we try to distinguish between moral justice and physical justice. While both terms include the word "justice," they are fundamentally different. The notion of physical justice is cultivated by political power to the point that it goes against its own elementary provisions of the understanding of justice. We are obviously referring to the provisions of physical justice that are decorated with the norms of democracy and international human rights and yet are essentially the presentation of certain physical military power over other subjects of moral justice internationally. Despite this, physical justice is not viewed as fair by its national standards. A clear example of this is the physical internal justice that is exercised against certain residents of the United States of America, Britain, or Israel who may have roots in other cultures.

I am only citing events that have been actually committed in the United States and have not yet referenced the large number of crimes committed by American governments against other nations of the world.[27] Reference can also be made to the British, French, German, Dutch, Australia and even Swedish hidden practices of physical justice against moral justice. This would give *de jure* legitimacy, at least for Palestinians, to initiate a case against the aforementioned governments for the damages and loss of life that have resulted from those nations' support of the criminal conduct of the Israeli government. Although the governments in the above enjoy their international legal personality, they are not permitted to aid, assist, or provide various kinds of help. They are therefore *de facto* in a state of committing international

[26] Consult also Bruce Broomhall, International Justice and the International Criminal Court: Between Sovereignty and the Rule of Law (2004); Farhad Malekian, International Crime of Blackboard-Barbarism ((New York: Nova Science Publishers, 2025).

[27] https://en.wikipedia.org/wiki/United_States_war_crimes.

crimes. Otherwise, ironically, we are forced to treat them with the principle of *doli incapax*, which is argued in the case of children, implying that they are incapable of criminal intent, and in this case, the international crime of genocide.[28] The fact is that all nations supporting the genocide in Palestine should be held accountable.[29] This is not only the order of moral justice, but also the order of physical justice, i.e., the ICC.[30]

2. Justice Ending in War

We do not believe that any nation that asserts that they are exercising moral justice is exercising it correctly. Simply claiming that we exercise justice correctly does not mean that we are doing so in reality. Since we can also claim in our judgments that all moral considerations have been taken into account in our relations with others, we may have violated the rights of others in our personal judgments, whether intentionally or unintentionally. This is what is normally seen in our social relations and is eventually forgotten about for one reason or another. As a result, we apply our own personal physical judgments to moral judgments and assume that the foundations of our judgments have respected the notion of morality, even though they have not.

Of course, we must emphasize that moral judgments are not about understanding one another, but rather about how we should deal with moral justice. However, this matter is always confusing and brings the concept of justice into question. It is therefore essential that moral law requires the education of every citizen in every civil society before allowing them to take active steps in the social contract. We need to incorporate this into our primary education. We do not need to impose any particular obligations on them in

---

[28] See also Farhad Malekian and Kerstin Nordlöf, *Confessing the International Rights of Children: The Basic documents with Analysis* (Cambridge: Cambridge Scholars Publishing, 2012); Farhad Malekian and Kerstin Nordlöf,'International Legal Status of Children' in Jay S. Albanese (ed.), *The Encyclopaedia of Criminology & Criminal Justice* (United States: Wiley-Blackwell (5 volumes, 2013), vol. III, pp. 1173-1178; Farhad Malekian, Kerstin Nordlöf, *Prohibition of Sexual Exploitation of Children Constituting Obligation Erga Omnes* (Cambridge: Cambridge Scholars Publishing, 2013); Farhad Malekian, Kerstin Nordlöf, *The Sovereignty of Children in Law* (Cambridge: Cambridge Scholars Publishing, 2012).

[29] Farhad Malekian, *Paralysing International Criminal Justice* (New York: Nova Science Publishers, 2021).

[30] Consult also Francesca P Albanese, Lex Takkenberg, Palestinian Refugees in International Law (2nd Edition, 2020); Study the report of Francesca Albanese file:///C:/Users/uub-b24-1502/Downloads/a-hrc-55-73-auv%20(1).pdf.

order to teach them the principles of moral substance or humanity. This can be achieved by understanding that we are all equal and have the same feelings. The argument also supports the theory of equalitarianism.

It is undeniable that men lack an understanding of each other's rights as well as a willingness to follow natural justice rules in relationships with each other. To address this, we have set up institutions or courts. This is the only remedy that can protect rights, and if this remedy does not work, then national relations may end in murder and international relations may end in war. Unfortunately, the systems of national and international justice function in this way. The system of justice is often paralyzed by the depravity of the majority of political parties, and consequently, it violates the preliminary rules of natural law justice as a whole. Therefore, the only means of securing the condition of good justice and increasing wicked justice is the truthful understanding of pure moral justice, which is, of course, the most difficult task of justice. Nevertheless, it is easy to understand why violations of the principles of justice occur. It is particularly clear regarding the international actions of the big powers, which are supposed to protect and promote the principles of human rights law and justice but do the opposite.

The notion of justice is equally necessary among all nations or populations of the world, as it is significantly important in relationships between individuals. Populations cannot really exist in peace without the appropriate implementation of the principles of justice. However, as soon as the rules of justice are united under the provisions of certain conventions or treaties, they relax and believe that they will be able to implement the principles of justice. Therefore, they are then able to cultivate certain relations with one another. However, they end up losing the guidelines in the content of the conventions when it is convenient and impose against one another their own interpretation of justice. It is seen that without presenting good reasons, they may refuse to accept arguments made by anyone not belong to their monopolized system of authorizing justice and, naturally, its existing content. As a result, principles of righteous justice may sufficiently regulate rules in a different manner that can be respected by all governments. This encompasses the misunderstanding and disagreements between various subjects of the law.

The body of justice undergoes various changes and strays from its original intentions. All these changes within the body of justice lead to the use of psychological force. Physical justice also often resorts to the use of military force and violates the rights of others. In such cases, it appears that the rules of force and justice are linked, or that the rules of force reveal the real nature of given justice. Consequently, we restrict the natural rights or liberty of humankind. It would not be difficult to apply this doctrine of the use of injustice to the doctrine of justice since the former has complete authority over the rules and roles of justice. Due to this, moral justice eventually dies. In other words, the spirit of justice ends up in the laboratories of governments that separate the real essence of justice from its practical high motivations.

As a result, many big criminals and super-military powers grant themselves impunity.[31] This also means the authorities do not view changes to the rules as being necessary and consequently, moral justice vanishes in the process of imposing physical justice. As a result, we reach a particular ambiguous situation concerning the interpretation and understanding of the terms of justice in our hearts, minds, and practices. In the end, hatred and evilness grow and work against those who have taken the power of justice or physical justice under their own control. A clear example of this is how the Zionist political government interprets the terms and provisions of justice, which in the end leads to protests and wars.[32] The reason is that the relevant government wishes to impose its own understanding of the system of international law and ignores the very established fact that it has taken over a country's legitimate rights to justice for several decades.

3. A Crashing Connotation

Physical justice always brings sorrow, depression, grief, mourning, and, in the end, the destruction of cities, civilisations, and populations around the world with it. These behaviours are surely against the systems of international human rights law and international criminal justice, wherein justice becomes a tool used to benefit the powertionist governments.[33] There is no reason why the system of justice should be missing its goals and producing catastrophic results that contradict the needs of justice and the spread of equality between all men. It is of considerable importance to carefully distinguish between the nature and needs of moral justice and the conditions of physical justice for the mechanism of natural justice.

The necessary moral justice and physical justice are both established institutions; however, one is the result of our natural existence, while the other

[31] Consult Farhad Malekian, *International Criminal Vacations: Tears of Justice* (New York: Nova Science Publishers, 2024).

[32] Immanuel Kant, Religion within the Limits of Bare Reason (1793).

[33] Farhad Malekian, *Powertionism in International Criminal Justice* (New York: Nova Science Publishers, 2022).

stems from the nature of our minimum production of reality and the collective force of man. Moreover, there are three different collective decisions for the establishment of physical justice. One demonstrates the existence of majority consent, while another presents the rules that minorities wish upon the majorities will. The final one is more dictatorial and harmful because of the will of a third state toward other nations. The third one is more often seen in the system of international relations. The natural justice may be said to be like a sacred law, which, without necessarily being involved in any spiritual or theological discussions, speaks outside their field about moral justice or moral necessities that were not established by particular legal or religious authorities and which have come into existence as the existence of the truth.

Thus, truth is itself the basic reason for the existence of the concept of moral justice in our discussions and the reason for the prevention of any immoral physical justice. However, I am also aware of the fact that we cannot entirely eliminate the immoral versions of physical justice. The only possible alternative is that we prevent its development and, if we are lucky, reduce its immoral rules. It is obvious that physical justice would not have found itself in a compromised situation if moral justice had been respected all along. This implies that the necessary measures have already been taken in the case of not destroying the basic law of all mankind. The fact is that the common idea of morality has completely different principles than what physical justice expresses and perpetuates.

Consequently, in regards to the principles of physical justice and moral justice, we have to understand that they function on different platforms and with different sources, and powers. Physical justice orders and demands its performance. This does not mean that it is necessarily wrong or right and it contains and exhibits the desires of the objects. These desires are sometimes voluntary and formulated based on the wishes of the population. This does not present a problem concerning its intentions. However, unavoidable conflicts arise when we encounter a situation where the physical justice system hinders the formation of natural legal order. This granite should not be violated at any time since it contains principles of moral justice, and these principles are the substance of the essence of humanity. This is the essential reason why human beings respect each other and work to the advantage of their existence as the value of humanity. The will or consent of universal synchronicity is the basis for moral justice.

The cornerstone of moral justice, or the strong undeniable existence of the granite of justice, is not only damaged and exploited by our physical justice, it is also vanquished by the atrocities of our military power.[34] Thus, to carry out the monopolisation of the power of moral justice, we prepare and conceal dangerous events with the sole purpose of occupying physical and moral justice. Although we may state that we are following democratic rules and supporting human rights law, the fact is that our weapons industry reveals the truth, and eventually, the system of physical justice not only becomes dominant in national relations, but also in international relations. This is why the provisions of international human rights contradict their nature. Therefore, acquiring rights and obligations is specific to authoritarian powers. This indicates that even though we bind ourselves, our consent to physical justice is much more typical than a matter of choice.

When physical justice becomes imperative in the place of moral justice, the question of choice becomes irrelevant and is replaced with the measures and values that are selected, drafted, and are the law based on the desires of certain political or national groups. A clear example of this is the international physical military force that has been directed by the British governments at various nations. These governments have ignored moral justice and still believe that they promote correct and good fundamental values. It is evident that such laws and physical justice cannot impose any binding obligation by force and are always invalid. Except for those rules of justice, which have very narrowly developed moral justice, finding moral justice in the physical justice of superpowers is similar to searching for justice in an ocean of injustice. Specifically, this is evident in the actions of the British, German, Dutch, and French colonial powers still today. It is therefore the maxims of injustice that extend their brutal operation on the victims of moral justice, physical justice, and international human rights justice.

4. Imposed Use of Consent

The notion of moral justice is the law of all men. It is primarily there to serve them and their needs based on their circumstances. This implies that

[34] Mark J. Osiel, 'Why Prosecute? Critics of Punishment for Mass Atrocity,' 22 Human Rights Quarterly 118 (2000); A. Bellamy, *Responsibility to Protect: the Global Effort to End Mass Atrocities* (Polity Press, Cambridge, 2009); David Wippman, Atrocities, 'Deterrence, and the Limits of International Justice,' 23 *Forham International Law Journal* 473 (1999); Farhad Malekian, *Powertionism in International Criminal Justice* (New York: Nova Science Publishers, 2022), pp. 231-237; Farhad Malekian, *Tour de force of Moral Virtue in International Criminal Justice* (New York: Nova Science Publishers, 2022).

everyone's interests are seen and respected by the moral substance of justice, and it intends to impart the knowledge of morality and its significant beneficial values to all individuals and not just private bodies. The spirit of moral justice is superior not only to physical law, but also to other notions of justice regarding its importance. This is because moral justice is more consequential than physical justice, which is formulated by legal or political authorities that are fulfilling the will of their masters. Nevertheless, fatal involvement in the questions of justice barely proves how little respect exists for those who direct the force of the law and do not promote the substance of pure justice. The principles of physical justice are implemented when authorities prioritise physical justice over moral justice in order to best serve their interests.

The real feature of justice is usually derived from the maxim of physical justice. This is also more evident regarding the implementation of the provisions of the United Nations, the provisions of the system of international human rights, and those of international criminal justice. In certain situations, physical justice neglects the position of its subjects and highlights the development of its force on the individuals of occupied countries by the rule of military advantages at all times. Therefore, there is no obligation to respect moral justice as long as physical justice can reach its intentions. Additionally, the same maxim forces the individuals of occupied counties to obey the orders of those in power.[35] This is how the system of justice, the system of law of nations, the system of human rights, and the content of physical justice gain strength without needing to respect the order of moral justice.

I must take into account the fact that the controlling powers establish the general rules and principles for physical justice as well as moral justice, and as a result, the latter becomes the instrument of the former. Thus, the moral justice that it provides in the direction of humanity and equality for all men encounters force and violations. Physical justice forces its subjects to accept its conditions and succeeds in obtaining unanimous consent. Although the legality of such consent is suspect, physical justice without any permission imposes its own method of morality on its subjects. This means that physical justice is a form of *sua sponte* that is imposed on subjects without being formally permitted. Governments that take control of internal physical justice as well as the system of international physical justice have certain intentions.

---

[35] Consult Farhad Malekian, 'Judging International Criminal Justice in the Occupied Territories,' 12 *International Criminal Law Review* (2012), pp. 627-869; Farhad Malekian, *'Islamic Law Justice Systems' in* Jay S. Albanese, *The Encyclopaedia of Criminology and Criminal Justice* (United States: Wiley-Blackwell (5 volumes, 2013), vol. III, pp. 1220-1225.

There are a large number of examples that indicate the very evil nature of physical international justice. On such example is the events of September 11th, which were framed as terrorist attacks on the United States. The actual events that led up to the attacks have shown that the US government, with the help of other countries, planned the attacks. We reference these events here not to speak about the crimes of the United States government, but rather to underline that the events are an integral part of evil physical justice that violates the values of moral justice, which in turn demand righteousness. In addition, this righteousness can simply and easily be monopolized by the physical justice.[36] This is why physical justice and moral justice normally have two different platforms and railways.

This is despite the fact that physical and moral justice run in the same direction, with the difference being that one destroys the basic underlying reasons of moral justice and enforces its own understanding of all forms of justice, which is not only dangerous for the philosophy of moral justice, but also for its own survival. This is why physical justice is continuously subjected to various moral, ethical, and political questions and modifications. Different wills and interests occasionally arise and bring the basic philosophy of moral justice under serious question in order to take control over the basic understanding of moral reasoning, which should naturally be more or less at the same level for all humankind. These are rights such as the right to live, the right not to be discriminated against, the right not to be killed, the right to have control over their own properties, the right to cultural or ethnic differences, the right to choose any religious belief, and the right to be treated equally within the procedures of the machinery of justice.[37]

---

[36] Examine Farhad Malekian, Concreting Righteousness in International Criminal Justice (New York, Nova Sciences Publishers, 2024).

[37] "The philosophy of both theoretical and religious disciplines, i.e., Christian and Islamic law, intends to reduce human mistreatment while not mistreating their own subjects. This is one of the most significant aspects of these theories that have misled or created confusion, whether intentionally or otherwise. A fact to be remembered is that both religious authorities have been mostly active when their subjects have been mistreated. Christians, for example, were demanding restitution when ISIS committed crimes against Christians, even though the entire concept of ISIS was created by westerners in order to strengthen their counter-terrorist ideologies. At the same time, they had not shown any particular sympathy to the genocide of Palestinians nor that of the Yemeni population. No Christian authority condemns the occupation of the Palestinian capital, Jerusalem. The city, without any historical doubt, belongs to both Muslims and Jews. Jerusalem's occupation using guns means the occupation of the peaceful theories of Christ through the power of military force, which Christ was predominantly against. The result of this criminal situation is that the political Zionism government is committing barbarous crimes against the population of

The vocabularies of various treaties and customs of international human rights law also talk about these principles and many others. Nevertheless, as it is not in the interests of the authorities who have the power to control physical justice under their own wills, the philosophy of moral justice is forced to modify its content as a result. It may be much more practical for the controlling power and its allies to witness the change of moral justice or international moral justice in order to direct and guide their controlling force with appropriate steps for the imposition of the power of physical justice.

5. Vulgar Maxims of Justice

Moral justice works against physical justice and intends to create the best and safest policy founded on the virtue of nature and its understanding of the rights of others and their respect. Moral justice is not only the master of law, but also the master of justice, and demonstrates how individuals, groups, nations, and governments realize the eloquence of the philosophy of the development of equality for all. Moral justice rejects the vulgar maxims that may be orchestrated by governments using physical justice. Thus, governments that commit injustices cannot contribute to moral justice, even if they are temporarily the conquerors or leaders of distributing the provisions of justice. *Here, the major difference rests on the fact that moral justice is built upon wisdom and not ignorance or the rejection of wisdom. However, physical justice acts in opposition and demands certain matters in accordance with its own interpretations.*

Concerning physical justice, we develop the entire philosophy of law based on various interpretations, deductions, reasonings, understandings, readings, clarifications, explanations, and descriptions. The goal is always to convince another party or parties of our arguments, even if the other parties may be correct in their interpretations. This is why physical justice can easily create a large gap between the reality of a case and the lies, thereby causing confusion. This is particularly evident with governments that maintain essentially a system of monopolisation, whether at home or abroad. Let me not renounce the pleasing hope of the powertionist governments who commit grave crimes and serious violations of the system of international human rights

---

occupied territories." Farhad Malekian, Exploitation of Christian Islamic International Criminal Justice (New York, Nova Sciences Publishers, 2024), p. 31.

and international criminal justice.[38] This means that there are almost no wise performers of wise justice in the inner structure of those governments.

Even when a wise man does appear, he is immediately silenced in some way. This is precisely what is happening in the sphere international relations with the current cases of Gaza and Ukraine, both of which are the result of the expansion of the authority of powertionist governments, and NATO, even if not explicitly.[39] There is thus a parallel process of physical justice being used in order to kill the theory and subjects of moral justice. This indicates that under the power of physical justice, wherever we go, we face the power of the controlling parties, and the *res judicata,* or the final appropriate decision of a court, a body, or the government, is under the control of the authoritarian subject.

In comparison, the theory of *res judicata* can be seen with the power of the Security Council, where the five permanent members are the judges of the court and are in control. Therefore, different approaches may be used to clarify the power of physical justice over moral justice or the essence of righteous justice. Thus, despite the existence of legal bases for moral justice, physical justice prevails, particularly when it comes to the evaluation of certain international conflicts. In the case of Gaza, even though the moral justice of the world is very strong, physical criminal justice has prevailed.

Justice is directed by bringing the provisions of physical justice into practice. This also leads to policies being made and massacres being carried out. Thus, in physical justice, the leaders in control are hoping for outcomes that benefit them and not the general public or the territories where they are promoting terror and carrying out atrocities serious violations. The intention of physical justice is to commit war crimes, crimes against humanity, genocide, rape, torture, and gross humiliations, with the clear intention of labelling the domestic authorities of the victim nations as criminals. This reflects international physical justice against international moral justice in practice.

The most important thing that should be addressed here is not how those crimes are committed by the big political or powertionist governments against other nations, but rather the infringements of the theory of international or

---

[38] Clara Nieto, Masters of War: Latin America and U. S. Aggression from the Cuban Revolution through the Clinton Years (foreword by Howard Zinn; translated by Chris Brandt, 2003); Farhad Malekian, *Powertionism in International Criminal Justice* (New York: Nova Science Publishers, 2022);

[39] *Id.*

universal moral justice based on *jus gentium*.[40] It is crucial for all governments and groups to respect this at all times. However, the phenomenon of moral justice is not respected, and the situation may result in different outcomes that are controversial and do not reflect the intentions of the basic essence of moral justice. This is particularly notable when physical justice forces moral justice to the edge, where there is no alternative except to die.

By virtue of the situation, physical justice intends to force its wills by various means, such as starvation and the destruction of houses and buildings. Due to these identical criminal measures, we affect the establishment or promotion of moral justice. Powertionist governments consistently prioritise physical justice over moral justice, which leads to a vicious cycle. A clear example of this is when a powertionist government frequently imposes sanctions on other governments or uses its veto power in order to squash any hope for the consolidation of moral justice.[41] The veto gives rise to the destruction of the principles of moral justice and its capacity and capability concerning the scope and applicability of its essence. That is why, in all our judgments, we must be conservative in our use of such embellishments of the principles of physical justice in order to ensure that the principles of moral justice are not violated.

6. Violators of Moral Justice

Without ever pointing at an otiose parade of judgments, we should seek to establish a preference for the principles of justice and the empowerment of the notion of moral justice, which aims at the rights of all peoples in the world, and does not encourage untruthful colours of justice. Certainly, the doctrine of justice and all relevant theories of justice are artificial as long as there is no significant example of righteousness in the practical application of justice.[42] This expression constitutes a principle, not a matter of choice. Thus, even though we may be professional lawyers, with a significant amount of court experience and various academic titles and even though we may be the deans of law, be famous for our academic writings, and have achieved different accolades, we still need to be truly righteous individuals.

---

[40] *Id.*

[41] *Id.*

[42] Farhad Malekian, Concreting Righteousness in International Criminal Justice (New York, Nova Sciences Publishers, 2024), 23-25.

None of this has any value if we do not understand the proper definition of humanity, international human rights, and the authentic definition of justice. I am referring here to moral justice for all and non-violation of the rights of others. The intention is to stop the destruction and brutal conduct of physical justice, and this cannot be achieved if we compare the detestation of moral justice with physical justice and fail to do anything except sit in our own position. *What is the point of being a lawyer that lies? What is the benefit of being a professional lecturer, but not supporting the crimes of governments? What is the advantage of being a good judge, but eating from multiple different hands? What is the point of being a professional writer when we do not apply our writings in practice? Additionally, what is the point of being educated at the most recognized universities only to commit various international crimes and kill millions?*

My final question is: what purpose do thousands of different provisions of international human rights law serve if they are completely ineffective and function as decorative norms of physical justice? A good father is not defined by his name, his looks, or his ability and experiences, rather he is defined by how well he protects his children, even to his detriment. Supporting a powerful government, protecting a criminal, and giving rights to many or those who commit crimes does not prove the morality of a father or a person, but the contrary. In other words, a lawyer, a professor of law, a judge, or an advocate who does not see the reality of the nature of physical morality acts like a dog that follows its master at all times. The theory is so simple that even cats could grasp the difference between a lawyer who does not trade the norms of justice and one who dresses in suits in order to silence justice. An evil mentality cannot cover the provisions of international human rights law.

It is easy to conform to the principles laid down by others for the sake of their own interests, but it is difficult to act contrary to the wills of brutal leaders. Most lawyers and those who engage in politics look for personal advantages with convenient opportunities. A wise man can, above all, endeavour to inspire a love of virtue for all human beings, regardless of their race or other artificial differences. The fact is that showing our patience and love to others does not come from isocracy or the opposite, but rather from the proper understanding of invisible norms of morality and not out of *fata morgana*, which is just a reflection of heat of the sun. By examining the crimes committed by superpowers all over the world, we can realize how unamiable the content of physical justice is. As to the rest of the jurisprudence of justice, the reasoning of moral justice is associated with the pillars of wisdom, insight, awareness, and vision. All this requires having a sufficient consciousness concerning the high value of human essence and not giving it away in the process of application.[43]

We should endeavour to avoid giving rights to big criminals by confirming their definition of justice. If justice is correct, it never requires explanation or exposition. Elucidations are normally required when we try to conceal the content of justice or the rights of individuals, groups, or nations. It is like the event of September 11th, containing accusations in order to plunder the content of moral justice with the orders of physical justice. We should appreciate the fact that moral justice is much more sensitive than a sacred rule respecting the truth or rights of others. *The common interests of the human race should always receive proper treatment instead of the personal interests of a handful of authorities, individuals, lawyers, politicians, or judges. In other words, finding a large number of charmers among lawyers is a very easy task, but finding lawyers that reject despotic power and base their principles on moral justice is difficult. Being a good lawyer is not less than being a mother of truth, of course, if there is any.*

Moreover, many of those who work with law or politics, are capable of knowingly or unknowingly prostituting justice to flattery. The power of physical justice is a reason why our system of international criminal justice has become a tool of injustice and consequently, moral justice has not been permitted in wars or courts. Thus, political bodies have become much stronger than legal or moral bodies. In other words, legal bodies controlled by politics and the intention of moral justice in order to unite human beings in promoting their common security and advantages through the mutual struggles of their combined strength are consequently paralyzed. Therefore, becoming a moral person who possesses sympathy for the victims is complicated, and eventually, the number of supporters of physical justice increases with the use of weapons. This means that we support the rights of victims, but the tools of injustice or the use of mechanisms of criminal justice are controlled by the big political governments. The situation becomes peculiar to itself and is susceptible to rights and obligations.

In order to establish a solid basis for the obligations and rights of all people in the world, we need to recognize the impact of our own decisions and statements and whether we are promoting the spirit of moral justice or strengthening the prostitute flattery of physical justice for the benefit of

[43] Examine the views of Richard Falk, John Mearsheimer, Avram Noam Chomsky, Jeffrey Sachs and Richard Wolff including colonels Douglas Macgregor, William Scott Ritter and Senator Richard H. Black. See John J Mearsheimer and Stephen Walt, The Israel Lobby and U.S. Foreign Policy (New York: Farrar, Straus and Giroux. 2007).

powers. Physical justice may therefore take over all aspects of moral justice, and this is made possible not only by the authorities, but also through our intentional or unintentional understanding of the policies of criminal governments.[44] The actions or statements of those who are blind and only focus on the consequences of violations do not reveal the reasons for violations or resort to armed forces. A clear example is when we know that physical justice is intentionally empowered by various weapons in order for one powerful state to get rid of another state and we ignore the fact that justice is nothing more than the power to do what is morally possible.[45]

7. Controlling Moral Justice

The concept of justice must be based on the knowledge of moral obligations incumbent on human beings that may lawfully require physical justice. *Pitting the notion of physical justice against moral justice can only cause anxiety and panic between the rights of man, and consequently, suffering as a result of war.* Nevertheless, a considerable number of writers do just this, and thereby ignore the basic reasons for certain conducts of certain individuals, groups, or nations of governments. A clear example is the present war in Ukraine and the presentation of various views concerning serious violations of international criminal justice by Russia while ignoring the fact that the war started as a result of the powertionist decisions of the United States in their attempt to gain more control in the region.[46]

At the end of the day, this means that the systems of international human rights law and international criminal justice are exclusively under powertionist governments their own political, economic, and military control. This indicates that the entire system of the United Nations is under the power of the

---

[44] Generally examine J. I. Ross, *Varieties of State Crime and its Control* (Monsey, NY: Criminal Justice Press, 2000); J. I. Ross, *Controlling State Crime* (2nd Edition, New Brunswick, NJ: Transaction Press, 2000).

[45] See Farhad Malekian, *Powertionism in International Criminal Justice* (New York: Nova Science Publishers, 2022); Farhad Malekian, *Conundrums of Paternalism i*n International Criminal Justice (New York, Nova Sciences Publishers, 2024); Farhad Malekian, Concreting Righteousness in International Criminal Justice (New York, Nova Sciences Publishers, 2024). Farhad Malekian, Exploitation of Christian Islamic International Criminal Justice (New York, Nova Sciences Publishers, 2024).

[46] Xinhua, U. S. Commits Serious Crimes of Violating Human Rights in the Middle East and Beyond (2022), https://english.news.cn/20220809/df33c619baf04b259981bcbba3961810/c.html.

American government.[47] Thus, the American government decides what is right or wrong, what constitutes the unlawful use of force or not, and where sanctions should be imposed.[48] This is how we view the system of international human rights systems and see the decorations that concern claims of controlling human morality, moral justice, and related provisions for the good of all nations in the world. Then, such thoughts, such wishes, and such interests are broadcasted with the intention of monopolizing power.

The US government does not permit other nations to establish military bases near their territories and yet will themselves violate the sovereignty of other nations to do just that. Moreover, the dismantling of Russia's military, political, and economic power has long been planned by the United States, Britain, France, and a number of other governments. The United States and its allies are actually responsible for the murder of innocent Ukrainians at the hands of the Russians.[49] The theory of physical justice, which is both direct and indirect, is in opposition to the principles of moral justice. In other words, if there had been no threat of NATO establishing a presence in Ukraine, then Russia would have never attacked, and civilians would not have died in both Russia and Ukraine.

In short, many of those who talk about the situation in Ukraine and the murder of almost half a million people do not take these matters into account and instead attribute the situation to the Russian government, even though the war was initiated by NATO in their attempt to militarily and economically destroy Russia and China. This is all strongly related to physical justice, which implies the practical application of constitutional or human rights rules whenever necessary for their own benefit. In other words, the reality of the situation in Ukraine is different from the narrative we are presented with. It is evident that justice should be derived from proper principles, and those principles must be based on moral justice. When physical justice does not follow the significant rules of moral justice, the very essential principles of humanity are violated.

It is an established point in the body of truthful justice that justice has to be based on the conscience of jurisdiction, and this conscience is the reason

[47] https://en.wikipedia.org/wiki/United_States_war_crimes.

[48] Examine Farhad Malekian, *Condemning the Use of Force in the Gulf Crisis* (Almqvist & Wiksell International, 1st ed., 1992).

[49] Consult Farhad Malekian, *Powertionism in International Criminal Justice* (New York: Nova Science Publishers, 2022), p. 139; Farhad Malekian, *Imperative Philosophy of International Criminal Justice: Visible Power – Invisible Essence* (New York: Nova Science Publishers, 2022); Farhad Malekian, *Tour de force of Moral Virtue in International Criminal Justice* (New York: Nova Science Publishers, 2022).

for existing justice. Otherwise, we should not look for justice but solely for the enforcement of the rules of powerful individuals or governments. That is why the intentions of physical justice contradict the intentions of moral justice, and as a result, subjects of justice are deprived of their rights without expressing any consent. However, despite the possibility of physical justice blocking the body of moral justice, the latter continues to be free and independent with regard to all physical justice principles. One example of this is how the French government plunders the sovereignty of African countries such as Niger. This implies that the rules of physical justice may hurt moral justice and be in charge. The evidence suggests that French governments have had control over a number of African nations for centuries.

We must therefore prioritize the principles of moral justice in order to discover what the obligations of governments are with the intention of preventing the monopolisation of justice at the national or international level.[50] As a principle, physical justice cannot be just and reasonable unless it meets the needs of its subjects and those needs cannot be proper if they are not made in a manner suitable to the spirit of moral justice. In all cases, we are comparing physical justice with moral justice. We should not forget the fact that we are in the age of the United Nations, which means that we should be promoting unity and not destruction. It is also the age of governing with humanistic philosophy, not anti-humanism. We thus want to establish a foundation of peace and justice and move away from inhumane policies of physical justice.

It is always the notion of physical justice that leads to the question of moral justice and brings attention to the disposing values of both theories. However, I am not still satisfied with my own statements based on the fact that moral justice is not a theory, even if we say it is. Moral justice contains the wills of nature and does not speak about the artificial facts of physical justice. Thus, moral justice seeks to establish harmony and understanding between the wills of men and man. Moral justice actually seeks peace and the establishment of contemplative mutual and multilateral relations in order to

---

[50] See Robert Cryer, *Prosecuting International Crimes, Selectivity and the International Criminal Law Regime* (Cambridge University Press, Cambridge, 2005); Farhad Malekian, *Trading Virginity of International Criminal Justice* (Nova Sciences Publishers, 2020); Farhad Malekian, *Imperative Philosophy of International Criminal Justice: Visible Power – Invisible Essence* (New York: Nova Science Publishers, 2022); Farhad Malekian, *Powertionism in International Criminal Justice* (New York: Nova Science Publishers, 2022); also Farhad Malekian, *Conundrums of Paternalism in International Criminal Justice* (New York: Nova Science Publishers, 2024); Farhad Malekian, *Concreting Righteousness in International Criminal Justice* (New York: Nova publishers, 2024).

prevent antagonism and self-reasons. That is why the institution of moral justice contradicts the personal wills of physical justice.[51]

[51] Examine Francesca P Albanese, Lex Takkenberg, Palestinian Refugees in International Law (2nd Edition, 2020); Study the report of Francesca Albanese file:///C:/Users/uub-b24-1502/Downloads/a-hrc-55-73-auv%20(1).pdf.

Chapter 3

The Millennium of Moral Justice

1. Diagnostic of Moral Justice

There is no notion of period of time in the case of moral justice since it is not the creation of man for man, but rather the will and substance of nature for human beings. Moral justice encourages men to work together for better understandings and divisions of the superficial material life in order to achieve a new solidarity of justice and judgment. Moral justice encourages men to delineate the true reasons for the satisfaction of all men and protection from evil vindication. Moral justice is based on an awareness of the needs of all men and rejects any paternalism or order of physical justice. That is why moral justice does not judge on the basis of power or wealth, but rather on the consequences of the outcomes. This means that we do not kill the spirit of the union of humanity, human rights, united needs, and united development of wills under moral justice.

It is therefore impossible to ignore the united essence of the will and nature of man under *jus gentium,* or universal moral justice. The origin and history of the idea of moral justice and its potential advantage for human society can be compared with the evil personality of physical justice. The value of justice can thus be better understood when looking at the international relations between nations and what the nature of physical justice is when it is evaluated under the use of force by authoritative power.[52] It is therefore in this connection that we search for an original natural definition of justice rather than a manmade one that is artificial and which compels the personal or collective interests of certain groups to be imposed upon others. Eradicating, restricting, or banishing the private interests of the big players of physical political justice is the most difficult task of moral justice.

In all these situations, man seeks to prevent conflicts arising from wills or interests. The aim is to cultivate the spirit of humanity, which is not defined by law, but rather by the nature of man himself. The morality of justice is thus

---

[52] Examine Ian Brownlie, *International Law and the Use of Force by States* (Oxford: Oxford University Press, 1996); Ian Brownlie, *Principles of Public International Law* (Oxford: Clarendon Press, 5th ed., 1998).

established without any use of force, without any need for speech, and without the occupation of other lands. In particular, the intention of moral justice is to prevent wars and the violation of rights. The logic of the theory of moral justice is peaceful and contains righteousness in its nature.[53] This means that moral justice, contrary to physical justice, intends to prevent war, atrocities, barbarities, murder, and the destruction of man's civilisation. These are the natural virtues of moral justice.

Consequently, moral justice tries to create possibilities for access to the necessities for all men and prevent destruction. In other words, equal access to all social needs is contained in the inner mechanism of moral justice, and achieving these matters is almost the whole duty of the notion of moral justice. The idea of equal justice is the first element and the first step in its sequence. Since the theory of moral justice does not contain evil provisions, there is no question about how to treat or defeat enemies. Speaking about how to treat or vanquish enemies is all about the particular characterisation of physical justice and its nature. This is why we try to draw out the various natures of physical and moral justice and bring attention to the evil nature of the former in comparison with the latter. The cause of these differences is bound up with the very characterisation of brutality or humanity, each for itself.

Friedrich Nietzsche clearly believed that:

> Justice (reasonableness) has its origin among approximate equals in power, as Thucydides (in the dreadful conferences of the Athenian and Melian envoys) has rightly conceived. Thus, where there is no demonstrable supremacy and a struggle leads to mutual, useless damage, the reflection arises that an understanding would best be arrived at and some compromise entered into. The reciprocal nature is hence the first nature of justice. Each party makes the other content inasmuch as each receives what it prizes more highly than the other. Each surrenders to the other what the other wants and receives, in return, its own desire. Justice is therefore a form of reprisal and exchange on the basis of an approximate equality of power. Thus, revenge pertains originally to the domain of justice, as it is a sort of reciprocity. Equally so, gratitude. Justice reverts naturally to the standpoint of self-preservation, therefore to the egoism of this consideration: "Why should I injure myself to no purpose and perhaps never attain my end?" - So much for the origin of justice. Only because men, through mental habits, have forgotten the

---

[53] Farhad Malekian, Concreting Righteousness in International Criminal Justice (New York, Nova Sciences Publishers, 2024), p. 124-127.

> original motive of so-called just and rational acts, and also because for thousands of years children have been brought to admire and imitate such acts, have they gradually assumed the appearance of being unegotistical. Upon this appearance is founded the high estimate of them, which, moreover, like all estimates, is continually developing, for whatever is highly esteemed is striven for, imitated, and made the object of self-sacrifice, while the merit of the pain and emulation thus expended is, by each individual, ascribed to the thing esteemed. How slightly moral would the world appear without forgetfulness? A poet could say that God had posted forgetfulness as a sentinel at the portal of the temple of human merit![54]

Our approach to justice is characterized by varying expectations. Obviously, with the term justice, we search for a clear understanding of the subject under consideration and whether or not the reasoning presented has roots in the essence of originality, fairness, objectivity, and the creation of equality for human beings both at the time of performance and beyond. It happens often enough, and always with great surprise, that the great powers of the world intimidate others and believe that it is their fault that international crimes such as crimes against humanity, war crimes, genocide, apartheid, torture, and terrorist acts are being committed.[55] They forget and wash their hands of corrupt physical justice and believe that the physical justice that is under their power is not only healthy, but also full of fairness and understanding. It seems to be something both ordinary and immoral in the content of physical justice and its application. The activities of such governments reflect and represent a serious tragedy in international criminal justice.

With this exclamation from the side of strong, powerful governments, the notion of justice, or the body of appropriate and fair justice in the international legal system, has gone through various challenges, and does not permit moral justice to grow within the international arena. The sole reason for this has been to control the wealth of the world and bring other nations under their own monopoly of power. They have no intention of questioning the evil nature of their physical justice and the killing of nations without any restrictions. That is why the nature of physical justice is always under serious question in the

---

[54] Friedrich Nietzsche, Human, All Too Human. https://www.gutenberg.org/files/38145/38145-h/38145-h.htm.

[55] E. S. Reddy, *Apartheid: The United Nations and the International Community* (1986).

national debates of all states in the world. The control and monopolisation of international justice by certain states for their own benefits is especially evident. And in fact, justice seems to be personalized under the power of military decisions. This means that the body of justice has not been approached with fairness and enlightenment of its will, but with the opposite.[56]

2. The Missing Ingredient of Justice

We are forced to look at the questions of justice much more closely in order to understand why the system of moral justice does not function at all. We can clearly see and understand that moral justice is disappearing from the surface of physical justice, even though it is very doubtful that it ever existed in the content of all national legal systems in the first place. This is especially notable with international physical justice, which has always been brutal and has led to many killings. A clear example of this is the situation with Saddam Hussein. Although he was accused of killing a large number of people in his own country, he was certainly not involved in the killing and injuring of millions - which the members of NATO cannot claim. We must then ask: have we reached the stage of humanity promised in the Declaration of Human Rights and the Charter of the United Nations?

The main reason for all these violations is that international declarations and instruments lack humanity. The other missing ingredient within all these international instruments is moral justice, which is the most essential principle for successful physical justice. This is why we have stated that the conflict between physical justice and moral justice is the most important part of the application of international justice.[57] A clear example of this is the fact that the ICC has been involved in the prosecution of African leaders for the crimes they committed in their countries since its establishment, and yet has never prosecuted big, powerful nations. Therefore, as a matter of principle, the ICC functions as a court to punish African nations rather than as a global court. Consequently, it may be argued that a soul for which we look for the spirit of justice has no free spirit in the real definition of the term "justice."

This implies the fact that the completeness of the principles of justice and morality is rarely present in the monopolized or binding provisions of physical

[56] C. Gray, *International Law and the Use of Force*, (2000); Farhad Malekian, *Concreting Righteousness in International Criminal Justice* (New York: Nova publishers, 2024).

[57] Bruce Broomhall, International Justice and the International Criminal Court: Between Sovereignty and the Rule of Law (2004).

justice. Physical justice, and in particular physical international justice, is always limited and presents the will and interests of the most powerful governments. This is one of the main essential reasons why the ICC does not function and cannot bring real criminals under its jurisdiction which includes individuals or governments.[58] This is why we see most Africans as violators of the systems of international criminal justice and international human rights law. However, the real criminals and the real governments committing serious international criminal violations against the rights of Africans are not in Africa and instead include nations such as France. Our conclusions are based on the assumption of the provisions of physical international justice. The fact is that the criminal hands of the political policies of those nations that have colonized African nations for centuries are behind all of the crimes that the population of Africa has committed against each other. The colonisation of African nations is still ongoing despite the artificial decolonisation that took place decades ago.

It is evident that the concept of physical justice and its actual nature are interwoven with choices and patronising qualities, depending on the government. In other words, the implementation of justice in the international legal system is not really a question of correct performance or the duty of the international criminal courts, but rather the choice between criminal conduct on one side and criminal conduct on the other. Thus, any notion of morality in the system of contemporary international criminal justice is meaningless and impossible to see. It also means that we involuntary recognize norms and practices because of the desire of the big powers to monopolize the body of justice at any price. All this indicates a dangerous curiosity concerning the economic sources of other nations. This is why the theory of physical justice contradicts the essence of moral justice. Additionally, this policy of physical justice is also a serious problem that could even destroy the promotion of justice. As a result, an independent notion of justice that is not controlled or influenced by the wills and interests of the big, powerful nations is rare and cannot be met.

The strength and will for self-protection and keeping the value of *somebodiness* of various nations decreases, and as a result, the nations of the

---

[58] R. Rosenstock, 'An International Criminal Responsibility of States?,' in United Nations/International Law Commission (ed.), *International Law on the Eve of the Twenty-First Century: Views from the International Law Commission* (United Nations New York, 1997), pp. 265–85.

world feel that they are in a state of *nobodiness* as it concerns justice.[59] This signifies that the sense of moral justice dies, and henceforth, the provisions of physical justice gain strength, the powerful dominate the weak, and the rules are imposed by the strong nations of the world. This is why moral justice suffers under the pressure of a sardonic laugh from the great powers. Therefore, they execute their criminal plan stealthily and are able to convince the majority of the world that they are fighting against terrorist groups or nations, while in reality, the real terrorists are the ones delivering physical international criminal justice with the power of their guns while calling it a lawful use of force.

3. Efficient Autonomy of Morality

Physical justice is sometimes the most dangerous form of justice because it can extinguish all forms of moral justice for its own benefit and annihilate a civilisation as a result.[60] *Governments commit the most forbidden acts in the system of justice to violate moral justice.[61] In this way, physical justice becomes the reason for the lack of morality in the world and ultimately controls the wealth it needs. Such reflections of physical justice not only (miss) guide the spirit of moral justice, they also increase violence and controversy in the system of our artificial human rights - which is solely based on one-eyed justice.[62]*

We should not forget that all nations have the same rights, even the militarily strong nations. Politics should not destroy or modify the societies of men that have a united essence for the purpose of promoting their common advantage and safety. This means that human nature and its development are both based on a joint venture. Any political power or government that fights

---

[59] Farhad Malekian, *International Criminal Law, the Law of Somebodiness, the Law of Nobodiness* (New York: Nova Science Publishers, 2021).

[60] On morality examine P. M. S. Hacker and J. Raz, (eds.), Law, *Morality and Society: Essays in Honour of H. L. A. Hart* (1977); Farhad Malekian, *Classical Morality in International Peremptory Criminal Law* (Newcastle: Cambridge Scholars Publishing, 2021); Joseph Raz, *Ethics in the Public Domain: Essays in the Morality of Law and Politics* (Oxford: Oxford University Press, 1994); Joseph Raz, *The Morality of Freedom* (1986); Robert Vischer K., *Martin Luther King Jr. and the Morality of Legal Practice: Lessons in Love and Justice* (2014).

[61] *Id.*

[62] *Id.*

to take over this interconnected union of man is not only the enemy of their own nation, but also the opponent of mankind.

The international society of men has norms that are based on the development of the conditions of all men and not just on a particular nation of government. *This means that we deliberate and adopt resolutions in the common interest of all societies; if this were not true, then we should not have established the United Nations. If this were not a fact, then we should not have adopted and ratified a large number of international conventions on the rights of man. If this is not reality, then we should not promote the idea that we must struggle for the establishment of moral justice in the content of those international conventions, the Charter of the UN, and particularly the resolutions of the Security Council and General Assembly. This means that moral justice aims at strengthening the moral attitudes of men against immoral and unjust physical justice. All these legal treaties, resolutions, protocols, and pacts are unique and susceptible to obligations and rights.*

In contrast to the idea of physical justice, the notion of moral justice is a science that imparts and communicates the rights within the inner structure of the universal natural rights of man, which I call moral justice, working against any provisions of physical justice that it intends to destroy. From here it follows that there are specific obligations for all states and their governments to regulate all their decisions in such a way that they do not violate the moral substance of the necessary obligations of humanity, justice, and respect. The theory of moral justice is very simple and understandable and not subject to various multiple interpretations. Men are forced to live with full dignity, and this force is nothing but the force of love for the distribution of moral justice.[63] Whenever we violate the real definition of morality, the force of love is ignored, and physical justice becomes the real substance for the demonisation of the power of moral justice.[64] This means that governments provide incorrect, malicious information in order to destroy and dismantle the value of moral justice. In order to establish the obligations and rights of all men on earth on a solid basis, we need to disarm physical justice and promote justice with the principles of equality and morality. This is the real reason for having various legal statutes.

We must remember that rights, fairness, justice, and righteousness reflect nothing more than the supremacy of doing what is morally possible and

---

[63] Farhad Malekian, 'The Canon of Love against the Use of Force in Islamic and Public International Law: Part II: The Anatomy of Love Against Violations,' 15 *International Criminal Law Review*, 2015), pp. 861-895.

[64] *Id.*

logical.[65] Thus, when we are only applying physical justice, we have not done something extraordinary, rather we have done what is right according to our sense of humanity and the duty to fulfil our moral rights. But what is appropriate and reliable according to our duties? It is obvious that rights are derived from particular obligations, whether for ourselves or for others. Thus when we have rights, we also have obligations that match. It is therefore necessary that physical justice not only requires obligations, but also mutually provides rights. Naturally, we need to acquire sufficient knowledge of the obligations incumbent on us and also on others. Without understanding our own obligations, we cannot demand rights based on the duties of others to physical or moral justice. We are therefore obliged to avoid all acts that are categorized as violations by moral justice—even if they are permitted by physical justice

Similar views can be expressed about the principles, elements, and obligations of the United Nations Charter, which means that moral justice requires respect for those obligations and physical justice should not adopt those obligations for its own benefit. Therefore, confirming the need for the righteous application of those obligations in the Charter is the duty of all members, which naturally points to the permanent members of the Security Council. However, as previously stated, the most frequent violators of those obligations are the permanent members, in particular the United States and the United Kingdom.[66] By virtue of the applicable obligations which are determined by the Charter itself, the permanent members are responsible for the prevention of the commission of international crimes and systematic violations of the body of international human rights.

They have particular legal, moral, and even oral obligations not to neglect obligations that are significant to the prevention of apartheid and discrimination.[67] Beyond all this, they have full responsibility to not hinder the self-determination of nations suffering under the illegal and immoral physical justice of the colonial powers. That is why the Charter encourages the settlement of international disputes through peaceful methods and the prevention of the implementation of unlawful physical force or physical

---

[65] Farhad Malekian, *Concreting Righteousness in International Criminal Justice* (New York, Nova Sciences Publishers, 2024).

[66] Andreas Schueller, The ICC, British War Crimes in Iraq and a Very British Tradition, https://opiniojuris.org/2020/12/11/the-icc-british-war-crimes-in-iraq-and-a-very-british-tradition/; see also https://www.icc-cpi.int/sites/default/files/itemsDocuments/201209-otp-final-report-iraq-uk-eng.pdf.

[67] J. K. Feimpong & S. Azadon Tiewel, 'Can Apartheid Successfully Defy the International Legal System?' 5 *The Black Law Journal* (1977), pp. 287-311.

justice. The Charter, therefore, has established a mechanism for settling disputes that ensures the proper implementation and application of the provisions of the charter for the establishment of the rights of victims. It is therefore important to respect the basic principles of the Charter and not create an adverse effect on the self-sufficiency or autonomy of the Charter, including the body of international law concerning authentic principles due to the requirements of certain key principles of the system of international law.

4. Convulsion of Physical Justice

We may be ordered to carry out certain acts that are, according to physical justice, correct and essential for the implementation of justice, but which are not in accordance with moral justice under the authority of physical justice. A clear example of this arises when the system of physical justice orders the application of capital punishment, which is also basically permitted in the provisions of the statute of criminal law. The performance of such punishment is fundamentally wrong and cannot be accepted. The performance of such an order of the law violates the provisions of the moral law, and therefore fundamentally has no value. As a result, we should avoid executing any legal order that is against certain rights. We should be aware of the fact that the principles of physical justice are made up of man-made law, but the natural rights of man are not selective and should also not be selected. *The intention of selectivity was condemned in a letter addressed to the Prosecutor of the ICC by several individuals, including Noam Chomsky, Moncef Marzouki, Rashid Khalid, Ilan Pappe, Sarah Leah-Whitson, and Avi Shlaim. Their strong condemnation stemmed from the prosecutor's approach towards crimes committed by the criminal powertionist governments of Israel against the Palestinians. "Many of us had hoped that the ICC investigation, started under your predecessor, would continue under your leadership. However, despite mounting evidence of crimes committed by the Israeli regime, your office has apparently taken no further action," said the signatories. "Since you assumed the position as the Chief Prosecutor of the International Criminal Court, no one has heard anything from you on the Palestinian case, while your office announced speedy investigations into the alleged war crimes committed by*

Russia during its ongoing war against Ukraine, and issued an arrest warrant for President of Russia Vladimir Putin."[68]

It is known that physical justice must be fair within the constitutions of all nations and, as a general rule, it must be identical with the purposes of human rights conventions, i.e., the basic principles of moral justice. When physical justice violates these essential constitutional principles of justice, which are natural, the basis of the law consequently collapses and crumbles into pieces of unacceptable physical justice. In addition to our previous example of capital punishment, there are numerous other examples, such as torture, unlawful imprisonment, the imposition of sanctions to kill, and forced displacement. Consequently, the arbitrary decision of a strong government against a nation cannot be regarded as valid by moral justice or physical justice.

Therefore, all men not only inherit rights and duties from the natural law or moral justice as a whole, but they also inherit them from the legal bodies of international human rights and any other international conventions dealing either directly or indirectly with human rights. Whether the body of physical justice and its authorities want it or not, there are certain inherited rights in the bodies of physical justice that have to obey certain obligations. Thus, even if we suppose that physical justice is independent from the principles and spirit of moral justice, those who perform the orders of physical justice are not. Therefore, a subject of physical justice cannot escape from their duties and responsibilities by arguing that they do not depend on moral justice norms.[69] In other words, we may be exempt from moral duties because of the order and power of physical justice. However, this exemption does not have a permanent role in the nature of our moral duties and we cannot forgive our crimes because the order or performance was made in accordance with the provisions of physical justice.

Thus, those who are involved in the enforcement of evil physical justice, which is in violation of the principles of human rights, international conventions, and particularly the body of moral justice, must be held criminally responsible under the relevant jurisdictions of the law. This is regardless of the fact that the relevant physical law has the power to enforce the provisions of the law. This means that any constitutional physical justice that violates the principles of moral justice is certainly responsible for all

[68] See ICC: pressure mounts on prosecutor to open probe into Israel war crimes (Israel, Middle East, News; June 13, 2023), https://www.middleeastmonitor.com/20230613-icc-pressure-mounts-on-prosecutor-to-open-probe-into-israel-war-crimes/.

[69] Farhad Malekian, *International Criminal Vacations: Tears of Justice* (New York: Nova Science Publishers, 2024).

violations, even if those violations are never prosecuted. The purpose of the motivation for prosecution is to prevent further violations and confess to the rights of the victims who have been the target of unlawful provisions of physical justice.

Moreover, when we speak about moral justice, which is absolutely free and independent with respect to all limitations created by physical justice, we are dealing with the body of the righteousness of justice. All men are subject to the laws of nature, i.e., moral justice, which in turn are independent of the obligations that have been drafted and established by any political, social, or other collective power. Since the rights and obligations of man are interrelated and cannot be separated from one another, we must therefore apply similar rules and obligations to all men concerning certain fundamental rights. That is why when we speak about the provisions of international human rights, we express that they have universally binding effect and are obligatory for all man-made powers.

Accordingly, we do not need to discover what the rights of all men are, but rather what the obligations of all governments are. Our governments thus ought to respect the provisions of moral justice and not argue or bargain for the mitigation of their obligations. Consequently, the body of moral justice law is simply the body of physical justice, insofar as the latter follows the provisions and the spirit of the former. This is because the application of the rules of moral justice is based on reasonableness, unless it is forced to change its direction by the unjust provisions of physical justice. Moral justice is precisely the same in every case and is not subject to different arguments. However, physical justice is often another subject of a quite different nature. There are therefore many cases in which physical justice may not be able to make decisions, except by force - which is naturally illegal. We must therefore know how to accommodate the application of the provisions of physical justice that should not violate the basic or moral essence of the law. Consequently, any arbitrary decision by authorities who enforce physical justice through different acts of violations, atrocities, barbarity, and brutalities is null and void and should not be respected at the national, regional, or international levels.

5. The Elephant of Physical Justice

The study of the philosophy of physical justice or the science of ethical justice based on constitutional or legislative boundaries presumes a familiarity with the principles of moral justice. This is what we assume physical law to be and what the constitutional provisions are. However, it is the influence of political authorities that proves the power of gravity in the system of physical justice in the end. Nevertheless, for the sake of those moral requirements of justice, there are certain provisions on the surface of physical justice that appear to protect the moral aspect of the law. When one looks systematically at the policies of almost all physical laws in the world, it will appear that it would not be remiss to say that all physical laws are driven by the control of power. This is particularly clear concerning dictatorial regimes.

The aforementioned policy is much more evident in international relations and when examining the greed of a government. There is essentially no hope of seeing any moral approach to the system of international criminal justice or international human rights. All the references to the system of international human rights are actually a form of political industry and present the axiom of incontestable lies and untruth. It is by virtue of moral justice that one can believe that the notion of fairness constitutes an integral part of justice. When physical justice does not have any sense of morality at the time of its performance, then speaking about the health of moral justice is rather unprofessional. This misuse of the faculty of justice, particularly in the case of international justice, has been clearly documented. Big political governments with different military and political strategies take the ties of international obligations with physical and moral justice under their control and interpret them to their benefit.[70]

We may then deduce that the principles of human rights presented by the big powers in the territory of other nations are correct, as the atmosphere of the situation gives such an impression. While the principles of international human rights were not drafted to be used for propaganda and politics, that is what happens in practice. A clear example of this is the provisions of the United Nations Charter, which aim to support human rights law through different meanings and terms, while in reality, the footprints of the colonial powers are still in the territories of their colonies. In order to create a new form of colonialisation using the norms of human rights, they have succeeded in crafting the most perfect provisions of human rights, human justice, non-discrimination, abolition of apartheid, and many others. This is how they use

[70] Farhad Malekian, *Trading Virginity of International Criminal Justice* (Nova Sciences Publishers, 2020); Farhad Malekian, 'Emasculating the Philosophy of International Criminal Justice in the Iraqi Special Tribunal,' *Cornell International Law Journal*, 58/5 (2005), pp. 677-678.

the framework of human rights in the name of justice and then reach their old colonial goals with new provisions that present their physical justice.[71]

There is no doubt that the sublime consideration of international human rights provisions misguides the general population, as it has done since the establishment of the UN. This practice consequently has misled the global population. All these disputes concerning physical justice fall within the scope of moral justice, although such disputes do not relate to the interpretation of the basic main requirements of moral justice. It is this propaganda machinery of international human rights that then enters the apparatus of international physical justice. However, we must emphasize that this process of justice is deliberately slow in achieving its goals and with being consistent with what it claims to be. As a result, there is no real sense of movement based on the fact that human rights provisions are monopolized and are not independent of the political decisions of their real directors.

6. Refusals of Physical Justice

Under this new system of international physical justice presented by the United Nations Charter, all evil notions of authoritarianism, domination, monopolisation, and mastery of military powers over physical justice, moral justice, and evidently human rights justice can be seen. Unfortunately, they are necessary for the specific development of power politics in moral justice. This means that the notion of morality is completely invalid. All this together constitutes and presents the physical justice of international society as dictated by the Security Council to others as an integral part of moral justice. At the end of the day, the elephant of physical justice is in the Council and no one can do anything about it as long as the power of the gun is guided by those who have monopolized the terms of justice as was seen in the Gulf Crisis in 1991.[72] There are rules and provisions concerning the use of force against nations, however their application is not allowed by the spirit of moral justice and is rejected entirely.

---

[71] Consult *Paris Declaration, International Conference on Sanctions Against South Africa (And Special Declaration on Namibia),* 27 May1981, Published by the United Nations Center Against Apartheid.

[72] Examine Farhad Malekian, *Condemning the Use of Force in the Gulf Crisis* (Almqvist & Wiksell International, 1st ed., 1992). James E. Hickey, *Challenges to Security Council Monopoly Power over the Use of Force in Enforcement Actions: The Case of Regional Organisations*, 10 Ius Gentium 75 (2004).

Nevertheless, this is not of any interest to the big governments. A clear example is the French government, which is the most brutal colonial government in Africa and still has political power there. The French government promotes propaganda about human rights norms in the name of democracy in Africa. This is one of the serious problems with modern human rights and its use against Africans. It would appear that it is only through the decisions of big powers that human rights are expressed, explained, and defined. As previously mentioned, while on the one hand we believe that Africans are free and independent from the traditional consequences of colonialisation, on the other hand they are still living under the conditions of slavery. The influence of the French government is particularly obvious when it comes to the murder of African leaders, such as Gaddafi. Similar problems of the monopolisation of physical justice can be seen with the American system of justice, which has supported the total destruction of the Middle East and the initiation of various wars in the name of human rights principles.

In addition, the French government has carried out the most heinous crimes against African nations. All violations of moral justice have been seen, and even simple rights in the vocabulary of physical justice are violated by all means. Thus, both notions of justice, i.e., physical and moral have been violated. Although the conduct of these big political and criminal governments is made in the name of implementing fairness and righteousness at a higher level, the facts prove the contrary.[73] The killing of the Libyan leader was planned long in advance because Gaddafi wanted to free Africa from colonialisation and establish an independent African continental sovereignty, such that the African nations would have the control over their oil, gold, and uranium instead of the superpowers or Western nations. His views were independent of his power over the entire country. Gaddafi idea was not welcome by Western authorities and was even opposed by certain African leaders who were the puppets of Western governments because they wanted to keep their political positions and impose their own physical justice despite enslaving their own population to Western countries. This indicates that moral justice was killed and monopolized physical justice was presented as moral justice. This also means that justice is not compatible with moral justice. The consistent application of rules is affected by inconsistent decisions about physical justice.

---

[73] Farhad Malekian, *Concreting Righteousness in International Criminal Justice* (New York, Nova Sciences Publishers, 2024).

We see that physical justice refuses to respect the integrity of man at different stages of the evolution of human civilisation because of our personal or political interests, which are always prioritized. Thus, while we may appreciate the nature of animals at all times, we may also kill a large number of human beings at one point. We are used to killing human beings in the millions and acting out our animal nature at the same time. My example may not seem eristic, but we have violated the full essence of humanity rather than for searching for truth. I am not degrading the nature of animals in my comparison, rather just the animal nature of man that is acting as animal and animal as human in lieu of its own character. In other words, the advantages that endow mankind with the substantive faculties of morality are essentially insignificant when it comes to the real practice and prevention of immorality in its nature and conduct. We are here referring to the capability of man to acquire moral justice only to reject it with the sole intention of earning a profit.

7. Harshest Physical Justice

Physical justice should be the consequence of the laws of conscience that have the intention of encouraging morality and avoiding the use of force and brutality against their subjects. The reason for regulating laws, constitutions, and legal statutes is not to have a series of rules, obligations, and duties. Rather, the intention is to come to a certain decision, action, or judgment, which can bring our immoral conduct into question. This is why certain conducts are considered to be illegal and condemnable by moral justice. Additionally, the laws of conscience that are considered significant in the legal philosophy of justice should naturally be developed from the notion of moral justice and be an integral part of the legal discipline. This means that legal authorities should express their consent to the provisions of righteous justice. They are bound to acquiesce to the basic meaning of justice and not prejudice one side against another.

Moreover, we should look for the notion of liberty in the foundations of all definitions of justice and not remain on the side of the violators of the law. That is why there is a significant difference between moral justice, physical justice, and the notion of legal discipline. In short, we should protest and not find the false statements of the political authorities to be lawful and enforceable for the victims of the unlawful use of force by the brutal governments, such as in Palestine.[74] Any assumption that justice should be performed contrary to moral justice is also contrary to the natural rights of man and should be condemned. Even though every nation is free to make their own decisions concerning the rule of law and justice, the independence of national physical justice does not grant permission to escape from the moral requirements of justice.[75]

Moreover, moral justice helps us measure the level of goodness and badness in a legal system, which is particularly significant in the case of physical justice. A national physical justice system that violates the universal needs or *jus gentium* of man is certainly against moral justice, and therefore its activities, decisions, and conduct must be questioned. This is regardless of the fact that national physical justice is acting under its own legal statute and not any other imaginable rules or regulations. However, we should remember that all laws and regulations are independent as long as they do not violate the primary requirements of international human rights laws. If this were not the case, then why did we codify a large number of provisions in human rights law? Certainly, our intent is to validate a large number of provisions in the international system that exclusively deals with the system of international human rights. We therefore also had the intention of creating certain obligations that should be followed by all nations, both big and small.

Furthermore, although we are free and independent of all requirements of the constitutions of other countries, there is still a certain obligation within the national laws of all nations that should be named physical human rights or, in the higher stages of interpretation, obligatory moral justice. This indicates the presence of a notion of justice that understands all laws and is familiar with all legal systems of jurisdiction. All nations dealing with physical justice realize that we cannot punish a child, even if we have proof that they committed a crime. This is because the sense of moral justice speaks about certain matters that have collective bounds between all nations, and the criminal legislation of all nations should recognize the fact that a young child cannot be held responsible or accountable for actions that they did not know the consequences of or actions that they did not know amounted to a crime.

---

[74] Examine Farhad Malekian, *Paralysing International Criminal Justice* (New York: Nova Science Publishers, 2021).

[75] Getting away results in impunity, and taking a vacation after committing barbaric international crimes also results in impunity. Examine William Schabas A., Justice, Democracy and Impunity in Post Genocide Rwanda: Searching for Solutions to Impossible Problems, 7 Criminal Law Forum (1996); Benjamin Ferencz B. 'Ending Impunity for the Crime of Aggression,' 41 Case W. Res. J, (2009), pp. 281-290.

Even the strictest form of physical justice must have certain limits concerning the attribution of criminal responsibility and the identification of criminal conduct.[76]

Although the aforementioned theory may be accepted or rejected by various parties, it is fundamentally true that we kill children through our international conduct.[77] Even in the application of international physical justice, we have been much more dangerous and brutal in the performance of our criminal decisions. A clear example of this is the killing of many innocent children by the Nazis during the Second World War.[78] According to various records, the Nazis killed a large number of children and called it a performance of physical justice.[79] Further examples include the killing of children in Vietnam, Afghanistan, Syria, Palestine, and Rwanda. Additionally, over the last nine months, the Israeli Zionist government has killed over 20,000 Palestinian children.[80]

---

[76] R. Rosenstock, 'An International Criminal Responsibility of States?,' in United Nations/International Law Commission (ed.), *International Law on the Eve of the Twenty-First Century: Views from the International Law Commission* (United Nations New York, 1997), pp. 265–85; Davis C. Michael, Dietrich Wolfgang, Bettina Schoolman and Sepp Dieter, *International Intervention in the Post-Cold War World: Moral Responsibility and Power Politics* (M. E. Sharpe, Inc., 2003); Farhad Malekian, *International Criminal Responsibility of States: A Study on the Evolution of International Responsibility of States with particular Emphasis on the Concept of Crime and Criminal Responsibility* (Stockholm, 1985); Farhad Malekian, *'International Criminal Responsibility,'* in *International Criminal Law* (M. Cherif Bassiouni, 2[ed], ed., 1999); Farhad Malekian, 'International Criminal Responsibility: International Criminal Responsibility of Individuals' in M. Cherif Bassiouni, *International Criminal Law,* Vol. *Crimes* (2[ed], ed., New York: Transnational Publishers, 1999); Martti Koskenniemi, 'Solidarity Measures: State Responsibility as a New International Order?' 72 *British Yearbook of International Law* (2001), pp. 337–56.

[77] On the law protecting the rights of children consult Farhad Malekian, *International Criminal Law of Children* (New York: Nova Science Publishers, 2021); Farhad Malekian, 'Prohibition Governing Child Soldiers Constituting an Integral Part of *Jus Cogens* and *Obligatio Erga Omnes*,' XVII World Congress of the International Association of Youth and Family Judges and Magistrates, Belfast, Northern Ireland, 27 August – 2 September (2006); Farhad Malekian, 'Conundrums of *Jus Cogens*: In Case Law' (Part II), No. 13 *Вісник Південного регіонального центру Національної академії правових наук України,* [No. 13 Journal of the South regional Center of National Academy of Legal Sciences of Ukraine] (2017), pp. 12-21; Farhad Malekian, 'Conundrums of *Jus Cogens*: in International Criminal Law' (Part I), *Вісник Південного регіонального центру Національної академії правових наук України* [No. 12 Journal of the South regional Center of National Academy of Legal Sciences of Ukraine] (2017), pp. 8-16.

[78] See Judgment of the International Military Tribunal at Nuremberg, 1 Trial of the Major War Criminals Before the International Military Tribunal, 365-66 (1947).

[79] *Id.*

[80] See Farhad Malekian, *Paralysing International Criminal Justice* (New York: Nova Science Publishers, 2021).

This is actually how we violate not only the system of national physical justice, but also that of international physical justice, both of which are against the high values of moral justice, which in turn should be respected at all times. When physical justice violates moral justice, it violates the essential nature of man, which should be respected by all men. However, focusing on the strength of moral justice does not work and is actually an injunction obtained from the order of physical justice, which is unfortunately not rejected by the national or international authorities. An example of this is the office of the prosecutor of the ICC, which is not only silent about the crimes committed against the Palestinians, but barely functions concerning its legal duties.[81] Obviously, we do not need to present more evidence of the brutality of the crimes committed against the Palestinians since the present events are evidence enough. The ICC practice has been too slow and too tardy to witness clear evidence of truth.

8. Realizing the Truth

The serious question here does not concern why the systems of physical justice or international physical justice are not successful in reaching their intentions, rather the very question of the mentality of man against their own united essence. Even though we suppose that man is incapable of understanding moral justice or justice as a whole, man should realize that all men have the same rights and the same basic needs. This realisation must be based on the wisdom of man. Even though we assume that man is not wise, even a fish realizes that they live together with other fish and that their existence is dependent on those fish. We cannot have a good life and address our needs without the existence of our essential nature. This is what the morality of the law, i.e., moral justice, requires from all its subjects. This point is particularly significant as it concerns righteousness in the moral philosophy of man.

Consequently, man is dependent on other men, who in turn are dependent on the existence of physical justice and the implementation and respect of morality for all that we call independent moral justice. The common law of all societies of man is therefore connected to this philosophy of existence, and without full respect for the theory of this philosophy, man is diminished. Therefore, every individual in every nation is connected to the central definition of humanity, which in turn is essential for the happiness and health

---

[81] See Farhad Malekian, *Conscience of Prosecutors in International Criminal Law, the Heart of the Matter* (New York: Nova Science Publishers, 2021).

of the community of nations. All these views present our own safety and common interests. In general, it is obligations bind the vast majority of nations in the world, not the major powers. Moral justice binds us to the observance of our duties at all times.

In other words, moral justice represents safety for all men, and it is the tool used against physical justice that threatens the integrity of humankind. This means that we should properly fulfil all moral requirements. If we did not care about these requirements, we would finally see our situation, and this is neither good nor recommended. Let us therefore attempt to promote the general joy of all mankind. It is easy to recognize what an exalted moral principle has for the good of all nations and the protection of their existence. Even though we suppose we do not want to share happiness with all nations, we should not take their happiness away through slaughter, destruction, and the plundering of their natural resources.

Moral justice promotes down justice for all, while physical justice that is not independent is harmful and cannot encourage wisdom in its subjects. Therefore, it is obvious that universal moral justice constitutes justice for all human races, regardless of their differences, i.e., *jus gentium*. This is why trust in the international physical justice of certain powers threatens the existence of wisdom and the establishment of a peaceful existence for the substance of humanity. The fact is that moral justice rejects violations and the commission of national or international crimes, while the notion of physical justice may demand more violations and inhumanity. This is why we use international physical justice for our own purposes in tandem with the power of guns and the commission of international crimes.

The function and enforcement of the system of international human rights may be encroached upon when it does not act for the protection of its subjects, particularly with reference to the body of international criminal justice. Although the system of international human rights exists, it is still suspended because of the particular approaches that powerful governments take. As a result, an effective system of justice is reduced to a state of imperfection. This indicates that the law does not follow its own rules, but rather the politics of the big, powerful governments. The system of international criminal justice becomes uncontrolled and entangled in the wills of certain governments. As a result, we perpetually confuse the situation of human rights and its intention to establish justice.

Due to this, we follow the structure of a system of human rights that is the result of the most trifling similarities that are lectured by those who are the masters of physical justice or who have its mechanism of application under their own control. Thus, moral capability to present reason for the better fulfilment of justice and prevention of harsh physical justice fails. We ignore the fact that the principles of justice should stem from the same set of truthful reasons during the process of development and implementation. While no formal rules are needed for the presentation of justice, except for the truth, there a lack of willingness to consolidate the proceedings of justice under the control of physical justice, and as a result, the face of the truth is hidden by lies, and its enforcement is consequently suspended. The desire for justice to be seen becomes unsuccessful. Overall, physical justice is unwilling to agree on consolidating the needs of moral justice, and the situation causes unbalance in national or international matters. We are even breaking the rule of complementarity in international criminal law.[82]

9. Autonomous Explanation of Justice

It may not be wrong to assert that the system of physical justice usually gains support from criminals. Additionally, the body of physical justice is often controlled by authorities that should be in the service of the law instead of serving their own interests. As previously mentioned, a clear example of this is the structure of the Security Council, which is supposed to be in the service of nations, however it is in the service of those who should serve it in order for a proper system of international physical justice to be applied. The same attitude exists regarding the imposition of international criminal justice, as we have witnessed on a number of occasions in instances where the system of international law is supposed to be applied to certain leaders who have grossly violated international law, but it is not. Of course, this is the case when powertionist governments are involved.

The example of the Saddam Tribunal, which was an American-made salami in reality, with the difference that it was not cut or served in Italy or

[82] William W. Burke-White, 'Implementing a Policy of Positive Complementarity in the Rome System of Justice,' 19 *Criminal Law Forum*, (2008), 59-89; Ondřej Svaček, 'The Human Rights Dimension of the ICC's Complementarity Regime,' *Czech Yearbook of Public and Private International Law*, 2015, Vol. 6, pp. 273-288; S. Fouladvand, *Complementarity and Cultural Sensitivity: Decision-making by the International Criminal Court (ICC) Prosecutor in Relation to the Situations in the Darfur Region of the Sudan and the Democratic Republic of Congo* (DRC), (2012). Kevin Jon Heller, 'The Shadow Side of Complementarity: The Effect of Article 17 of the Rome Statute on National Due Process,' 17 *Criminal Law Forum* (2006), available at file:///C:/Users/admin/AppData/Local/Temp/SSRN-id907404.pdf.

the United States but under Iraqi legislation, and was used to confuse the world of moral justice and pretend that physical justice was acting as moral justice.[83] In this case, physical justice was employed as the master key of private justice and led to the death of an individual who could have presented a powerful testimony before an international criminal court in The Hague. Thus, confusion and a lack of eligible international organisations available to control the case led to the deaths of millions. The political power that controlled international physical justice invented habitual lies under the process of justice - the savagery of which has not been forgotten. Physical justice marked its brutality with lies and nonsense, invaluable legal statements from sheer exhaustion, in order to take the rights of others.

Moreover, the implementation of physical international criminal justice with the complicity of a number of governments, such as Great Britain and France, confirmed our theory that physical justice is under the control of militarily powerful governments. Physical justice is dangerous and infringes on the peaceful sphere of moral justice. This was also seen in Abu-Ghraib prison and throughout Iraq. Despite this, the brutal torture and slaughter of 600,000 people was commended by the physical justice of the powerful nations, both regionally and internationally.[84] Certainly, we all remember this savage and atrocity of the United States, United Kingdom, and France.[85] This situation reflects the inadequacy of distinction and error in judgments contained in the theory of physical justice, smashing in pieces the theory of moral justice and, as a result, ignoring the facts.[86]

In addition, the preposterous idea of the system of international physical justice is even more wrong when the system appears to function properly for powertionist governments and only condemns those who are on the hit-list of the powerful nations.[87] The simple question then is: who is really preparing

---

[83] Marc Weller, *Iraq and the Use of Force in International Law* (Oxford: Oxford University Press, 2010); Christian P. , Scherrer, *Iraq: Genocide by Sanctions* (2011); Ramsey Clark, *War Crimes - A Report on United States War Crimes against Iraq* (Maisonneuve Press, 1992); Farhad Malekian, *Trading Virginity of International Criminal Justice* (Nova Sciences Publishers, 2020); Farhad Malekian, 'Emasculating the Philosophy of International Criminal Justice in the Iraqi Special Tribunal,' *Cornell International Law Journal*, 58/5 (2005), pp. 677-678.

[84] Farhad Malekian, 'Emasculating the Philosophy of International Criminal Justice in the Iraqi Special Tribunal,' *Cornell International Law Journal*, 58/5 (2005).

[85] *Id.*

[86] The Special Iraqi War Tribunal neglected this fact concerning the barbaric crimes committed by Americans. ***Id.***

[87] Farhad Malekian, *Powertionism in International Criminal Justice* (New York: Nova Science Publishers, 2022).

those lists of international criminals, and why is the theory of physical justice being sold? I am not here to present the plea of *tu quoque*. Certainly, it is unacceptable. But the important question is how can those who plan the most dangerous crimes against the civilisation of man, kill millions of people, and have power over the visible and invisible parts of the system of international criminal justice still claim to be innocent? The savagery of their conduct casts a shadow of permanent darkness in the house of the victims. Are we really protecting the rights of victims of international criminal justice? Are we really leaving the provisions of international human rights out with our dirty physical justice of political laundry? Obviously, I am not searching for a specific answer, but we have to acknowledge that we are ignoring the magnificent picture of moral justice entirely due to our inability to be wise and accept that moral justice looks for purity and purity searches for truthfulness.

We clearly recall a dream of a child who had a home and parents. We surely cannot listen to the situation of the victims and still believe we are right since we have arrested and killed a criminal while ignoring the fact that we caused the situation in the first place in the pursuit of our interests, and consequently modified the existence of moral substance in the terms of physical justice. We are certainly taking the wrong steps and we believe these steps should be accepted since we want to bring the theory of justice under our control in order to control the resources of other countries and dream about taking other nations as our own. Due to the implicit faith the victims have in their own dreams, they are going to have control over their properties and plundered rights one day. However, the theory of physical justice turns a blind eye to the facts and hopes that its lies concerning equalities will not be seen.

If the notion of moral justice cannot be seen as more than a matter of physical justice requirements, and if physical justice does not respect certain principles, then the violations of the basic reasons for justice do not exist. Power politics is the only moral tool that powertionist governments have, and it is the only tool that is the subject of discussions and contradictions in the system of justice. This means we are fighting between the consequences of moral justice and physical justice without achieving any result. The conditions that we have created with the system of international human rights law are so painful and dangerous that even earlier generations of mankind could not have foreseen their consequences due to the rapid advancement of the weapons industry.[88] The fact is that international human rights are only found in hallucinations described in the UN Declaration but not in practice.[89]

[88] Examine J. Dhanapala, *Under-Secretary-General for Disarmament Affairs United Nations, International Law, Security, and Weapons of Mass Destruction*, (New York, 9 May 2002).

[89] Farhad Malekian, *Condemning the Use of Force in the Gulf Crisis* (Almqvist & Wiksell International, 1st ed., 1992).

Chapter 4

Provocative Roles of Physical Justice

1. Pleading for Justice

Our system of international criminal justice harms the nervous system of moral justice and provokes the statutes of international human rights and international conventions that deal with justice and humanity. Indeed, the constant agitation in the system of human rights in practice clearly indicates the absence of morality in our legal system and its various painful wounds - not only in the bodies and hearts of the victims, but also in the mental body of moral justice, which suffers as a result of the conduct of powerful governments. This has certainly not been the purpose of international criminal justice, nor of human rights conventions. Although almost all of the organs of international criminal justice should act independently and intensely for the victims, they are doing the opposite and instead engaging in the commission of serious international crimes. The blood of the victims has been spilled, and yet we are still thinking about our profit and positions or titles that we have received from our kings without taking the fact that they are stained with the blood of millions of victims. What is wrong with our positions, thoughts, and judgments that causes us to give privilege to the principles of evil and disregard the principles of moral justice? We should understand

> There is no difference between Jews, Muslims, Christians, Buddhists, Baha'i, and the people of any other religion in the world. Everyone is equal regarding their heritage and entry into the heaven of God, and in terms of justice and love. The disappearance of love in theory would surely kill the entire goodness of God's philosophy. *Ergo*, if the love of God means killing, let us arrest the God of all Gods and bring him before the ICC for the crimes he has committed with full *mens rea* in the name of Gods. If this does not work, then we – in the name of justice, in the name of peace, and on behalf of the United Nations Security Council – should announce that God is condemned to die by crucifixion for all the atrocities and brutalities committed in his name with the intent of carrying out his cruel theory.

> *The murder of God would certainly bring peace, and take away the need for the ICC and, ultimately, vanquish our cruel Declaration to commit genocide against the Palestinians. Then God himself would have committed genocide against all members of the group, no one would live, and the United States and the government of Israel would have reached the greatest extent of their inhumanity, justice, and peace. Is this the heaven promised to us by Jesus and Mohammed, achieved through the Security Council and the instruments of human rights law?*
>
> *Here, I have certainly wrestled* with *my* faith, with my heart, with the rights of indigenous people, with the rights of Palestinians, and with the rights of our Gods. I am certain that if there is one God, He is the same for all people, and does not approve of violations of the system of international criminal law and justice. This is independent of the name and provisions of the judiciary, whether Islamic or non-Islamic, whether European or non-European. No doubt, if God exists, it will not help us to kiss the Holy Quran at international conferences and keep it in our pockets. The same applies to Judaism. The swaying of believers at the Wailing *Wall* also brings no peace, if transparency between religions is at war with God.
>
> The notion of heaven is coupled with an entrance to enlightenment through a garden of love, justice, generosity, happiness, awareness, wisdom, of the attainment, of non-punishment, of the existence of solely one decree, and the proportionality between means and end. In the heaven of divine law, there no longer exists a propensity for evil deeds in the nature of man. The soul is free from positive law. Thus, if we can correctly imagine the meaning of heaven, we can also understand the connotation of justice with love. The term "heaven" is the complete concept of humanity with justice, however such a heaven may not exist in reality.[90]

Please allow me to face justice within the words and prosperity of moral justice. *Please* permit me to discuss fairness and human rights. *Please* agree with me to dance on the platform of ingenuous human rights provisions. *Please* join me in singing about the true nature of humanity and the law of human rights. *Please* let me cry for the perished rights of the victims, and *please* understand my mourning for the non-existent tombs of innocent Jews killed during the Second World War by Nazism; on the vanished graves of the victims of the Vietnam War who were burned and killed by the United States

---

[90] Farhad Malekian, *Paralysing International Criminal Justice* (New York: Nova Science Publishers, 2021), pp. 237-238; Malekian, *The Heaven of Justice with Love*, note 260, p. 5.

criminal armed forces; on the sepulchre of the Palestinians who have been killed by the brutal criminal conducts of the Zionist regime; and please also allow me to grieve for the millions of children who have been killed all over the world, including but not limited to in Iraq, Afghanistan, Libya, Syria, and Yemen under the orders of the brutal terrorist governments of the United States, Britain, France, and their allies.

It is fitting to quote the song Children of the Grave here:

Revolution in their minds the children start to march
Against the world in which they have to live
And all the hate that's in their hearts
They're tired of being pushed around
And told just what to do
They'll fight the world until they've won
And love comes flowing through, yeah

Children of tomorrow live in the tears that fall today
Will the sun rise up tomorrow bringing peace in any way?
Must the world live in the shadow of atomic fear?
Can they win the fight for peace or will they disappear, yeah

So you children of the world,
Listen to what I say
If you want a better place to live in
Spread the words today
Show the world that love is still alive you must be brave
Or you children of today are children of the grave, yeah[91]

All this indicates that the theory of physical justice that is exercised in our sovereignty does not follow human rights standards and is dictatorial. This is particularly evident regarding violations of the system of international human rights, which contains the spirit of moral justice and yet is meaningless in practice. Additionally, national physical justice contains some of the attitude of the parts of the body of moral justice but is not effective. All the elements of justice that are in line with the slogan of humanity unfortunately use the principles of human rights to impose one-eyed justice. With every passing day, more arms are produced, and then we propagate human rights laws that are not respected and violated. In addition to our previous examples, another

[91] The art of Black Sabbath, released in 1971.

example here would be the presidents of France, all of whom have engaged in grave criminal activities in African nations in the name of justice, humanity, and peace. Their actions in Africa have violated the understanding of physical justice and moral justice.[92] Much more remarkable is the situation of the children of Palestine, who are being starved by the Nazi-Zionist government and are facing a Holocaust and massacre.[93] This implies that the concept of moral justice is not only being vigorously violated, but the conduct of the relevant government savagely violates the terroristic reasonings of any authoritarian physical justice as well.

2. The Instrumentality of Justice

Under the sphere of physical justice, in particular within the realm of international relations, the intent of physical justice is not to reach justice and create equality between all states, but to resort to the domination of power. Its application in this context assumes that states do not have equal status since the provisions of Chapter VII of the Charter and its practice over several decades prove that the states with more power concerning weapons are those that determine what the principles of physical justice are and are meant to be. In very rare situations, justice has been achieved, and not because of the will of the power-hungry governments, but rather because of great international movements against physical justice. A clear example of this is the abolition of Apartheid after decades of the white South African government committing the crime with the assistance and complicity of the United States, the United Kingdom, and Israel, among others.[94]

Thus, for example, whoever demands and wants justice is condemned for violating and disrespecting the principles of justice. This means that we are prevented from protesting the handicapped position of the system of physical justice, whether national or international. We should not do this because otherwise we are responsible for the system of prosecution and punishment of physical justice in big-power politics. This is particularly seen in the system

---

[92] Such as are Charles de Gaulle (1959–69); Georges Pompidou (1969–74); Valéry Giscard d'Estaing (1974–81); François Mitterrand (1981–95); Jacques Chirac (1995–2007); Nicolas Sarkozy (2007–12); François Hollande (2012–17); Emmanuel Macron (2017–).

[93] Examine Farhad Malekian, *Paralysing International Criminal Justice* (New York: Nova Science Publishers, 2021).

[94] J. K. Feimpong & S. Azadon Tiewel, 'Can Apartheid Successfully Defy the International Legal System?' 5 *The Black Law Journal* (1977), pp. 287-311.

of international criminal justice, and if the protest grows, then international physical justice can take direct action against the population of the relevant state, which ends in the commission of crimes against humanity, war crimes, aggression, genocide, and torture. Physical justice has no moral virtue and is not familiar with any virtue at all, except for demanding without limit. This has been observed and demonstrated throughout the history of civilisation.

Authorities have either asserted that their requirements for physical justice were not met or that the subjects of physical justice have been aggressive terrorists and violators of their sanctions. This is how physical justice intends to monopolize its subjects under the national legal system or monopolize subjects of international law through accusations. This means that every matter of international physical justice is pending the decisions of the authoritarian, power-hungry government. Thus, we cannot choose the implementation of moral law or fair justice for all in a rational manner. Naturally, every matter is dependent on our particular interests—whether we accept the force of physical justice or fight against it. The latter choice may not only lead to imprisonment, but could even lead to death. Therefore, everything depends on the pressure posed by time and prudential engagements.

Consequently, the cogs of moral justice are in motion, even if the powerful authorities may not see or confirm their existence. This is regardless of the fact that the main headlines of physical justice object to their existence and prevent its demands. The authorities may therefore argue that moral justice is the subject of the provisions of our constitutions, and since it has been voted on by the representatives of the people and for their interests, it is the law of the state, and its provisions are therefore imperative as long as they are not modified by a collective government decision. Therefore, they sanction the use of the law and its legal order on all occasions. At first glance, this may seem like a hypothesis posed by the powerful authorities. However, a complementary political artistic picture is always created when the law is ordered by those in power and the order becomes the real law.[95]

Thus, arguments concerning the constitution of physical justice are just like sea snakes, which swim in a particular shape. They are superior to any reaction concerning a package of the laws that reduce their authoritative power. It is the snake that decides and enforces the law. This argument is particularly true regarding international criminal justice and human rights law.

[95] Examine A. Jacovides., *Treaties Conflicting with Peremptory Norms of International Law and the Zurich-London 'Agreements,'* (1966).

Our intention here is not to deny the values of the principles of justice that are integrated into *de lege lata* in the system of international law or into the general principle of law within the preliminary meaning of physical justice. However, the theory of moral justice held the normative standard of faithfulness and sympathy to the rights of all nations, in particular those which have been the victims of armed conflict created, supported, and carried out by the artillery of powertionist governments. As I have written earlier:

> The global criminal justice system has a long history of committing crimes according to barbarous laws imposed by the judges of criminal religious courts. As a result, criminal justice jurisprudence has faced a variety of judgments, punishments, attributions of criminal responsibility, and overall accountability of various criminals. This is one of the reasons why legal jurisprudence has made more and more discoveries about religious mental criminality as well as political mental barbarism over time.[96] *One may even assert that the 30 years of religious war in Europe culminated in the Second World War against the Jews. This war was not only a political war but also – more significantly in this context – a religious war waged by a specific faction of Christians against minority religious groups, ending with the annihilation of millions of people in Europe. A source of shame for human history is that a group of "enlightened" European Christians exterminated entire groups within their society with blasé and egoistic selfishness. The barbarity of medical experimentation during this time period diminished the value of medical ethics and future development. Ironically, these obvious criminal conducts were not considered sin. Even today, murdering the entire population of Palestine by the Zionist political government is still not viewed as a sin, but rather as a way to achieve the theory of God.*[97]

---

[96] It is also documented that both religions divided he concept of war to just and unjust war. Consult Ian Brownlie, International Law and the Use of Force by States (Oxford, 1963), pp-5-6.

[97] Under the contemporary historical context of civilisation, the Zionist political regime engages in war crimes, crimes against humanity, and genocide against the inhabitants of occupied territories.

3. Mechanisms of Monopolisation

The circumstances model, as imagined based on the conditions around the subject matter of justice and whether the arguments are presented by the protesters, can be largely met by the authorities. Otherwise, physical justice becomes harsh and aggressive and may lead to the brutal murder of the protesters in accordance with its legal system. *This is because physical justice is not a law in reality, but rather a system that compels its subjects to follow the law and its orders. It is therefore based on its impact on the rights of its subjects, instead of fulfilling their demands, which are under the order of the system. This is similar to the cosmic order of the day and night. This is why the presented physical justice may go against the moral substance of the law and violate its mechanism of applicability.*

The question then is: how has physical justice survived for centuries with minimal modifications to its framework, even though it is the main rival of moral justice and its violations? Physical justice never strays from its intentions concerning the manipulation and monopolisation of the principle of moral justice. Physical justice being supported and safeguarded by the authorities and their military power might be a key factor against its opponents. Authorities are habitually cautious, vigilant, and observant when it comes to the control of the demands of moral justice by its opponents and, at the same time, they are conservative in dealing with hypotheses of moral justice, which can diminish or hinder their interests. These are some of the reasons why the plausible hypothesis of the opponents does not get credit in the system of physical justice. They know that the theories of the opponents are basically correct and have no doubt that the arguments of the opponents acknowledge the basic foundation of their tyrannical existence. Consequently, they do not need any explanation or any particular measure, as the true explanation can cut off the very existence of physical justice and its supporters. This is especially clear when the big powertionist governments apply the provisions of international criminal justice and international human rights.[98]

We must also remember that tyranny, atrocities, brutalities, barbarities, mass killings, crimes against humanity, war crimes, genocide, torture, and rape are the result of the direct or indirect long-term plans of the powers in

[98] Farhad Malekian, *Powertionism in International Criminal Justice* (New York: Nova Science Publishers, 2022); also Farhad Malekian, *Conundrums of Paternalism in International Criminal Justice* (New York: Nova Science Publishers, 2024); Farhad Malekian, *Concreting Righteousness in International Criminal Justice* (New York: Nova publishers, 2024).

control upon physical justice, the philosophy of which is contrary to the basic existence of moral justice. The intention of moral justice cannot be destroyed at any rate or degree. *Moral justice builds, while physical justice generally destroys. Moral justice is against the industry of human rights. Moral justice does not produce weapons of mass destruction. Moral justice contains love for humanity, while physical justice stunts and destroys civilisation.*[99]

This is why the system of justice does not work, regardless of how it defends itself. This is also why we are still suffering from the effects of physical justice within the territories of a large number of nations that have been the targets of the immoral conducts of physical justice. Consequently, the savage nature of big political power shows the same tendency in the operation of their will and interests in the name of human rights, international criminal justice, or international humanitarian law in armed conflicts.[100] However, we must not put aside the fact that the system of international human rights creates and imposes an atavistic relic of humanity at the international level, manifesting the real nature of our modern time.[101] The question is how

---

[99] Farhad Malekian, *Jurisprudence of International Criminal Justice* (Introduction by Professor Benjamin B. Ferencz, the former Prosecutor of the Nuremberg Tribunal (Cambridge: Cambridge Scholars Publishing, 2014); Farhad Malekian, 'Comparative Substantive International Criminal Justice,' in Ronald Slye (ed.), *The Nuremberg Principles in Non-western Societies: A Reflection on their Universality, Legitimacy and Application* (2017), pp. 10-44; Antonio Cassese, Albin Eser, Giorgio Gaja and Robert E. Conor, *Justice at Nuremberg* (1980); Kevin Jon Heller, *The Nuremberg Military Tribunals and the Origins of International Criminal Law* (2010); Farhad Malekian, 'The Canon of Love against the Use of Force in Islamic and Public International Law: Part I: The Chamber of Love within Legal Discipline,' 15 *International Criminal Law Review*, 2015), pp. 591-628.

[100] Examine Susan O'Connor, 'Up in Arms: A Humanitarian Analysis of the Arms Trade Treaty and Its New Zealand Application,' 11 *New Zealand Yearbook of International Law* (2013), pp. 73–105; Antonio Cassese, (ed.), *The New Humanitarian Law of Armed Conflict* (Naples: Editoriale Scientifica, 1979); Karima Bennoune, 'As-Salamu 'Alykum? Humanitarian Law in Islamic Jurisprudence,' 15 *Michigan Journal of International Law*, (1994), pp. 605-643; Antonio Cassese, 'On the Current Trends Towards Criminal Prosecution and Punishment of Breaches of International Humanitarian Law,' 9 *European Journal of International Law* 2 (1998); Jason S. DeSon, 'Automating the Right Stuff? The Hidden Ramifications of Ensuring Autonomous Aerial Weapon Systems Comply with International Humanitarian Law,' 72 *Air Force Law Review*, (2015), pp. 85–122; John Carey and John R. Pritchard (eds.), *International Humanitarian Law: Origins, Challenges and Prospects* (2000); Kesolofetse Lefenya, 'Use of Explosive Weapons in Densely Populated Areas: Implications for International Humanitarian Law,' *African Yearbook on International Humanitarian Law* (2014), pp. 68–86; Adedokun Ogunfolu, Oludayo Fagbemi, 'I Have a Drone: The Implications of American Drone Policy for Africa and International Humanitarian Law,' 23 (1) *Revue Africaine de Droit International et Comparé* (2015), pp. 106–128; Thomas. G. Weiss, *Military-Civilian Interactions: Humanitarian Crises and the Responsibility to Protect* (2nd ed., Rowman & Littlefield Publishers Inc, Lanham (MD), 2005).

[101] *Id.*

our international lawyers can argue that the system of international human rights law, and particularly the humanitarian law of armed conflicts, contains the new and modern provisions of human rights law and its magnificent rules, when we still carry ancient traditions of previous generations with us - massacres.[102]

How can we accept that the system of international criminal justice has a true nature of humanity and justice when its sole function is to determine when moral justice has been violated? It seems that immorality is an integral part of the international criminal justice system. The existence of justice, which is based on immorality within us, shows the value of the faculty of justice. This means that the nature of physical justice is stained by the blood of victims. We could actually start wars between nations using the system of international human rights, however we have no substance in humanity that can develop moral justice and the principle of love for humanity that can include all mankind, i.e., all nations.[103] The dispute in this case might seem abusive to the system of international human rights, however no protest emerged upon closer scrutiny of systematic violations of the rights of victims by those who are supposed to prevent serious violations of the body of physical justice. In other words, the entire system of international criminal justice demands the appropriate and objective implementation of physical justice, however current events reflect the opposite. The ongoing mistreatment and genocide of the entire population of Palestine is a clear example of this.[104]

---

[102] *Id.*

[103] Farhad Malekian, 'The Canon of Love against the Use of Force in Islamic and Public International Law: Part I: The Chamber of Love within Legal Discipline,' 15 *International Criminal Law Review*, 2015), pp. 591-628.

[104] On genocide and atrocities examine William A. Schabas, *Genocide in International Law, the Crime of Crimes* (2000); William L. Hurlock, 'The International Court of Justice: Effectively Providing a Long Overdue Remedy for Ending State-Sponsored Genocide (Bosnia-Herzegovina v. Yugoslavia),' 12 American University Journal of International Law and Policy (1997); George J. Andreopoulos, (ed.), *Genocide: Conceptual and Historical Dimensions* (Philadelphia, 1994); Machteld Boot, *Genocide, Crimes against Humanity, War Crimes: Nullum Crimen Sine Lege and the Subjective Matter of Jurisdiction of the International Criminal Court*, (2002); Christopher Browning, *The Path to Genocide: Essays on Launching the Final Solution*, (2002); Christian P. Scherrer, *Iraq: Genocide by Sanctions* (2011); Richard Falk, *Slouching Toward a Palestinian Holocaust*, www. transnational.org/Area/Falk Palestine Genocide.html, 20 October 2010.

4. Justice as Money

We are so thoroughly restrained in the system of international human rights that all our words and thoughts are connected to the marvellous character of its nature. However, in reality, every norm or provision of human rights, and of international criminal justice, has the character of dollars, euros, and gold bullions. This is how the system of international criminal justice and human rights is seen in the eyes of lawyers. This is how we reach our dreams and use a body of law that was created to be free from economic interests and protect the victims but is used to do the opposite. That said, how I interpret the systems of international human rights and international criminal justice is insignificant. Hungry lawyers or pretended faithful lawyers do not give a damn. International human rights lawyers are exempt from human rights duties and responsibilities. This is because they must earn an income, and it does not matter to them who is paying it or what price it comes at. Most human rights lawyers are similar to politicians and their opinions change every day. How can we speak about the implementation of the provisions of international human rights when the entire theory of human rights is for sale, even in the international office of human rights and prosecutor of the ICC? Several lawyers have bargain the system of international criminal justice under certain circumstances and ignore genocide or barbarity such as William Schabas,[105] Michael Scharf,[106] and Geoffrey Nice.[107]

> If there be in nature such a principle as justice, it is necessarily the only political principle there ever was, or ever will be. All the other so-called political principles, which men are in the habit of inventing, are not principles at all. They are either the mere conceits of simpletons, who imagine they have discovered something better than truth, and justice, and universal law; or they are mere devices and pretenses, to which

---

[105] Muslim Rohingya of Myanmar case in ICJ.

[106] Iraq tribunal case. Study Farhad Malekian, 'Emasculating the Philosophy of International Criminal Justice in the Iraqi Special Tribunal,' *Cornell International Law Journal*, 58/5 (2005), pp. 67.

[107] At the Uyghur unofficial Tribunal, Geoffrey Nice criticized the Chinese government for allegedly perpetrating crimes against humanity against the Uyghur population. However, he failed to acknowledge the gross crimes committed by Tony Blair or the presidents of the United States governments in Iraq or Afghanistan. The following reports demonstrate how governments, such as Britain, tend to cover up their own genocide. Evidence of the double morality of lawyers. https://researchbriefings.files.parliament.uk/documents/CDP-2022-0009/CDP-2022-0009.pdf.

selfish and knavish men resort as means to get fame, and power, and money.[108]

The fact is that international human rights and ICL lawyers pretend to work for humanity, justice, and peace, while the contrary has been proven to be the case, and almost any lawyer of human rights or criminal justice who supports humanity will change their mind for the right price. This reflects what we call the interminable stage of the evolution of the provisions of international human rights and international criminal justice around the world. *Thus, the fanciful and facile form of philosophy that is being asserted in support of humanity is the magical form of dreams for the victims. In reality, the pillar of national, regional, or international justice that is most often missing is the absence of morality and human rights as a whole. This is what I call the humiliation of the substantial nature of humankind. This is how we reach the central power of human rights for the promotion of the harm to nations and their children.*

How can we believe that the victims of our armed conflicts can receive justice and that they will regain what they have lost? How can the lost members of a family be brought back? How can the population of a nation return when millions of them have been murdered or displaced? Even true or imaginary prophets of any religion in the world are incapable of bringing back a single individual.[109] My arguments and philosophies may be rhetoric, pomposity, or, let's say, speechmaking, and they do not sound logical in the physical system of justice. Nonetheless, they are important to the understanding of physical justice and how its attitudes differ in comparison with the system of moral justice. *I do not actually need to face or meet the many demands for trained lawyers who are arrogant enough to work for justice but continue to play different sides. Such lawyers will act in accordance with the wills of those who pay the most, while also pretending to promote human rights law and its application. Certainly, those lawyers do, and there is no doubt about it, but the payment should not be modified or prevented by any means, even at the cost of the deaths of millions.*

The fact is that the system of international human rights law teaches lawyers about when they should close their eyes, where they should look, and when they should pretend that they are blind and unaware. Even the politicians

---

[108] Lysander Spooner, Natural Law; or the Science of Justice (1882) in https://oll.libertyfund.org/titles/spooner-natural-law-or-the-science-of-justice-1882.

[109] Farhad Malekian, *Exploitation of Christian Islamic International Criminal Justice* (New York: Nova Science Publishers, 2024).

of big nations do the same. A clear example of such a politician is Tony Blair who, after killing several million people in different countries in compliance with the policies of the United States, stated that he did not know the statements of Bush and others were malicious and contained false physical justice. This argument is similar to the story of *Pinocchio,* with the difference being that Pinocchio's nose grows every time, while Blair does not need to care about the length of his nose since the *British queen* covered for him.[110] The systems of international human rights and international criminal justice involve a specific category or reasoning that should be respected at all times and should not be violated. The displaying of political and legal arguments that are in opposition to the fundamental arguments of physical or moral justice should not be permitted.[111]

Our mission in the implementation of international human rights and international criminal justice is to reduce the conflicts and open our eyes to the reality that international criminal justice does not function due to violations and is instead based on moral justice and the implementation of correct and useful justice that does not violate the rights of its subjects to the benefit of others. Here again, the imagination that our system of physical justice, in particular the international one, is good and fulfils the notion of moral justice is continually interposing its own images of rights. This is to the extent that it participates in the incorrect development of principles of justice and ultimately leads to violations. Based on these considerations, we can realize how philosophical thoughts, logical beliefs, and the true conception of the cause of justice can be changed through the imposition of physical force, physical justice, and physical ignorance of the substance of the value of established rights for mankind. Here again, the unity of physical justice does nothing for the unity of humanity and moral justice and instead achieves the contrary. As a result, the statue of justice crumbles to pieces.

5. Killing Opportunities for Justice

The philosophers of the systems of international human rights law and international criminal justice are in the habit of situating every single provision

[110] Andreas Schueller, The ICC, British War Crimes in Iraq and a Very British Tradition, https://opiniojuris.org/2020/12/11/the-icc-british-war-crimes-in-iraq-and-a-very-british-tradition/; see also https://www.icc-cpi.int/sites/default/files/itemsDocuments/201209-otp-final-report-iraq-uk-eng.pdf.

[111] *Id.*

of law in place of the active norm. This is particularly regarding international law, which sees justice as the vocabulary of who wins the case and not who asserts the right norms of justice. The philosophers believe that the phenomenon of justice is achieved by convincing the other side of their arguments, regardless of the facts underlying the philosophy of drafting and codifying provisions and norms concerning certain very significant questions of law and justice. Whether the law in force is really meeting the basic conditions of the philosophy of law, and particularly the reasons of law, in order to practically enforce the notion of moral justice is another serious argument. We refer here to the truth and the rights of human beings as a whole. If the definition of justice presented by the reasons of the philosophies of law does not meet the primary needs of its subjects, it is obviously violating the shared sphere of the definition of the existence of the law.

But what are the primary needs of the subjects of the law? Does primary need refer to the usual philosophical manifestation and reasoning? Does primary need mean uncovering the basic truth of every case and consequently prioritizing the principle of righteousness?[112] Does it mean preventing any version of the law that presents a form of monopolisation of the system of justice, whether through physical justice or through use of the provisions of physical justice by its applicants who have the central power of the law under their own control? This colouring of the provisions of the law by its philosophers or by lawyers is often resorted to in order to reach a conclusion regarding the true object of morality of the law, and it is confused and muddled by personal advantages. Based on this reasoning, an unrestrained interpretation of the law can be inferred - as long as we stay away from the main purpose of adapting and codifying the law and its provisions.

This process is generally regarded as sufficient clarification for the existence of the law. In other words, philosophers and lawyers discuss what the purposes of the existing law are and who must help achieve them. Many philosophers, and particularly lawyers, get lost within the provisions of the law and become involved in negative promotion of the provisions of the law. This can be done knowingly or unknowingly, and accepting that they were involved unknowingly in the process of unqualified justice is indeed meaningless with reference to the fact that the task of philosophers and lawyers is not to get lost in an untruthful process. The concept of the metaphysic needs an appropriate understanding of the formulation of the law

[112] Farhad Malekian, *Concreting Righteousness in International Criminal Justice* (New York, Nova Sciences Publishers, 2024).

and to draw attention to the hidden faces of the law and make them visible to all subjects of the law. This is particularly important in the case of international human rights and international criminal justice.

However, all our regulations and enforcement are conditional, which means that they cannot be enforced or empowered without the orders of the political powers. This means that we are forced to accept the orders of power, which in reality means the will of those who orchestrate the hidden mechanism of justice, which is argued to be the essential metaphysic for the existence of the law. Thus, we should not ignore the underlying circumstances that reflect the philosophy of justice in the process of applying the law or as it concerns the accountability of the subjects of the law.[113] This is because many authorities all over the world ignore their own erroneous fundamental origins of morality and righteousness and approach human rights principles in accordance with their own interests. This means that their own moral justice may be presented as physical justice. This is why the system of international criminal justice, and particularly its body of human rights, is always unhealthy and is actually the reason for most violations and for the call for the annihilation of the existence of mankind, such as with the ongoing genocide in Gaza.[114]

---

[113] Richard Falk, 'The Accountability of Leaders: A Challenge to Civil Government and Society' in Jeremy Brecher, Jill Cutler, Smith Brendan, *In the Name of Democracy: American War Crimes in Iraq and Beyond* (American Empire Project), (New York: Metropolitan Books, Henry Holt and Company, 2005); Allen Buchanan, 'Toward a Drone Accountability Regime,' 29 (1) Ethics and International Affairs (2015), pp. 15–70; Karin Arts and Vesselin Popovski (eds.), *International Criminal Accountability and the Rights of Children* (Heidelberg: Springer, 2006), pp. 37–52 and 53–65; Farhad Malekian, *Gravity of Wisdom in International Criminal Law* (New York: Nova Science Publishers, 2021), pp. 43-44; Farhad Malekian, *Orchestrating Diversity in International Criminal Justice* (New York: Nova Science Publishers, 2021).

[114] Farhad Malekian, Paralysing International Criminal Justice (New York: Nova Science Publishers, 2021), pp. 220-221. Examine also See also JTA, "Kassams hit Israel after terrorist killed," 16 December 2008, available online at: http://jta.org/news/articleprint/2008/12/16/1001575/kassams-hit-israel-after-terrorist-killed?TB_iframe=true&width=750&height=500; PCHR, "Weekly report on Israeli human rights violations in the Occupied Palestinian Territory," No. 49/2008 (4-17 December), available at: http://www.pchrgaza.org/files/W_report/English/2008/18-12-2008.htm; Al-Jazeera, "Israeli missile kills Gaza man," 18 December 2008, available online at: http://english.aljazeera.net/news/middleeast/2008/12/2008121721428340460.html: PCHR, "Weekly report on Israeli human rights violations in the Occupied Palestinian Territory," No. 50/2008 (18–23 December 2008), available at: http://www.pchrgaza.org/files/W_report/English/2008/24-12-2008.htm; Reuters, "Hamas declares end to ceasefire with Israel in Gaza," 18 December 2008, available online at: http://www.reuters.com/article/topNews/idUSLI75623220081218; PCHR, "Weekly report on Israeli human rights violations in the Occupied Palestinian Territory," No. 51/2008 (24–31 December 2008),

Thus, physical justice monopolizes the terminology of international criminal justice, and therefore achieving the simple logic of moral justice becomes impossible in practice. As a result, the enforcement of moral justice requires great effort, since the opposite of physical justice does not always have the situation under control and is also empowered by arms. Therefore, speaking about moral justice in the context of physical justice is dangerous. Those who present the sphere of moral justice are always under serious question and it requires significant effort to fight against the injustice of the law and its supporters.

The fact is that the principles of physical justice, and particularly the systems of international human rights and international criminal justice, have not only been monopolized and plundered, but the systems have even transmitted the imposition of power to us and remain a treasure trove of significant legal provisions. Consequently, speaking about free and independent human rights or criminal justice systems at the international level is indeed a lie. This unfortunately means that value stems from the decisions of authorities and not from the essence of moral justice, which should be the real natural treasure for human civilisations.

The situation of the ethical philosophy of moral justice is in such danger that hardly anyone can foresee any change in the system of application of international criminal justice, which functions solely on the principle of military guns and interests.[115] Since it could not eradicate the influence of the heritage of dictatorial power at any time in the history of human civilisation, the civilisation of mankind is always in a state of war for various reasons, which is unnatural and violates international human rights and international criminal justice. Therefore, there is no opportunity to gradually cultivate moral justice to grant us some kind of protection, at least for the time being.[116] The facts, however, remain the same: powerful governments do not feel responsible for the immoral situation in the world and are not.

---

available online at: http://www.pchrgaza.org/files/W_report/English/2008/pdf/weekly%20report%2051.pdf; Mr. Fadi Qawasme, testimony at the public hearing in Geneva, 3 July 2009, and PCHR, "Weekly report on Israeli human rights violations in the Occupied Palestinian Territory," No. 26/2006 (29 June-5 July 2006), available online at: http://www.pchrgaza.org/files/W_report/English/2006/06-07-2006.htm.

[115] Joseph Raz, *Ethics in the Public Domain: Essays in the Morality of Law and Politics* (Oxford: Oxford University Press, 1994); Joseph Raz, *The Morality of Freedom* (1986); Farhad Malekian, *Classical Morality in International Peremptory Criminal Law* (Newcastle: Cambridge Scholars Publishing, 2021).

[116] *Id.*

6. Abusing the Essence of Justice

Authoritarian physical justice has a very conclusive nature of its own, implying that it only accepts its own arguments during proceedings and does not accept moral arguments. Instead, it prioritizes the authorisation of the use of force by the controlling power. This is the case in both the national and international spheres of law. Overall, all powers certainly find themselves to not be responsible for the violations of the rights of victims. There are many reasons for this lack of responsibility, which is generally based on the power of physical justice, which has occupied all possibilities of reaching justice in a nutshell.[117] Naturally, if the basic principles of justice are not free from expropriation or exploitation, then the mechanism of justice will not receive appropriate treatment and ultimately fail to fulfil its main intended purpose.

The original and basic goal of justice and its duties towards others depend very much on its duties towards itself. Whereas moral justice is weak because of all mental and physical fights against its true nature and the rejection of conspiracies against other nations by physical justice, moral justice is ultimately hindered.[118] As a result, we must treat the obligations and rights of nations as inaccessible and thus unfulfilled. This can be seen in the case of Palestinian rights under the brutal occupation of a terrorist government. We are not seeking any remedies concerning how to prevent this brutal regime of the Zionist criminal government, rather we wish to stop the violations of the systems of international human rights and international criminal justice that are against all nations of the world. The main problem here is not just the imposition of unlawful international physical justice, but decades of violations of faith in justice and the abuse of the elements of moral justice.[119]

The general and fundamental rule of creating justice concerning our duties towards ourselves is that every principle of moral justice ought to exist in a manner compatible with its nature. This is especially significant regarding the understanding of moral justice. There are then practical decisions of governments as such, wherein they are concerned with their national character and which are either suitable or opposite to what international criminal justice or international human rights law indicates. It must be emphasized that the

---

[117] Farhad Malekian, 'Judging International Criminal Justice in the Occupied Territories,' 12 *International Criminal Law Review* (2012), pp. 627-869.

[118] *Id.*

[119] Richard A. Falk & Burns H. Weston, The Relevance of International Law to Palestinian Rights in the West Bank and Gaza: In Legal Defense of the Intifada, 32 Harvard International law Journal (1991), pp. 129-157, at 148-149.

preservation of a political power and its authority to control the physical constitution rests in the strength of its adherence to the theory of rightful justice and not its falsification. Therefore, the intentions of the political association by which it reached power and occupied the power of the constitution of the country can no longer survive if the relevant power in force has constantly violated the system of international human rights law or its necessary demands.

However, my previous statement is not really significant since the most powerful governments in the world violate the system of international human rights and still remain in power. This is because *speaking about human rights principles and their value capable of obtaining and maintaining the perfect rights of man is essentially irrelevant because when more rights are violated, the political power gets stronger and more aggressive, and it is the nature of this policy that makes sense in the philosophy of physical justice. For these reasons, we must promote moral law and justice in order to supply possible misunderstandings of the theory of justice with better outcomes of parallel physical justice. For any action to be legally, physically, and morally good, we need to be pure concerning all areas of the law.*

Therefore, speaking about moral justice cannot have any essential value when the only thing that matters to the authorities is staying in power. This means that we may never arrive at a perfect institution of justice and this is why there is no perfect government in the world, and as a result, there is no rightful and authentic application of international human rights or international criminal justice. In other words, when the principles of justice are based on physical force, physical interpretation, friendly relations, rejections of the rights of victims, and the military force of the authorities, then the principles of justice have surely failed and the nature of evil injustice prevails.

One of the essential reasons for the international conflicts between moral and physical justice is that the United Nations is essentially a facade and does not promote the value of man as it claims to. There is no such thing as the principle of equality in the charter of the UN, and every provision that refers to equality is just symbolic and has no substantive meaning at all. The fact is that the United Nations has directed the use of force and the strength of arms to be based on connections and the strength of the military. Thus, the sole and most essential vocabulary of the organisation is the term "use of force," i.e., the armed use of force.

7. The Heteronomous Determination of Justice

As we approach the systems of international human rights and international criminal justice, we can see that the Charter of the United Nations is not a perfect agreement and is based solely on the decisions of the powerful political authorities of the organisation. The theory that the organisation creates equal international legal personality between its members is simply a legal lie. The organisation is empowered to maintain justice - and not only physical justice, but also moral justice. We are not encouraging the rejection of the existence of the Charter of the UN, rather we are referring to the fact that the physical constitution of the organisation is orchestrating different terms and phrases, the final form of which is resorting to use of force and carrying out the orders of the big political parties such as the NATO. Failure to comply can result in losing legal and political standing. This is the philosophy of justice, as long as it is not modified or rewritten for the sake of all parties at the same level and degree.

Even a state that binds its political and legal existence to the orders of a superpower or military power does not exist in reality and carries no weight in the philosophy of physical justice except for obeying the rules and roles of paternalist governments. The question then is: what is the end, or even the beginning, of the system of physical justice? The answer to this question may initially be that there is no beginning or end to the philosophy of physical justice, in particular in the United Nations concerning international physical justice. In other words, the end or object of physical justice is to procure full satisfaction from the plans of the superpower states. It indicates that even the intention of mutual defence against all violations occurring under the power of a militarily powerful government is unsuccessful.

This will always be the case because the corpus of violence is the final policy of the United Nations. Therefore, we cannot assert that physical justice contains moral justice because it does not. This is reflected in the UN, which speaks about the equality of all states and yet promotes inequality as a principle. There are therefore no reciprocal engagements on the theoretical, ideological, or philosophical notion of physical justice other than in the most significant and vital times of violations. These principles or measures of the United Nations are meant to address the potential needs of power-hungry governments. Accordingly, there might be inconsistent decisions concerning certain conflicts brought before the Security Council.

However, this inconsistency does not help with solving conflicts as long as the big powers have different understandings of physical and moral justice.

The justice of the United Nations is justice without justice, thereby indicating the full risk that accompanies personal or governmental interests. This is particularly clearly demonstrated by the powertionist government of the United States vetoing the resolutions of the Security Council, one after another. The use of veto rights has killed thousands of Palestinians and deprived them of their immutable right to self-defence.[120] As a result, there are immeasurable costs for the American government to assist the Israeli criminal Zionist government in carrying out a Holocaust against the innocent occupied population of Palestine.[121] Additionally, the same issues of monopolisation of physical justice have been carried out throughout the history of the United Nations.

We have officially succeeded in establishing wars, violations, and murder as the main pillars of the United Nations by abandoning the system of moral justice. We have reached the point where the concept of morality is the idea of non-existence, and ultimately, wars are the main principles of discussions around negotiation desks.[122] This implies the fact that wherever the negotiators parties do not agree, waging war is the next form of negotiation.[123] This is why

---

[120] See and read the earlier shameful United States National Security Advisor John Bolton statements about the victims. Bolton Warns ICC not to go after Israel, Confirms Closure of PLO's DC in The Times of Israel (10 September 2018, 8:30 pm), Office https://www.timesofisrael.com/bolton-warns-icc-not-to-go-after-israel-confirms-close-of-plos-dc-office/.

[121] Farhad Malekian, 'Judging International Criminal Justice in the Occupied Territories,' 12 *International Criminal Law Review* (2012), pp. 627-869.

[122] Consult also Joseph Raz, Ethics in the Public Domain: Essays in the Morality of Law and Politics (Oxford: Oxford University Press, 1994). Consult also Roland Dworking, *Justice for Hedgehogs* (2011). For a deep analysis of morality consult P. M. S. Hacker and J. Raz, (eds.), *Law, Morality and Society: Essays in Honour of H. L. A. Hart* (1977); Farhad Malekian, *Classical Morality in International Peremptory Criminal Law* (Newcastle: Cambridge Scholars Publishing, 2021); Joseph Raz, *Ethics in the Public Domain: Essays in the Morality of Law and Politics* (Oxford: Oxford University Press, 1994); Joseph Raz, *The Morality of Freedom* (1986); K. Robert Vischer, *Martin Luther King Jr. and the Morality of Legal Practice: Lessons in Love and Justice* (2014); Fuller Lon Luvios, *The Morality of Law* (Virginia: Yale Law University, 2nd, ed., 1969); A. R. C. Duncan, *Practical Reason and Morality* (Nelson, 1957); M. J. Detmold., *The Unity of Law and Morality: A Refutation of Legal Positivism* (Canada: Law Book Co. of Australasia, 1984); Lea Brilmayer, American Hegemony: *Political Morality in a OneSuperpower World* (1994); Adil Ahmad Haque, *Law and Morality at War* (2017); Kenneth Himma and Brian Bix (eds), *Law and Morality* (2005); David Lyons, 'Moral Aspects of Legal Theory' in Kenneth Himma and Brian Bix (eds) *Law and Morality* (2005).

[123] *Id.* See also Teklewold Gebrehana, *Duty to negotiate: An Element of International law* (1978); T Gebrehana, Arbitration - An Element of International Law (1984). Moreover, "to focus some attention on certain packets of the globe, where nations who have failed miserably to create consensus both nationally and internationally are attempting to preach the doctrine of gun at the expense of bread, for the purpose of either covering up their internal weakness

physical justice is based on military justice, and military justice is based on how we should negotiate the tactics of war and not how to prevent them. Completing these arguments implies the fact that the whole idea of the United Nations is based on some hidden essential elements, and those elements are the very essential reason for excluding or narrowing the definition of justice. They essentially restrict the philosophy of moral justice and impose the will and interests of the controlling power of physical justice.

There are many reasons for this, as we have previously discussed. Thus, the big political parties of the United Nations Security Council, particularly the United States and its allies, are not allowed to sit in the Council to present good physical justice or give power to the elements of righteousness. They have hidden intentions.[124] They have taken a seat in order to achieve their evil intention of monopolizing the heritage of all nations. This shows heteronomous determination, or taking actions based on personal desires instead of moral justice. It reveals that authorities do not work to prevent the use of force and promote good physical justice and instead they engage in the heteronomous empowerment of their own private political interests, which indicates an end to the system of moral justice and its total monopolisation. That means treating the priorities of their own interests with the burglary of the wealth of other nations. It is not irrelevant to say that thousands of American soldiers avoided participating in the Vietnam War and the killing of the Vietnamese. Therefore, they avoided being the tools of heteronomous determination and supporting the interests of the government rather than the reason or moral duty of the persons acting in the war. Their decisions reflect the philosophy of German philosopher Kant.[125]

---

or of pursuing a course of hegemony. The grass roots of every nation are beginning to question the wisdom of their leadership. " *Id*, Arbitration, p. 40.

[124] Xinhua, U. S. Commits Serious Crimes of Violating Human Rights in the Middle East and Beyond (2022), https://english.news.cn/20220809/df33c619baf04b259981bcbba3961810/c.html.

[125] For Kant theories consult Immanuel Kant, 'Religion within the Limits of Reason Alone,' in *Religion and Rational Theology*, ed. and transl. Allen Wood and George di Giovanni (Cambridge University Press, 1996); Immanuel Kant, 'Religion within the Limits of Reason Alone,' *in Religion and Rational Theology, ed. and transl. Allen Wood and George di Giovanni* (Cambridge University Press, 1996); Immanuel Kant, *Answering the Question: What is Enlightenment?* (1784); Immanuel Kant, Critique of Judgment (1790); Immanuel Kant, *Critique of Pure Reason* (1781); Immanuel Kant, *Groundwork of the Metaphysic of Morals* (1785); Kant Immanuel, *Metaphysical Foundations of Natural Science* (1786); Immanuel Kant, Opus Postumum (1995); Immanuel Kant, *Perpetual Peace, and Other Essays on Politics, History, and Morals* (1784); Immanuel Kant, *Perpetual Peace: A Philosophical Sketch* (1795); Immanuel Kant, *Practical Philosophy* (editor: Mary J. Gregor, 1999); Immanuel Kant, *Prolegomena to Any Future Metaphysics* (1783);

The recent decision of the valiant American soldier, Aaron Bushnell, to protest against the American government is a clear example of the rejection of the heteronomous determination of the powertionist government. Although some Zionist supporters called his actions mentally sick, this is not surprising given that physical justice wants to destroy the moral justice norms and humanitarian and correct understanding of the case.[126] Those who resist or protest national or international crimes have always been labelled as being mentally disturbed. Runaway slaves were said to have *drapetomania*; suffragettes fighting for women to get the right to vote were called *hysterical*; and Soviet dissidents were all branded as mentally ill. This is how physical justice invalidates dissenting voices. It may be because the world is realizing what physical justice does when it has the power of law in its own possession without any responsibility.[127] This is how the system of international human rights works. Certainly, the violence of the Israeli military is beyond reason. The number of Palestinians killed thus far has exceeded 50,000; survivors are actively starving while also fighting against international crimes. Why not tell the Israeli Zionist criminal government to stop the occupation? It is not at all easy to struggle against heteronomous determination.

8. Taking Advantage of Negotiations

The fact is that the United Nations Security Council promotes and permits wars, and monopolisation of moral justice in the cases of:

a. The element of negotiating war;
b. The element of negotiating the strategies of war;
c. The element of negotiating coalition policies;
d. The element of negotiating how to steal, destroy, and kill;
e. The element of framing crimes as being necessary;

Immanuel Kant, *Religion within the Bounds of Bare Reason* (1793); Immanuel Kant, *The Critique of Practical Reason* (1788); Immanuel Kant, *The Metaphysics of Morals* (1797); Immanuel Kant, *The Only Possible Argument in Support of a Demonstration of the Existence of God* (1763); Immanuel Kant, *The Science of Right* (1790).

[126] Examine Antonio Cassese, (ed.), *The New Humanitarian Law of Armed Conflict* (Naples: Editoriale Scientifica, 1979); Thomas G. Weiss, *Military-Civilian Interactions: Humanitarian Crises and the Responsibility to Protect* (2nd ed., Rowman & Littlefield Publishers Inc, Lanham (MD), 2005).

[127] https://www.dn.se/kultur/amat-levin-hetsen-att-sjukdomsforklara-aaron-bushnell-ar-ren-desperation/.

f. The element of creating and imposing sanctions against those who do not submit themselves to the decisions of the powertionist governments;
g. The element of empowering one state against other states;
h. The element of the use of NATO to isolate other powers;
i. The element of declaring states which do not agree with the decisions of certain powerful criminal government of the Council as criminals;
j. The element of condemning any notion of morality;
k. The element of increasing the number of victims of international crimes;
l. The element of use of engaging in acts of torture and causing starvation;
m. The element of waging wars in addition to manufacturing and trading weapons;
n. The element of supporting the Zionist government and threatening those who are against them;
o. The element of committing acts of terrorism and designating others as the true terrorists.

Thus, the entire philosophy of the system of international criminal justice establishes the theory of negotiation by different means in order to kill and destroy. This is how theory of physical justice has been exercised in the UN.[128] Negotiating is essentially the art of convincing other parties with lies and then repeating our lies with more lies. Negotiators thus generally speak about the correctness of their measures and their intentions of bringing peace to a particular region, while the real political policy is hidden. For example, negotiations took place between the United States and the Soviet Union concerning certain political matters in Europe. One of these negotiations concerned the situation in Ukraine. However, the United States governments violated the agreements of the negotiations and they ended up empowering the neo-Nazis of Ukraine in 2014, which ultimately led to the current war in Ukraine and the deaths of over one million people. This means that moral justice is marred and mutilated in the process of negotiations, and negotiators do not care about their lies or how many people die—instead they only care about their pay check.[129]

---

[128] See also Teklewold Gebrehana, *Duty to negotiate: An Element of International law* (1978); T Gebrehana, *Arbitration - An Element of International Law* (1984), p. 23, 130-131.
[129] *Id.*

We are not speaking here about any particular process for negotiating since all negotiations are based on man-made roles and rules. This is because physical justice has no rules for negotiations.[130] In other words, wherever securities of interest are guaranteed, the system of international negotiation is considered correct and without any shortcoming.[131] However, wherever the rights of the strong party are not achieved, the system of negotiation means devolves into a system of waging war. This is why we insist that negotiations are the best way to achieve the monopolisation of the provisions of international human rights and international criminal justice by all means. The idea is not to condemn the system of the United Nations but to underline the fact that the statute of the organisation is essentially based on one term, "negotiation," which indicates the trade of moral justice with the evil strength of physical justice.

However, this term of negotiation is just a method by which the authorities can interpret the provisions of the organisation flexibly, like a rubber band, which is really a collection of provisions, rules, norms, and phrases that have different definitions hidden in the structure of the charter.[132] In theory, their definition is visible, but in practice, they are inaccessible as long as the powerful negotiator does not reach its interests. This indicates the fact that speaking about human rights and justice is really a game between different political parties and not the question of righteousness in the mechanism of the Charter. Although my conclusion may be interpreted as a very negative interpretation of the system of justice under the Charter of the United Nations, the fact is that the entire system of organisation is based on negotiating justice. In other words, the Charter encourages negotiation in the meetings of the General Assembly and the Security Council. This also implies the fact that physical justice negates moral justice and follows the orders of the big powers in the UN.

We fulfil our goals, not through equal treatment of all members of the organisation, but with the high privilege of having the power of negotiation under our control. The characterisation of the consciousness of the state parties or their relevant governments reasoning and presentation of the facts at the table of negotiation do not matter. Reasoning correctly has the least amount of power in negotiations, and instead it is more important who supports who and who is afraid of who. The provisions of the United Nations are only powerful

---

[130] *Id.*

[131] *Id.*

[132] Consult Teklewold Gebrehana, *Duty to negotiate: An Element of International law* (1978); T Gebrehana, *Arbitration - An Element of International Law* (1984).

when it concerns minor matters. As a result, the whole body of the Charter of the United Nations is just full of aspirations and not the actual remedy. One who looks after remedies for a peaceful settlement of differences must not only not understand the notion of justice and its various demands, but must also be naïve regarding the facts and reality of political justice, physical justice, military justice, as well as moral justice and the control of all these justices by the powertionist governments.[133]

9. Charter as a House of Cards

Surely, the moral capacity of the provisions of the Charter is not valid. The obvious evidence for this is that the Charter of the United Nations does not follow the philosophy of reason in critical situations, but instead follows the power of reason. This indicates that the strongest and most logical reasoning concerning the most vital questions is the theory presented by the most powerful government.[134] Hence, every government has to follow the fake order of the system of international human rights if it wants to survive politically, militarily, and economically, and if it wants to protect its international legal personality. This means that the notion of international personality found in the body of various systems of international laws is just a political ploy used to control the political and economic capacities of every government in the world with legal cards.

The systems of international human rights and international criminal justice found in the body of the Charter of the United Nations and the Statutes of the International Criminal Court are actually like playing cards with different suits. The Ace of Spades, which is also known as the spadille or death card, is held by powertionist government. This proves that even if there is another Ace of Spades, the powertionist governments have their own death card in the end.[135] Thus, preventing the use of force, achieving justice and equality with peaceful methods, and organizing and supporting the rights of

[133] Farhad Malekian, *Powertionism in International Criminal Justice* (New York: Nova Science Publishers, 2022), p. 132.

[134] A. Pellet, 'Vive le crime! Remarques sur les degrés de l'illicité en droit international' in United Nations/International Law Commission (ed.), *International Law on the Eve of the Twenty-first Century: Views from the International Law Commission* (United Nations New York 1997), pp. 287–315.

[135] Farhad Malekian, *Powertionism in International Criminal Justice* (New York: Nova Science Publishers, 2022).

self-determination are all jokes. Consequently, the United Nations Charter is like a house of cards that blows over with the smallest gust of wind.

Therefore, all negotiations within the United Nations, and even other international bodies, are largely for show rather than tools for achieving real justice. The powerful political power that has the power to exercise physical justice and control the discussions around the negotiation desk is also the one that dictates which acts and decisions are right. There is no need for more reason, which means that we decide about the strength of physical justice and its hidden content against the international legal systems as a whole. We view the principles within in the provisional body of the system of international human rights as the presentation of a good characterisation of justice, while in reality, they are used by certain powertionist governments to antagonize other parties and called the implementation of physical justice and respect of the basic essence of morality. This means that the military inclination is the will of the strong over the weak.

Their inclination to enter the system of equal rights of nations is due to the absence of equal international legal personalities among the governments at the negotiation table. The notion of equality among governments is a legal dream. The international legal forum is faced with violations of their perpetual rights to their resources in every matter. This is what physical justice does not want to face, and is also one of the reasons why moral justice is not welcome in the legal region of physical justice. The result is that the latter identity occupies its universal natural priorities. The conflict between these two justices continues and reveals the desires of powertionist governments. This does not mean that we need to awaken for the determination of moral justice in order to conquer physical justice monopolized power. There is no doubt that awakening exists among most governments of the United Nations, but there is a strong lack of willingness to go against the power of international physical justice - i.e., the justice of military strength imposed by the powertionist government of the Security Council.[136]

There is in fact a spiteful competition of self-importance and ego among several powers around the negotiating tables, and this spitefulness is not something new and has a long story of its own. This reflects the desire to gain authority over law enforcement and, naturally, the power to control world wealth to the benefit of the super powerful governments. The result is that the

---

[136] Examine also A. Orakhelashvili, 'The Impact of Peremptory Norms on the Interpretation and Application of United Nations Security Council Resolutions' 16 (1), *The European Journal of International Law* (2005), pp. 59-88.

system of human rights is monopolized under the physical strength of justice, and moral justice faces the unlawful power of man under its lawful natural strength at all times. The natural impulses to empower equal moral justice die as a matter of the evil conduct of certain governments.[137] These are the result of the greed of the superior for the development of his powers. Then it will not see any government enviously overturn its political or military power. As a result, a considerable number of problems arise and the love for justice and peace is replaced with hate and antagonism.[138] This in turn leads to the deaths of millions of people. This is the result of our peaceful negotiations and the curriculum vitae of international human rights and justice, with an ample number of wars, crimes against humanity, genocide, war crimes, rape, and torture. While governments claim to be knowledgeable about human rights, their actions deny it.

---

[137] Examine Spooner Lysander, Natural Law; or the Science of Justice: A Treatise on Natural Law, Natural Justice, Natural Rights, Natural Liberty, and Natural Society; showing that all Legislation whatsoever is an Absurdity, a Usurpation, and a Crime. Part First. [1882], available at http://oll.libertyfund.org/titles/spooner-natural-law-or-the-science-of-justice-1882 (Accessed: on 18 December 2017).

[138] "If justice be not a natural principle, governments (so-called) have no more right or reason to take cognisance of it, or to pretend or profess to take cognisance of it, than they have to take cognisance, or to pretend or profess to take cognisance, of any other nonentity; and all their professions of establishing justice, or of maintaining justice, or of regarding justice, are simply the mere gibberish of fools, or the frauds of imposters. But if justice be a natural principle, then it is necessarily an immutable one; and can no more be changed - by any power inferior to that which established it - than can the law of gravitation, the laws of light, the principles of mathematics, or any other natural law or principle whatever; and all attempts or assumptions, on the part of any man or body of men - whether calling themselves governments, or by any other name - to set up their own commands, wills, pleasure, or discretion, in the place of justice, as a rule of conduct for any human being, are as much an absurdity, an usurpation, and a tyranny, as would be their attempts to set up their own commands, wills, pleasure, or discretion in the place of any and all the physical, mental, and moral laws of the universe." *Id.*

Chapter 5

Challenges in the Core Curriculum of Justice

1. Empowering Injustice Constituting Justice

The system of justice in general and the system of international criminal justice in particular are facing the most difficult treatment of their foundations as a result of our greed, whether personal, collective, or governmental. This means that we are missing the real definitions and basic needs of justice. The history of civilisation has never witnessed a true understanding of the content of justice and its imperative need for the integration of the notion of morality in order to reduce injustice and cultivate the essence of equality among all men without any particular distinction regarding their rights and values. The concept of justice thus has serious problems of identity that can equally fulfil the needs of its subjects. The solution to this problem is therefore not easy and requires a reinterpretation of our system of justice and the integration of moral justice in place of unjustified physical justice.

Here, we are focusing on the equal liberty of every member of the United Nations. Therefore, both national and international justice should guarantee the personal integrity of all men.[139] This is what I have called the notion of *somebodiness* in our existence, which implies that physical justice should not violate our natural connection with the system of moral justice.[140] Physical justice has proven that, in many aspects, people have been harsh and committed crimes at the national or international level, but those crimes have not been identified as crimes by the perpetrators, but rather through the imposition of justice. This means that a perfectly civil constitution can be administered according to the principles of right, under which it seriously violates the rights of its citizens while still claiming to be just.

For example, the conditions imposed by a considerable number of physical justice systems in a large number of states promote *nobodiness* for their civilians or subjects.[141] As previously mentioned, a clear example of this

[139] Examine Bruce Broomhall, *International Justice and the International Criminal Court: Between Sovereignty and the Rule of Law* (2004).

[140] Farhad Malekian, *International Criminal Law, the Law of Somebodiness, the Law of Nobodiness* (New York: Nova Science Publishers, 2021).

[141] *Id.*

is the constitutions of the United States and Israel, which appear to be fair, and yet they violate the rights of members of other races. As a result, this policy of physical justice rejects moral justice in the sphere of international legal developments. This is particularly clear when comparing the relations of powertionist Western governments with those of non-Western ones. This is the ideal of the criminal NATO and the theory behind the United States, Great Britain, and France and their minion states including the Netherlands, Sweden, Denmark, Norway, and Finland. The theory of moral justice has been compromised by their policies which have resulted in lies and the highest level of practical delinquency.

In sum, promoting criminal activities with physical justice is equivalent to intentionally committing crimes. I am not accusing any state directly, but rather addressing the fact that directly or indirectly supporting the crimes committed by the powertionist government itself constitutes a commission of crimes, assistance, aid, help, support, and complicity. The direct cause of these acts by governments is the killing of innocent victims, including children. The problem is that physical international criminal justice leads to lawlessness in international relations, and as a result, reaching moral justice becomes impossible. Everyone should be treated compassionately and humanely- this is the minimum standard that must be respected by the rules and provisions of the system of international physical justice.

However, the system does not have any understanding of the rights of populations in other states when it is executed by the big powers. The system is typically violated by the super powerful states of NATO to the detriment of non-Western governments that do not yield themselves to the criminal decisions and conduct of American, British, and French criminal governments. In such cases, it does not matter that the value of physical international justice loses its legal power, even though it is supposed to protect all men. In practice, it is unfortunate that when the powertionist governments engage in the commission of international crimes, it may take several decades for the evidence to be discovered.[142]

We should remember that justice, proper justice, and moral justice, do not exist if we collude with criminals for personal gain, whether at the individual or governmental level. Much more clearly, harsh physical justice does not leave the platform of moral justice voluntarily and does not go away independently, as long as our complicity is colouring its existence. The

---

[142] Farhad Malekian, *Powertionism in International Criminal Justice* (New York: Nova Science Publishers, 2022).

establishment of physical justice, particularly in strong governments, has always been done by military force. It is the private interest of self-preservation or self-interest that, in all situations, kills the interests of the public. A clear example of this is the situation during the Second World War and the Germans' interest in annihilating the Jewish population. Another contemporary example is the policy of the Zionist government concerning the Palestinian population and their territory, which has been occupied by the Israelis, who plan to seize the entire territory.[143] These acts go beyond those seen during the Holocaust, thereby giving rise to the international crime of *blackboard-barbarism*. It is also significant to mention:

> … the tears of the victims of the Second World War. I refer to the victims on all sides. A much earlier example is the history of the African continent and the extermination and mass murder of Africans by Western colonial authorities across centuries. For instance, Leopold II established Belgium as a colonial power in Africa and owned not only the land but also its people, like animals. His brutal, widespread atrocities were committed against the population of the country. Consequently, it is recorded that between 10 and 20 million people were mass murdered in Congo. However, we recognize Hitler as the most infamous criminal figure in history, while that should not hold true when we compare Belgium's crimes against Congo's population. This was similar for France, which colonized African nations thorough mass murder and extreme humiliation.[144]

The interest in exterminating the Palestinian population even exists in the political plans of other European countries. This means that physical justice occupies the sphere of moral justice. We must remember that physical justice gets its strength from its supporters, and it is the collective power of supporters that prevents the establishment of proper constitutional international justice and respect for the principles of international human rights law. Thus, the right to impose decisions and sanctions on other states is under the control of those with the power of Chapter VII of the Charter. These states unfortunately have the right to initiate or continue to investigate a case under the authority of the

---

[143] Farhad Malekian, 'Judging International Criminal Justice in the Occupied Territories,' 12 *International Criminal Law Review* (2012), pp. 627-869.

[144] Farhad Malekian, *International Criminal Vacations: Tears of Justice* (New York: Nova Science Publishers, 2024), p. 23.

Security Council without the say of any member of the United Nations - except for those who are considered permanent members of the body.

2. Survival of the Institution of Justice

The institution of physical justice cannot survive on its own without the interests of certain wealthy individuals and groups. It may therefore be asserted that physical justice is capable of turning the most qualitative norms into unjust norms. Physical justice commits crimes beyond crimes and then pretends that they are not crimes but rather the implementation of human rights. This is because physical justice thrives on the development of its own ideologies, and these ideologies are extensions of the occupation of rights. In other words, when rights are occupied, wealth automatically follows. This is the reality in all matters concerning the development of the power of physical justice. An example of this is the establishment of the International Criminal Court in The Hague.

Physical justice first occupies the rights to implementation and then takes all powers of decision under its monopolized control. As a result, the powerful nations become the real directors of the Court, even though the judges of the Court may have different skin colours and ethnic backgrounds. This is just a political game and nothing more. For example, the prosecutor of the ICC, Karim Khan, works for the powertionist governments and therefore keeps their position and believes they are protecting international human rights law and international criminal justice.[145] However, the powerful governments conceal the true reality. The survival of the International Criminal Court is decided by the British and American governments. Thus, nothing more can be said and the cases heard by the ICC strengthen our statement's accuracy. The same is true about the presentation of reasons and facts in the Security Council.

If the system of justice of the ICC was not controlled by the powertionist governments, impunity would not increase.[146] The reason for this is very simple: the criminals who are prosecuted in the ICC are not American, French,

---

[145] See Farhad Malekian, *Conscience of Prosecutors in International Criminal Law, the Heart of the Matter* (New York: Nova Science Publishers, 2021); Farhad Malekian, *Conscience of Judges in International Criminal Law, the Heart of Judgements* (New York: Nova Science Publishers, 2021); Farhad Malekian, *Conscience of Lawyers in International Criminal Law, the Burden of Doppelgängers* (New York: Nova Science Publishers, 2021).

[146] Farhad Malekian, *International Criminal Vacations: Tears of Justice* (New York: Nova Science Publishers, 2024).

or British. This indicates that the ICC permits the big criminals to walk free with impunity.[147] For instance, Biden has murdered millions of individuals, and yet the Swedish prime minister still meets him and gives him a warm hug. Since Biden's crimes cannot, and will not be recorded, he will not be prosecuted. This is because his government controls the provisions of international physical justice and there is nothing more to say. Thus, we base our primary understanding of the systems of international human rights and criminal justice on who can control the mechanisms of the survival of the institution of international criminal justice and to what degree.

Consequently, this situation demonstrates that the theory of instrumentality in the system of the ICC is a fact and is not a self-independent power, but rather the creation of physical control in the system of justice. As a result, wherever we push aside the spirit of moral justice, it does not lead to stunning and natural justice but to the contrary.[148] Additionally, those who speak about moral justice are very rare. The result of this is that the system of moral justice constantly struggles against the ignorance of man and greed, whether of an individual, family, group, nation, or even a government.[149]

---

[147] The unfortunate fact is that the former president of the ICC - - Sang-Hyun did nothing for the prosecution and punishment of leaders of powertionist governments such as Israel, the United States, and the United Kingdom, to name but a few. Did he not protect imperialist governments during his terms in office? Nonetheless, Sang-Hyun Song emphasizes that "Without the rule of law, impunity reigns. By punishing violations of international legal norms and by promoting adherence to these norms, the ICC and the wider Rome Statute system play an important part in advancing the rule of law, thereby reducing impunity. This role is critical given the nature of the specific norms that the Rome Statute concerns—norms aimed at preventing crimes which "threaten the peace, security and well-being of the world."[13] The acts and omissions which fall under its jurisdiction are so heinous, so destructive, that every effort towards their prevention is worthwhile. Accountability is important not only for the sake of the past, but for the future as well. Where impunity is left unaddressed, it provides fertile ground for the recurrence of conflicts and repetition of violence." The Role of the International Criminal Court in Ending Impunity and Establishing the Rule of Law, https://www.un.org/en/chronicle/article/role-international-criminal-court-ending-impunity-and-establishing-rule-law. Farhad Malekian, *International Criminal Vacations: Tears of Justice* (New York: Nova Science Publishers, 2024).

[148] Read Spooner Lysander, Natural Law; or the Science of Justice: A Treatise on Natural Law, Natural Justice, Natural Rights, Natural Liberty, and Natural Society; showing that all Legislation whatsoever is an Absurdity, a Usurpation, and a Crime. Part First. [1882], available at http://oll.libertyfund.org/titles/spooner-natural-law-or-the-science-of-justice-1882 (Accessed: on 18 December 2017).

[149] "Man, no doubt, owes many other *moral* duties to his fellow men; such as to feed the hungry, clothe the naked, shelter the homeless, care for the sick, protect the defenceless, assist the weak, and enlighten the ignorant. But these are simply *moral* duties, of which each man must be his own judge, in e ach particular case, as to whether, and how, and how far, he can, or will, perform them. But of his *legal* duty - that is, of his duty to live honestly towards his fellow men - his fellow men not only *may* judge, but, for their own protection, *must*

However, justice witnesses the events of war, and justice at the end is arrested under the power of guns. Although as natural beings our actions, conduct, and decisions must be in conformity with the law of nature and its vital values for the respect of man's integrity, we are incapable of achieving the requirements of our universal essence of justice and its moral norms. The essence of justice is therefore ignored.

The problem with ignorance is that it establishes a perfect constitution and power for tyrannical governments. That is why if we search in the system of international criminal justice, we often see how the collective greed of man has succeeded in destroying and vandalizing the rights of others and establishing tyrannical injustice beyond the rights of victims. This means that ignorance does not function in accordance with the principles of rights ownership, but rather with the forceful ownership of man in order not only to control the power of law and justice, but even the physical body of individuals, i.e., slavery. *Which international lawyer, which international legal system, which power of justice, which collective force of mind, and which religious, philosophical, and ethical argument does not agree that the existing system of international human rights does not promote millions of lies concerning violations that have been committed in the name of justice? The intention is not to question the system of international human rights law and its legal values, but rather to question whether its existence is utopic and a fallacy.*

3. Pleasure of the Skeletons of Justice

The definition of justice is being squandered in a utopia that violates the *jus cogens* norms of international law. That indicates that there is a place where nonsense reigns supreme.[150] The fact is that the general constitution of justice

---

judge. And, if need be, they may rightfully *compel* him to perform it. They may do this, acting singly, or in concert. They may do it on the instant, as the necessity arises, or deliberately and systematically, if they prefer to do so, and the exigency will admit of it." *Id.*

[150] On *jus cogens* consult Czaplinski, Wladyslaw 'Concepts of *Jus Cogens* and Obligations Erga Omnes in International Law in the Light of Recent Developments' 23 *Polish Yearbook of International Law* (1997–1998), p. 87; G. Danilenko, 'International *Jus Cogens*: Issues of Law-Making' 2 (1) *European Journal of International Law* (1991), p. 42; A. D'Amato, 'It's a Bird, It's a Plane, It's *Jus Cogens*' 6 *Connecticut Journal of International Law* (1990), p. 1; AJJ de Hoog, 'The Relationship between *Jus Cogens*, Obligations Erga Omnes and International Crimes: Peremptory Norms in Perspective' 42 *Österreichische Zeitschrift für öffentliches Recht und Völkerrecht* (1991), p. 183; E de Wet, '*Jus Cogens* and Obligations Erga Omnes' in de Wet, E and J. Vidmar (eds.), *Hierarchy in International*

promotes injustice and confusion. This condition of physical justice is obviously not the presentation of moral justice; otherwise, we would not continue to witness the killing of millions of individuals by the armed forces of those who claim to be the masters of human rights law, justice, of understanding fairness, protecting the rights of children, and the masters of protecting refugees. It is important to note that their wicked practice of international human rights and criminal justice has terribly blemished the bones of victims. That is the sign of their morality. Due to this, the essential system of international law known as *jus cogens* or the significant body of *erga omnes* is being ignored.[151]

An example of this is the French, British,[152] and American governments' international crimes committed from corner to corner of the world, but

---

Law: The Place of Human Rights (2012); P Dupuy, 'Some Reflections on Contemporary International Law and the Appeal to Universal Values: a Response to Marti Koskenniemi' 16 *European Journal of International Law* (2005), p. 131; C. Focarelli, 'Promotional *Jus Cogens*: A Critical Appraisal of *Jus Cogens*' Legal Effects' 77 *Nordic Journal of International Law* (2008), p. 429; M. J. Glennon, 'De l'Absurdité du Droit Impératif (*Jus Cogens*)' 110 *Revue Générale de Droit International Public* (2006), p. 529; Robledo Gómez, A El Ius Cogens Internacional (Estudio Histórico Crítico) (1982); A. Gómez Robledo 'Le *Jus Cogens* International: Sa Genése, sa Nature, ses Fonctions' 9 *Recueil des Cours de l'Académie de Droit International de la Haye* (1982), p. 172; L. Hannikainen, *Peremptory Norms (Jus Cogens) in International Law: Historical Development, Criteria, Present Status* (1988); M. W. Janis, 'The Nature of *Jus Cogens*' 3 *Connecticut Journal of International Law* (1988), p. 359; A. Kawasaki 'A Brief Note on the Legal Effects of *Jus Cogens* in International Law in International Law' 34 *Hitotsubashi Journal of Law and Politics* (2006), p. 27; A. J. J. de Hoog, 'The Relationship between *Jus Cogens, Obligations Erga Omnes* and International Crimes: Peremptory Norms in Perspective' 42 *Österreichische Zeitschrift für öffentliches Recht und Völkerrecht* (1991), p. 18; M. Byers, 'Conceptualising the Relationship Between *Jus Cogens and Erga Omnes* Rules' 66 *Nordic Journal of International Law* (1997), p. 211; A. Cassese, 'For an Enhanced Role of *Jus Cogens*' in A. Cassese (ed.), *Realizing Utopia* (2012); C. Chinkin, '*Jus Cogens*, Article 103 of the UN Charter and other Hierarchical Techniques of Conflict Solution' *Finnish Yearbook of International Law* (2008), p. 63.

[151] E. de Wet, '*Jus Cogens* and Obligations Erga Omnes' in, E de Wet and Vidmar (eds.), J *Hierarchy in International Law: The Place of Human Rights*, (2012). A. J. J. de Hoog, 'The Relationship between *Jus Cogens*, *Obligations Erga Omnes* and International Crimes: Peremptory Norms in Perspective' 42 *Österreichische Zeitschrift für öffentliches Recht und Völkerrecht* (1991); A. de Hoogh, *Obligations erga omnes and International Crimes: A Theoretical Inquiry into the Implementation and Enforcement of the International Responsibility of States* (Kluwer The Hague, 1996). See also Erika de Wet, 'The Prohibition of Torture as an International Norm of *Jus Cogens* and its Implementation for National and Customary Law,' 15 (1) *European Journal of International Law* (2014), Vol. 15, No. 1, 97-121.

[152] "In the context of war crimes committed by British forces in Iraq, the UK has not secretly shielded its high-ranking personnel from accountability, but done so in a blatant and aggressive manner. It has attacked those representing Iraqi victims and witnesses with the aim of destroying the evidentiary value of their testimonies in an unprecedented approach

painting all crimes as the result of fighting against the atrocities of certain regimes.[153] These tyrannical or colonial governments use the same means of protection and justice as they did in the past in order to bring about a state of human rights, justice, and morality. In other words, they define their own governments. It is more surprising that even the governments that claim to have created an advanced democratic system engage directly or indirectly in committing crimes, all while still claiming that they are following the principles of international human rights law. Once again, I should bring up the example of the Swedish government and the serious political mistakes it is making at this time.

How could the prime minister of Sweden say that she appreciated Biden's commitment to helping Sweden achieve its membership in the criminal organisation of NATO? How could she not be aware of the fact that Biden is one of the evil criminals of the twenty-first century? How could the next prime minister and foreign minister make the same mistake? A president who, together with several other presidents of the United States, has carried out the most terrorist attacks in the history of civilisation, even against their own nation, in order to convince the world about the hypothetical terrorist attacks of September 11th.[154] On March 7, 2024, the Swedish government and its foreign minister completed their membership in the criminal organisation of

---

that it continues to pursue across a range of cases even today. By taking legal actions and calling claims "vexatious" and law firms "ambulance-chasing" (para. 461), the state's executive branch has attacked the domestic justice system, as such, and successfully brought down many of those seeking to enable victims' access to justice. The Ministry of Defense supported and applauded the Solicitors Disciplinary Tribunal's decision that, in the end, led to the closure of Public Interest Lawyers and left hundreds of Iraqi victims without legal representation in the UK, without witness support during their interviews with IHAT, and without the possibility to exercise their rights as part of investigations. Further, investigative mechanisms like IHAT were shut down in an extremely hostile climate. The Prime Minister at the time and several Secretaries of Defense over the years have openly attacked the idea of holding any form of investigation into British soldiers, let alone commanding officials, and have pressured investigative bodies to shut down all cases as soon as possible." Andreas Schueller, The ICC, British War Crimes in Iraq and a Very British Tradition, https://opiniojuris.org/2020/12/11/the-icc-british-war-crimes-in-iraq-and-a-very-british-tradition/; see also https://www.icc-cpi.int/sites/default/files/itemsDocuments/201209-otp-final-report-iraq-uk-eng.pdf.

153 For example consult Clara Nieto, Chris Brandt, Howard Zinn (Foreword), Masters of War: Latin America and U.S. Aggression From the Cuban Revolution Through the Clinton Years (2003).

154 Noam Chomsky, The Crimes of U.S. Presidents, https://www.youtube.com/watch?v=5BXtgq0Nhsc; https://en.wikipedia.org/wiki/List_of_wars_involving_the_United_States. See also Farhad Malekian, *Trading Virginity of International Criminal Justice* (Nova Sciences Publishers, 2020), p. 35.

NATO by submitting their final book to Antony Blinken, one of the most well-known perjurers and criminals of all time.

The fact is that the constant preparation for possible wars has been a demonstration of the provisions of international human rights by big, powerful governments.[155] Any campaign or the heavy burdens of injustices by the big powers have long been the primary threat to other countries, even democratic ones such as Sweden. Simply put, the Swedish government accepted going into the mouth of the wolf in order to avoid potentially being attacked by Russia. As a result, we are being fed to those who have killed millions and still believe that we are the most democratic country in the world. I am referring here to the country that controls the weapons industry and sells weapons to its customers to kill the principles of democracy, human rights, and criminal justice in the Middle East.[156]

Without hesitation, the goal of all wars is to diminish the theory of justice, ethical understanding, and moral requirements while strengthening the theory of brutality for trade purposes. The fact is that within the system of the United Nations, there exists a garden of wars, a garden of fire, a garden of trading injustices, a garden of reaching the most unlawful measures of humanity, a garden of occupying the territories of others, and a garden of the criminal policies of democracy that can only be reached by criminals or those who support the criminal conducts of others as the presentation of human rights principles. This is why we continue to succeed in convincing one another that physical justice is the most profitable justice for humanity and that moral justice does not exist and its principles are hypothetical. As a result, we establish a federation of all-powerful governments and their followers as the mechanism for the promotion of perpetual justice, fairness, and the creation of a gate to peace. This constitutes the end of physical justice, which is enforced by military force and, if necessary, by the content of the resolutions of the Security Council and the imposition of unilateral sanctions.

---

[155] *Id.*

[156] Examine also Jean Allain, *International Law in the Middle East: Closer to Power then Justice* (2004); see also Jean Aflain, 'Orientalism and International Law: The Middle East as the Underclass of the International Legal Order,' 17 *Leiden J. International Law* 391, 392 (2004); Robert Cryer, The Boundaries of Liability in International Criminal Law, or 'Selectivity by Stealth,' 6 *J. Conflict & Security Law* 3, 3-6 (2001). Examine *also* Farhad Malekian, *Imperative Philosophy of International Criminal Justice: Visible Power – Invisible Essence* (New York: Nova Science Publishers, 2022); Farhad Malekian, *Tour de force of Moral Virtue in International Criminal Justice* (New York: Nova Science Publishers, 2022).

4. The Tyrannical Obstacle to Justice

Justice is hampered by a tyrannical obstacle. When the inequality of arms in the United Nations becomes the first principle of human rights instruments or the powerful terms of the largest international organisation, rights and justice go on sale, and the customers are those who are kissing or hugging the international physical justice of criminals and believe to bring democracy to the world with the industry of weapons. It is not without reason that it is said that injustice and immorality will reign over nations as long as we believe and trust that physical justice has the potential to prevent wars. However, this neglects the fact that physical justice is detrimental and utterly destroys the legally and morally perfect constitution of human rights in the world. The question is: what is wrong with our human rights provisions? Adopting more human rights norms is akin to putting more decorative Christmas trees in the court of justice and denying that all these trees point to the same unreachable carnival that does not exist in reality and that when the festivities have ended, the trees will die. This means that although nothing is wrong with human rights provisions, they still contain the wills of criminals.

The house of justice, the court of justice, the house of victims, and the house of judges must all mean the same in the jurisdiction of national and international criminal justice if justice is to be done correctly. We cannot establish peace and truthful justice for the population of the world, and particularly for the victims, if perpetual international peace is under attack by evil authorities in the national or international physical constitutions of the world. When unjust and evil directors are in charge of international constitutions or laws, talking about moral fairness is meaningless. Otherwise, we are killing the nature of morality.[157]

What will this attitude of justice establish when the institution is at war with its subjects? Even the most peace-loving human rights provisions cannot avoid war when the main enemy is the constitution itself or what physical justice demands. This seems to be what is required in terms of physical justice and, to a certain extent, immoral rejuvenation for man. There must be pure trustworthiness in international criminal justice within the boundaries of the definition of its provisions if justice is going to serve all men and their future generations. However, imperialists, autocracies, tyrannical regimes, and those

---

[157] F. Klein Wilkes & Daniel, United Nations Draft Statute for an International Criminal Court: An American Evaluation, in *International Criminal Law 526* (Gerhard O. W. Mueller & Edward M. Wise eds., 1965).

who wish to be masters of all wars and authoritarian utilitarianism do not consider what is happening to the victims of their crimes. Instead, they only think about the benefits they are deriving from their criminal enterprises. This is the end of moral and physical justice, and it is nobler than any other notion of justice. All pleasures of killing and destruction are worthy for authoritarian utilitarianism as long as they contain the maximal nature of their interests.

The fact is that good faith interpretation and fulfilment of the provisions of any physical justice is not a matter of bargaining, and is instead about what should really be done. In addition, justice must have honest justice in its possession, and that cannot be anything other than moral justice, which does not want to win in the process of justice but solely seeks to promote a fundamental understanding of the rights of man as closely as possible in accordance with the spirit of right for all men. Obviously, we are not forced to create moral justice in international social relations, even though we are forced to accept brutal physical force. Examples of this include the wars that have been carried out over the past few decades by the United States. For example, the lies presented by Blair, Biden, Obama, and Hillary Clinton, one of the ugliest liars in the world, can even be recognized as such by children.[158] All these are questions of the self-interest of individuals who have killed millions in violation of the most basic ethical description of philosophical justice.[159] However, identifying their crimes lies not in the hands of moral justice, but rather in those of international physical justice, which is under their control.

The system of physical justice, which does not desire the enlightenment and equality of its subjects, is tyrannical. This is because equality is the primary principle of healthy national and international societies. Therefore, if the ICC is not empowered to prosecute all criminals, then it is instead empowered to promote a sense of inequality and assist criminals. This is because we naturally search for justice and equality of arms in the court of justice, and when justice is not served with respect to the integrity of its subjects, speaking about equal justice would be in itself humiliating. More highly developed international criminal courts must be more conscious of their obligations to serve their subjects. In the unawareness and cruelty of physical justice, the greatest obstacle is to control the power of the law and eventually justice. This power sees other nations or governments as uncivilized or

---

[158] Noam Chomsky, The Crimes of U. S. Presidents, https://www.youtube.com/watch?v=5BXtgq0Nhsc; https://en.wikipedia.org/wiki/List_of_wars_involving_the_United_States. See also Farhad Malekian, *Trading Virginity of International Criminal Justice* (Nova Sciences Publishers, 2020), p. 35.

[159] *Id.*

underdeveloped and therefore as subjects who must obey the orders of the brutal developed government. Thus, it does not matter from which perspective we interpret the law and its provisions, as long as the law reflects the brutal government and the brutal government is the law. This is because wherever we go, we are under the same tyrannical physical justice order.

5. Moral Faculties of Justice

What can be done about all of the injustices that are being committed by these or other political authorities in the name of democracy? The history of the international legal system and its monopolisation demonstrates that our moral ability is typically zero and cannot be humanized by any means due to avarice.[160] The fact is that the realisation of a hidden strategy of moral justice for the sake of man is undeniable - albeit impossible to enforce because of the political, military, and economic interests in the system of physical justice. This means that the sole element under which the faculties of morality or justice can be fully developed is the awareness of the population of the world concerning the fact that the present international order is not honest with its subjects and has left them with an evil mentality of political powers. Therefore, the question is: does the experience of different nations in the world that have been subjected to plundering support the present theory of international physical justice?

We may have different responses, clarifications, and modifications to the given questions, but we must all reach similar conclusions. The present iteration of justice does not function properly, and therefore it should be changed or abolished. The absolute aim of all victims and other parties must be to be released from dynastic physical justice. As a result, we have no alternative other than to reject all powers of monopolisation to protect the population of the world. We must then condemn any form of military monarchy dictated by political powers that seek to wage perpetual imperial wars. We must realize that the powerful nations do not leave the body of justice or international human rights alone because these bodies feed their greed.

---

[160] Consult Farhad Malekian, *The Monopolisation of International Criminal Law in the United Nations, A Jurisprudential Approach* (Stockholm: Almqvist Wiksell International, 1st ed., 1993, 2nd ed., 1995).

In order to reduce the power of injustice, we are forced to unite ourselves concerning the implementation of moral justice and the cultivation of its principles within ourselves, gradually extending to family members, clans, and ultimately, the entire nation. Achieving such a goal is not easy and requires that we make strong decisions about our self-development. Thus, we are forced to start with the belief and confidence that love for moral justice is the only alternative to fighting peacefully against the injustices of physical justice. Without question, the love for working with moral justice, which is grounded in principle, can slowly close the gates of injustice or at least minimize its catastrophic consequences. Justice is actually the inspiration of love for the truth and it strengthens and the practical ability of moral justice. This is because moral justice is not political or legal power. It is neither the surface of a court, nor a very significant part of our existence as human beings with needs for similar protections. The fact is that uniting our love for moral justice and working together to that end means we have nothing to lose and will all be victorious in gaining a common understanding of our needs.

Obviously, we cannot guarantee our existence as beings. However, we can guarantee that our present being is human, and thus we need to be treated as respectable subjects of physical justice by all authorities. There may be other factors for the existence of man that we do not reach, but the fact is that moral justice intends to secure both the visible and invisible rights of man, whether through growing the consciousness of humanity or through settling a conflict with honesty and prosperity. The sphere of moral justice keeps destructive physical principles and their effects away. Moral justice, contrary to physical justice, signifies the properties of man, while the latter plunders people's rights in various regions of the world and forces them into a new form of slavery.

The criminal activities perpetrated by the American government in the Middle East and the French government in Africa are a clear example to illustrate this point. The French government is a colonial power that speaks about human rights, human justice, peace, and the protection of the rights of nations, all while refusing to withdraw from Niger long after the abolition of slavery and the establishment of Niger's sovereign international legal personality - simply because the dependent puppet and fake government of the country, which was protected by the French government to plunder the Niger uranium, gold, and other resources, has been removed by the revolutionary government. The French government is actually violating UN laws and legal order. It violates the provisions of all international conventions concerning human rights of all natures. This is how the system of international physical justice orchestrates its unlawful motivations and still believes itself to be on the side of democratic rules. The protests against the French government are occurring at a time when the vast majority population of Niger has been suffering for centuries and struggling to just survive.

The fact is that European governments are so closely bound together by political, historical, traditional, military, and commercial interests that they are remain silent on current matters. This is certainly a violation of international human rights and their own constitutions, which speak about the rights of man but not the rights of the victims of genocide, crimes against humanity, and slavery at the hands of most European governments. One does not necessarily need to engage in the commission of those crimes, but one who purchases and uses the cargo resulting from those crimes is certainly aiding in the commission of said crimes. Slavery was established as a result of European law, and European governments consume the products of the French government, which in turn were originally developed to steal the resources of African countries. The idea of physical justice and its brutal nature can be seen clearly here. This is why we insist that the idea of moral obligations does not coincide with physical obligations. This is certainly true in the case of obligations that have the virtue of *jus gentium*. We are here speaking about the faculties of justice, morality, righteousness, and faith in relation to the basic rights of all men.[161]

6. Occupying Inherited Rights

Throughout the history of civilisation, the notion of moral justice has been ignored within all societies because of economic interests. However, many changes have been made, not because man has become rational, but because violations and suffering have been the most significant factors in finding solutions that can give humankind peace, justice, and equal understanding. Consequently, man has tried to express his will and rights within certain documents, conventions, agreements, and constitutions. The chief function of these constitutions has been to create certain rules and obligations that should be binding on all members of the given society. However, we should emphasize that all these regulations have not been attainable in practice, and obtaining rights has been particularly complicated when it comes to certain matters, in particular political rights and freedom of expression.

[161] Farhad Malekian, *Concreting Righteousness in International Criminal Justice* (New York, Nova Sciences Publishers, 2024), p.

It is the notion of attainability that proves that rights exist. That is why a considerable number of constitutions list a number of rights that are, as a matter of fact, impossible to achieve. Similar conclusions may be drawn about the system of the United Nations, the Statute of the International Court of Justice, the system of the International Criminal Court, and, in general, all human rights and criminal human rights conventions and agreements. The primary intention of all these instruments and bodies has been to promote the rights of man by establishing rights and preventing governments from committing crimes against those rights.[162] However, the fact is that most of these legal and humanitarian provisions are unattainable in reality. The ideas in the content of these documents are idealistic, but they have put less value on the rights of man when the policy of war, occupation, threat, or use of force has been placed on the desk of justice.

This is not the end of justice, but we must realize that the ideas of regulative principles of physical justice have been instrumental and do not have objective validity. This means that the nature of the obligations of the authorities has not been consolidated in reality, and these obligations have been free from the general practice of physical justice. This indicates that obligations have been beneficial for the legal and political authorities. Hence, we are alarmed at how physical justice has disregarded its real function and strayed from its initial intentions regarding the establishment of the rights of man. That is why, in the system of international criminal justice, the voices of the victims are not given any value over the voices of victors.

A very clear example is the Palestinian voice, which holds no value for the system of international criminal justice or human rights law. Although we have the means to uphold their rights, the weakness of international lawyers and the fact that they are sold means that we are unable to help those people who have been deprived of their rights.[163] This is the nation where every single

---

[162] Consult the new judgment of the ICJ concerning the genocide in Gaza. https://www.un.org/unispal/document/summary-of-the-icj-order-icj-19jul24/. See also Hurlock William L., "The International Court of Justice: Effectively Providing a Long Overdue Remedy for Ending State-Sponsored Genocide (Bosnia-Herzegovina v. Yugoslavia)," 12 *American University Journal of International Law and Policy* (1997).

[163] Consult also Nina Jørgensen, *The Responsibility of States for International Crimes* (OUP Oxford 2000); A. de Hoogh, *Obligations erga omnes and International Crimes: A Theoretical Inquiry into the Implementation and Enforcement of the International Responsibility of States* (Kluwer The Hague, 1996); J. Crawford, S. Olleson, 'The Continuing Debate on a UN Convention on State Responsibility' 54 *ICLQ*, (2005), 959–71; Robert Cryer, 'The Doctrinal Foundations of International Criminalisation,' in M. Cherif Bassiouni, ed., *International Criminal Law*, Vol. 1, (2008), pp. 107-128; Joseph Hoover, *Moral Practices: Assigning Responsibility in the International Criminal Court*, 76

individual has a moral duty to demand their rights from the authorities who have a constitutional or international responsibility to implement physical justice. First, the evil mentality of physical justice must be prevented. Second, the rights that have been stolen as a result of criminal activities need to be restored.[164] The question then is: what are the general conditions of international human rights and the legal personality of states that do not exist for certain nations because of the needs of political powers?

The negative circumstances surrounding the system of international physical justice require our full attention, not only in the assemblies of the United Nations, but also on the platforms of international courts, both civil and criminal. Even though the situation may jeopardize friendly relations between nations, we are already in danger from the armed forces of political powers. The fact is that a considerable number of politicians and writers are afraid to talk. These conditions have been seen on occasion and require truthful examination. The different situations in which hostilities occur against the rights of Palestinians are therefore very controversial and painful to the body of moral justice and underline the very immorality of international physical justice.

Again, any nation can commit international crimes both within and outside of its territories, but what this undefended nation is doing is indeed equal to international crimes committed by Germany and a number of European states against the innocent Jewish population of Europe. This situation clearly demonstrates that the victims of yesterday are the criminals of today. Here we are not standing against the rights of any Jew, but rather stating that the situation must be seen and addressed by those speaking about human rights and justice in all forms of legal institutions. The danger of actual conflicts arising between nations because of the tension of physical justice *versus* moral justice should not be ignored based on the provisions of their constitutions and the power of their parliaments to use their own interpretations concerning those provisions.

It is always these exaggerated and unconstitutional interpretations of the system of international human rights, international criminal justice, and the

---

Law and Contemporary Problems (2014), pp. 263-86; Farhad Malekian, 'Armenian Genocide and the Questions of Responsibility of the Turkish Government,' *House of Commons Conference on the Armenian Genocide, Armenian Solidarity, British-Armenian All-Party Parliamentary Group, No Security Publication* (2007), pp. 31-9; Farhad Malekian, *System of International Law: Formation, Treaties, Responsibility* (Uppsala, 1987); Gracia-Amador, 'The Crime of Apartheid: Responsibility and Reparations,' *Review of Contemporary Law* (1981), pp. 31-38.

[164] *Id.*

body of international relations that pit governments against each other, just like dogs fighting in the streets of armed conflicts. The system of international law does not permit the right of occupation, intervention in political situations, or other priorities to destroy and steal the economic rights of a nation based on our constitutional physical justice. Even the UN Charter avoids permitting the rights of intervention in the political affairs of other states as much as possible. The essential reason for this is that states have inherited certain independent rights concerning their territories in a way that subverts their political, economic, military, and cultural independence. That is why every sovereign acts independently concerning its international legal personality. For a similar reason, physical justice cannot be hired or used with the intention of destroying the sovereignty of other governments.

7. Intervention in Moral Justice

There is nothing new in the basic understanding of the principles of justice except our constitutions and relevant interpretations. This means that with the assertion of rights, we advance our personal or governmental collective deductions and take them as guarantees for our arguments. The right to use moral arguments therefore disappears, and physical justice and its powerful interpretation become common law. Thus, as a result of knowing more than others, we bring our arms and military arms into action with the full intention of pursuing our governmental interests. In the same manner, we have to use the system of international human rights as our basic arguments developing universal hospitality, cordiality, and friendliness against nations that seek to occupy other countries in order to access their resources such as oil, uranium, and gold.

Therefore, the situation requires resorting to the use of force under the provisions of the Charter of the United Nations and according to the priorities of our votes in the Security Council. Guaranteeing any form of justice based on equality of rights loses any support in the course of the negotiations. That is why I have insisted that a constitutional unlimited power based on physical justice is unfair and represents an intervention in the theory of moral justice. It is the conflict between the wisdom of moral justice and the unwise decisions of big political power that becomes the starting point for conflicts. The right to demand equal justice in the practice of United Nations members and, in general any government, is the idea of truthfulness in the application of equal justice. Again, the fact that all governments, both strong and weak, should have a constitution that is in accordance with the principles of international human rights is the main point of all arguments.

In order to make this possible, the provisions of our constitutions must be reasonable and not sanction a complete separation of constitutional provisions from their practical ones. That is why problems may arise in the application of democratic rules and provisions of constitutions when physical justice reigns as a despot in a democracy. Clear example of this can be seen with two different Iranian governments, one of which was overthrown in 1953, and the other in 1979. Both times, Iran was robbed by the British, American, and French physical justice. They brought the Persian King to power, but they also removed him from power. In addition, the clearest example is the democratically elected Nazi leaders and the annihilation of millions of Jews by the democratic despots. The Palestinians are also currently being deported from their traditional lands due to the brutal plans of powertionist governments.

A good domestic constitution of any government should be firmly established on the principles of the rights of both its own citizens, as well as the citizens of other countries. This means that a good constitution does not want to increase the strength of its power, neither domestically nor internationally. Such a reasonable constitution does not solve its problems with the murder of other nations and the occupation of their resources. It would, in reality, be more harmful if it destroyed the sources of other nations for its own profit. This is because the end of most wars proves that the aggressive government that has employed the principles of international physical justice, or, in other words, international human rights, for its own benefit is actually the loser in the history of civilisation. A clear example is the apartheid case in South African. However, we do not deny that waging war under the system of international criminal law is an established phenomenon of government immorality today.[165]

---

[165] On international criminal law, see Georg Schwarzenberger, 'The Problem of an International Criminal Law,' 5 Current Legal Problems (1950) 265; Edward M. Wise, 'Prolegomenon to the Principles of International Criminal Law,' 16 New York University Law Review (1970) 562; Farhad Malekian, *International Criminal Law: The Legal and Critical Analysis of International Crimes* (2 vols. 1991); Farhad Malekian, *Principles of Islamic International Criminal Law: A Comparative Search* (2011); Farhad Malekian, *The Monopolisation of International Criminal Law in the United Nations: A Jurisprudential Approach* (2nd ed., 1995); M. Cherif Bassiouni (ed.), *International Criminal Law* (5 vols., 1999); Farhad Malekian, 'International Criminal Responsibility,' in M. Cherif Bassiouni (ed.), *International Criminal Law*, (1999).

Constitutional provisions have unlimited use, which strongly conflicts with the principles of moral justice. However, conflicts may be prevented or reduced if physical justice is not based on the unlimited strength of its provisions and is instead based on the wisdom and power of love for justice. *The central idea of moral justice is truth, and above all, truth for the establishment of rights of others and the consolidation of the principle of equality of arms based on moral principles and not friendship. This must be seen as the final stage in Menfolk's progress.* The problem here is that we do not understand the principles of moral justice and the very vital rules in the establishment of justice. This would possibly be the surest presentation of those who enforce physical justice, but it is almost impossible to see moral justice as privileged over physical justice, and the latter is more often an undesirable legal mechanism.

Certainly, moral justice condemns any idea of a universal physical justice that is dominant and promotes a system under which the rights of national individuals or international ones are frozen. The only column in an indubitable system of justice is therefore the one in which humanity in its true form is respected for the reasons of humanity and not for the reasons of law or justice. Here, I am referring to the union of understandings of the vital and perpetual principles of justice that should not be used for personal advantages. This scheme of a perpetual system of principles of peace, justice, equality, and love is therefore the master key to reducing the suffering of both domestic and international victims. Although our arguments may still be regarded as controversial, the progress of this idea of moral justice is not, and opposition to it comes mostly from those who are supporters of dictatorial physical justice. Beyond this, there exists a necessary evil in any physical legal system that must be fought against or rejected through wisdom.

8. Grief for the Consequences of Injustice

It is the attitude of the modern system of justice that always speaks about international human rights. This attitude can also be seen in the discussions and meetings of international organisations and governments. The greatest champions of the war on physical and moral justice have nothing to lose in reality, based on the fact that admitting that moral justice or physical justice are the leading principles of justice serves no purpose. This is because both notions of justice address the philosophy of taking the provisions of human rights as the master key of their discussions into consideration.[166] However, there is a significant gap between the policies of both legal systems. One addresses the correct and equitable concept of international human rights, which in turn states that implementation is necessary and equal to elements of humanity and not to violations of their rules.[167]

At the same time, reference to human rights in the body of physical justice does not necessarily also ensure the application and respect of human rights norms. Such situations indicate that all powers and orders of the law equally support significant provisions of human rights with the basic support of morality. However, references to physical justice in human rights norms are synaptic and heretical. With the synaptic reference to human rights, we mean that the relevant provisions of the Convention on Human Rights function like a nerve cell under the orders of political powers. This means that politicians will use these provisions when it suits their form of political justice.

The theory of physical justice, insofar as it pertains to nations of the world, contradicts the real feature of moral justice, which demonstrates that it is the physically unhealthy imposition of the provisions of manmade law that creates war and anxiety among the subjects of constitutions globally. Physical justice orders injustice against moral justice as a method of extermination, while moral justice guides us in the direction of humanity. Physical justice norms are wild and are not educational instruments of justice, rather they are untreatable warts on the legal system. When treated, the warts simply grow in other areas of legal justice, and these warts are easily cultivated in the internal affairs of other nations with the full intention of monopolizing their resources. The same policy shows the real strengths and weaknesses of the system of physical justice, in particular the international standard, which is combined with violations and barbarities in certain traditional areas of human civilisation.

With this last clarification, most lawyers will probably be inclined to agree that physical justice is more often the presentation of power and occupation of territories by other nations, based on the pretext of the principles of humanity.

---

166 Consult Ruth Gavison, ed., *Issues in Contemporary Legal Philosophy: The Influence of H. L. A. Hart* (1987); Heidi Hurd, 'Challenging Authority,' 100 *Yale Law Journal* 1611 (1991); G. Hughes, 'Validity and the Basic Norm,' 59 *California Law Review* 695 (1971); H. L. A. Hart, Essays in Jurisprudence and Philosophy (1983); Joseph Raz, *The Morality of Freedom* (1986); J. W. Harris, *Legal Philosophies* (2nd edition, 1997); John Austin, *The Province of Jurisprudence Determined and the Uses of the Study of Jurisprudence* (1954); Gerald J. Postema, *Bentham and the Common Law Tradition* (1986); Julie Dickson, *Evaluation and Legal Theory* (2001); H. L. A. Hart, *The Concept of Law* (1961).

167 *Id.*

It therefore seems to be a necessary character of physical justice which treats the backbone of its own structure badly in the name of humanity. The question then is: how can physical justice, which destroys all its opponents, and even in certain situations, foreigners, want to be recognized just? It is very obvious that we are degrading the notions of morality and humanity with the sole intention of reaching our own goals and ignoring the misery, pain, and grief that come with war. The great magical forces of international human rights that we recognize go nowhere because of our weak humanity principles and their divorce from the notion of moral justice as a whole.

The great moral influence of humanity, which has already been adapted into our legal system of international human rights, therefore sees no light and contributes nothing to the fundamental principles of humanity because of the political prevention of the rights of victims. This is particularly obvious when the function and principles of international human rights reach the stage of disparity. My explanations may be rather vague to those who wish to confuse the subjects of human rights in order to reach their hidden goals. Thus, they do not want to see a successful notion of human rights that is very close to its definition because that would hinder their pursuit of their political and economic wills and interests. There are many good rules in the system of physical justice, however there is also evil within the system. I am referring here to the system of international physical justice and its powertionist governments, including those in NATO. The organisation is at war with its existence. We should not forget the fact that the notion of morality may be less than a sentiment for many and ignoring the fulfilment of morality or righteousness in our judgments should be an integral part of our physical justice duty.[168]

9. Questioning the Statute of Justice

The illusive excitement of a goal or a desire to promote international human rights principles in practice has long since died within contemporary international relations. The fact is that we cannot speak about human rights values and their very significant intentions while at the same time having other visible and invisible goals. The very encouraging glory of implementing international human rights cannot be effective when we have a number of

[168] Farhad Malekian, *Concreting Righteousness in International Criminal Justice* (New York, Nova Sciences Publishers, 2024).

different political and economic intentions regarding the glory of power, force, and injustice. If I am wrong concerning my statements, then the reader should apologize to me for not being on the side of their powerful criminal governments. Certain matters are very serious and will remain so for me forever.

a. How can the governments of the world engage in the weapons industry and still speak about human rights values?[169]
b. How can a government be proud of the democratic principles within its constitutions and still be involved in the production of weapons?[170]
c. How can a government claim to respect the fundamental basic values of human rights but be the very reason for the colonisation of African continents?[171]
d. *How can a government* plunder the uranium, oil, gold, cultural heritage, and many other resources of different countries and still believe that it is supporting the rights of the people?[172]
e. How can governments commit international crimes and still claim that they are supporting and protecting international human rights principles?[173]
f. How can a government value the new colonial legal systems in Africa and believe they support human rights norms?
g. *How can a government* sign, ratify, and enforce the international conventions on children's rights and privileges in its constitution and still be supporters of powertionist criminal governments?
h. How can governments speak about children's rights while engaging in the trade of weapons that will be used to kill children during aggressive wars?
i. How can your government be proud of itself when it hides its crimes?
j. How can our government be proud of itself when it does not protect the rights of the population of the occupied countries against criminal actions?[174]

---

[169] In 2023, the World's largest arms exporters were United States; Germany; China, France, Italy, Russia, United Kingdom, Israel, Spain, South Korea.
[170] Such as Sweden, Netherlands, and Denmark.
[171] Such as British criminal governments.
[172] Such as French government.
[173] Such as the United States, The United Kingdom and France.
[174] Farhad Malekian, 'Judging International Criminal Justice in the Occupied Territories,' 12 *International Criminal Law Review* (2012), pp. 627-869; Claus Kress, 'Aggression and the Use of Force in International Law,' *Proceedings of the 108th Annual Meeting of the*

k. How should I satisfy the body of your human rights law when it cannot see that almost all organized criminality is planned, directed, and committed under the authority of criminal powertionist governments in the name of the implementation of human rights?
l. How should we convince ourselves that the terrorist attacks on September 11th that were created by brutal powertionist governments were actually carried out by other parties?[175]
m. How should we believe that the ISIS criminal organisation was not created by the imperialist powers?
n. How should we deny the horrible acts of torture committed in the *Abu Ghraib* prison by the terrorist government?
o. How can we close our eyes to the inhumane acts of torture being carried out in the Guantanamo Bay detention camp?
p. How should we admit to the brutality of detaining Julian Assange for simply supporting human rights and the hidden truth is necessary for the basic structure of international physical justice?[176]
q. How can the position of your government touch the very essential principle of moral justice when the notions of morality and humanity in the actions of your government are a utopian dream?

Despite all these questions, the reality still remains the same: we are left with something that has been artificially constructed as peaceful and which does not reflect the real picture behind human rights norms. We have actually moved towards the complete ruin of our human rights principles, whether in the body of international conventions or in the structure of the United Nations Charter. All this indicates the existence of our physical justice and its pretend

---

American Society of International Law (2014), pp. 325–346. See also Proof Obama Lied!! The Terrifying Truth Behind Obama Chef's Disappearance, https://www.youtube.com/watch?v=0j1botxJnXw.

[175] David MacGregor, 'September 11 as 'Machiavellian State Terrorism,' in Paul Zarembka, *The Hidden History of 9-11-2001* (New York: Seven Stories Press, 2008); Paul Zarembka, *The Hidden History of 9-11-2001* (New York: Seven Stories Press, 2008); Thierry Meyssan, 11 September 2001: L'effroyable imposture (2002); Arthur Naiman, *9/11: The Simple Facts - Why the Official Story can't Possibly be True* (US: Soft Skull Press, 2011); John Farmer, *The Ground Truth: The Story Behind America's Defence on 9/11* (New York: Riverhead Books, 2009); Don Paul and Jim Hoffman, *Waking Up from Our Nightmare, the 9/11/01 Crimes in New York City* (New York: I/R Press, 2004); Paul Zarembka, *The Hidden History of 9-11-2001* (New York: Seven Stories Press, 2008); Michel Chossudovsky, *War and Globalisation: The Truth Behind September 11* (Global Outlook, 2002).

[176] He was released after being forced to agree that it was not the right way to disclose the truth about political terrorists, which is punishable according to the United States' view of human rights.

values. Can we really not see how physical justice extinguishes the very high values of moral justice? We shall have to get rid of all wars that are organized and orchestrated by civilized governments, whose civilisations bring destruction to other nations. We should soon be able to cover the expenses of all wars, but not the expenses of our human rights law. Almost all notions of humanity are present within our human rights convention, but not the conditions for preventing our own criminal actions. Almost all positions have been recognized in the punishment of criminals, but not the fact that the majority of crimes that are committed by our own governments. In sum, the big criminals, big perpetrators of international crimes, and big terrorists of humanity are all on criminal vacations.[177] It is appropriately put into words that "each war crimes trial is an exercise in selective justice to the extent that it reminds us that the majority of war crimes go unpunished."[178] This is how the practical body of international criminal justice functions concerning physical justice - i.e., without any notion of reasonableness.[179]

10. Decentralisation of the Values of Justice

The body of moral justice is strong and easy to understand, however its policy of application is not only weak, but also impossible to implement when physical justice keeps the body of law under its own control. With the development of the system of international criminal justice, one could suppose that the requirement for moral justice, universal essence, and various rights would receive more support in the sphere of international physical justice; however, the opposite is true. In fact, the application of the notion of morality or righteousness has become more difficult, and the law has become more instrumental than ever before. This means that the instruments of the destruction of the civilisation of nations have advanced, and waging wars and

---

[177] Farhad Malekian, *International Criminal Vacations: Tears of Justice* (New York: Nova Science Publishers, 2024).

[178] Gerry J. Simpson, *War Crimes: A Critical Introduction, in The Law of War Crimes: National and International Approaches* (T. L. H. McCormack & G. J. Simpson, eds., 1997).

[179] "The final duty of the tribunal is thus to arrive at a reasonable understanding of the rules of international criminal law, apply them to a given case, and if the person is found guilty of committing an international crime, impose an appropriate punishment. The principles of international criminal justice are thus those principles of the system of criminal law that must be respected in the examination of a given case and should not be selected or ignored by the tribunal." Farhad Malekian, 'Emasculating the Philosophy of International Criminal Justice in the Iraqi Special Tribunal,' *Cornell International Law Journal*, 58/5 (2005), pp. 67.

occupying the territories and resources of other nations has become bloodier than ever before. This very increase in the provisions of international human rights and international criminal justice has actually made the rights of powerful war-mongering governments much stronger with reference to the fact that it used the legal development of the law as the political reality of the law and the way of argumentation to convince other governments around the world.

It was believed that after the extension of the principles of international human rights and the ratification of a number of international criminal conventions, moral justice and physical justice would walk hand-in-hand in the same direction and promote the development of the principles of humanity, while proving that their basic elements are far from being in accordance to truth and are actually far from understanding morality and its ability to promote peace and the respect of legal personalities. The authorities of physical justice do not question such matters and they are actually of no interest in their political policies of monopolisation of power. Therefore, the modern system of international wars has come to the conclusion that killing and destroying the civilisations and populations of other nations is now necessary for the continuation of their policies. Consequently, governments are much more reluctant to approach the philosophy of moral justice, which would address the underlying reasons for international wars.

Surprisingly, wars are considered necessary for the greater dignity and military powers of the governments that are seeking and propagating the provisions of their own definitions of justice. They are more earnest about consolidating issues such as their own desires, and speaking to powers about the necessary obligations of the system of international human rights is indeed impractical. The prophecy around moral justice and its existence within our universal justice has come to the point where speaking about morality in the offices of judges, prosecutors, and advocates of international criminal justice has indeed become fanatical and even ridiculous. The reason for this is that every matter is connected to profits instead of to the concept of morality. Having large profits, occupying positions, and being known as a well-established lawyer have become the most necessary reasons for the existence of law. Thus, all matters in the battles of war and in the offices of those involved with legal norms are only compared to the profits.

The much more serious problem is that we extend physical justice and wars by intervening in different countries, bringing different dictators into and out of power. However, we are completely silent when our favourite national leader commits crimes, as long as they do not violate our international criminal policies or jeopardize our stake in their national resources. A clear example of such a situation is the last king of Iran who came to power with the help of powerful criminal governments. He was then deposed by the same governments and replaced by the new Islamic regime with the hope of preserving the interests of the Western governments. The same Western governments now want to change the region by ushering in another set of new leaders who follow their orders. This is how international physical justice works in reality and how it rejects any concept of moral justice and its implementation upon the righteous principles of democracy.

Therefore, there is a greater reluctance among political and legal authorities of great powers to engage in the interpretation of international human rights and international criminal justice with righteous principles. This is why the system of international justice remains unchanged concerning the imposition of injustice in the practice of great powers. The clear examples are the British and French governments, which have exercised brutal international policies against various nations. In fact, their international military corps act at the behest of the United States government wherever needed. *This is why all dynastic or imperialist wars are carried out with their military arms and, if needed, by mercenary troops. Thus, physical justice has tried to overcome moral justice in various ways. However, the main motivations for the authorities of physical justice have been love for control of the power of law, love to monopolize the power of justice, love to exploit the power of peace, and love to fight against any government that does not accept the supremacy of its government. It is in the settled contemplation of evidence that the most essential factor for physical justice has essentially been love for victory.*

How could we then suppose that physical justice is the practical demonstration of human rights law and that such justice does not embrace many different elements of moral justice? There are governments that hold that physical justice was established on the basis of a collective understanding of the population and the redistribution of the territory of law and jurisprudence. However, these governments reject the principles of human rights, which demand complete respect for the rights of objects of law on equal natural values. This indicates that disputes about the rights of various physical justice subjects are primarily personal and not centered on the rights of men. To what extent are these monopolized principles of physical justice useful or practicable? This is an essential question that arises when the sphere of monopolisation of law, human rights law, and particularly moral justice, depend on arbitrary decisions.[180]

[180] Farhad Malekian, *The Monopolisation of International Criminal Law in the United Nations, A Jurisprudential Approach* (Stockholm: Almqvist Wiksell International, 1st ed., 1993, 2nd ed., 1995); Study the report of Francesca Albanese file:///C:/Users/uub-b24-1502/Downloads/a-hrc-55-73-auv%20(1).pdf.

Chapter 6

Bitterness of the Supervisors of the Hegemony of Physical Law

1. Substitute Tools of Physical Justice

There is a strong sentiment in favour of the fabrication of the system of international criminal justice among governments that insist that they uphold human rights provisions. Thus, one-sided decisions, one-sided judgments, and one-sided implementations of punishment are the only reasons why most physical justice survives. The governments are either the decision-makers or the puppets of those decision-makers. This means that, on the part of all classes of international society, including both weak and strong nations, we face the circumstances under which the framework of justice is determined and controlled by the perpetrators of crimes. This is most notable in the case of international crimes. It is dishonourable to wage a bloody war in order to earn bloody profits from our weapons industry. The question then is: why should we seek peace, why should we insist on the implementation of human rights provisions, and why should we dig to see whether the provisions of physical justice contain the significant rules of moral justice? When money is the deciding factor for every action, then there is no reason to fight and struggle for peace.

It is our judgment of what is good or bad that determines the nature of good and bad. It is the verdict of a court that says whether a person is a criminal or not. It is also the decisions of politicians that express what constitutes interests and what does not. As a result, the position of physical justice is always changing. Modifications of physical justice might be permitted if they are not obstructed in any way by those in charge. However, when modifications depend on the decisions of highly influential individuals or groups, it represents a complete monopolisation of the legal order and a more uncertain and incomplete security of the law. Human rights and morality are then at stake. The consequences of living an immoral life in accordance with laws that are against moral principles may be more harmful than departing from the order of the supervisors of the hegemony of physical law.

The principles of justice governing peaceful relations may be seen as defective when they do not uphold the conditions of peace set by both sides and only cater to the strong party. Thus, any dispute concerning the determination of the scope of physical justice involves additional matters, which is surely a violation of the philosophy of justice. Such a situation may generate significant political questions without providing answers, there is actually no single instance of a supreme conflict empowering the morality of justice regarding international questions - even though that could be useful regarding the fundamental questions of law. We may neglect the fact that, in some cases, involving the state or the military may be useful as long as their intention is based on the presentation or integration of equal justice and they fight against all forms of foreign occupation. The reason for this is that we must not neglect the problem of finding an objective judge to evaluate questions of justice and move away from any mistreatment of natural regulations.

Even though we realize that finding rational solutions for the questions of justice might be extremely difficult, it is still in the interests of physical justice to not extinguish the needs of justice in order to gain as much moral understanding of the given case as possible. When the principles of justice bring about flames of war, immorality cannot be stopped. However, because both justices aim to provide equal justice and see themselves as belonging to the same body in the sphere of moral justice, the morality of justice cannot be stopped by the immorality of the law. Physical justice has a number of substitute tools and arguments for waging wars. That is why we only encounter immorality in the sphere of international criminal justice, even though all the humanitarian support given to the victims is superficial. This is because of the basic foundation of our reasoning. Humanitarian support becomes moot when we are supporting the production of weapons, powertionist governments, and criminal organisations such as NATO, for example.[181] We massacre victims to support our allies' goals and then pretend that we have come to save the victims.

The various criminal acts that have been committed under the supervision of powertionist governments within the context of peacekeeping missions are

[181] Farhad Malekian, International Crime of Blackboard-Barbarism ((New York: Nova Science Publishers, 2025). Consult *also* Bruce Broomhall, International Justice and the International Criminal Court: Between Sovereignty and the Rule of Law (2004); see *also* J. Dhanapala, *Under-Secretary-General for Disarmament Affairs United Nations, International Law, Security, and Weapons of Mass Destruction*, (New York, 9 May 2002).

a clear example of this.[182] Peacekeeping missions were not established in order to help maintain peace among certain African nations, rather they were established as part of the legacy of imperialism in former colonies and to promote a new modern method of colonialisation. The question then is why, despite the significant development of international human rights and their role in helping developing states, the conditions in these countries have not changed. This becomes particularly significant when we realize that the continent of Africa is one of the richest areas of the world as it is imbued with various natural resources such as gold, uranium, and oil. The presence of European governments, including the United States, is above all imaginable. Consequently, there is not really true independence or a healthy international legal personality covering and protecting the rights of African governments. If immoral international physical justice is not imposed upon the African population, then it is surely at least within the gates of its foreign or internal puppet systems.

Nonetheless, looking away from such vital queries of moral justice to prevent wars, the unlawful killing of individuals, and the plundering of their resources, there can be little difference of opinion about the serious violations of the systems of international human rights and international criminal justice under the supervision of international physical justice. This is the most intricate and strange situation relating to the imposition of injustice in place of justice. Historically, wars have been waged against the parties who do not support Western hegemony and colonialisation. We assert that the provisions of international human rights are significant and that any violation of those rights is an injustice. Is it not true that the same rights have multiple interpretations? We have one definition for ourselves, and then one for nations that do not agree with our intentions and plans that we have created within our false system of international physical justice.

Therefore, we violate our moral duty in all forms, despite the gross violations that occur during the implementation of physical justice, which itself does not contain any trace of moral justice and its united essence for humanity. This position of physical justice and the commission of genocide against other nations serve as a standard for humanity. For example, the Swedish government, like many other European governments such as those of France, Britain, Germany, and the Netherlands, is a strong supporter of the provisions of international human rights and their implementation. However,

---

[182] Farhad Malekian, *Powertionism in International Criminal Justice* (New York: Nova Science Publishers, 2022).

the same government has not signed nor ratified ratify the UN Convention on Certain Conventional Weapons (CCW). *The wars of aggression waged by big, powerful governments are designated as acts of self-defence in response to terrorist attacks, while the defensive wars waged by the victims against occupied powers are designated as acts of terrorism.*[183] *This is one of the serious problems with the current form of practical international physical justice, which is based on the power of militarily strong nations instead of on the substance of moral justice. In this system, the motivations behind defensive wars are ignored.*

2. Hypocrisy of Justice Versus Victims

It's crucial to remember that healthy justice cannot be based on lies and a desire to erase the dictionary of truth; such justice is not true justice and is instead just a combination of lies, the use of the vocabularies of law, and criminal jurisdiction. This is not my own interpretation of the system of justice, but rather a wider ethical and political reality concerning the state of international human rights. We cannot judge the questions of international criminal justice under the auspices of the big political parties and according to their will because doing so would be morally and legally wrong. All judgements must be objective and not predicated on the military or political strength granted by the Charter of the United Nations. For instance, the majority of Western countries believe that the present conflict between the Israelis and Palestinians was motivated by a terrorist attack carried out by Palestinian authorities.

Thus, the Palestinians have been designated as terrorists, despite the fact that Palestinians and Palestine have been the targets of brutal terrorist attacks

---

183 For different views on terrorism see Ahmed, N. Mosaddeq, "Terrorism and Statecraft: Al-Qaeda and Western Covert Operations after the Cold War," Zarembka, P. (Ed.) *The Hidden History of 9-11-2001.* (Research in Political Economy, Vol. 23, 2006), Emerald Group Publishing Limited, Bingley, pp. 149-188. https://doi.org/10.1016/S0161-7230(06)23005-0; David MacGrego, 'September 11 as 'Machiavellian State Terrorism,' in Paul Zarembka, *The Hidden History of 9-11-2001* (New York: Seven Stories Press, 2008); Louis Kos-Rabcewicz-Zubrowski, The Creation of an International Criminal Court, in *International Terrorism and Political Crimes* 519 (M. Cherif Bassiouni ed., 1975); M. Cherif Bassiouni, (ed.), *International Terrorism and Political Crimes* (1975); Johannes Husabø Erling, Ingvild Bruce, *Fighting Terrorism through Multilevel Criminal Legislation: Security Council Resolution 1373, the EU Framework Decision on Combating Terrorism and their Implementation in Nordic, Dutch and German Criminal Law* (Martinus Nijhoff Publishers, 2009).

carried out by the British, American, and Israeli governments for hundreds of years. These countries have waged wars against Palestinian independence and called it self-defence. This is how the system of physical justice functions and how we modify the system of human rights to serve the interests of Western countries. In fact, the British criminal government created Israel in order to have control over their politics and lies. The Western world has been silent about the deaths of thousands of Palestinians, and when the Palestinians fight back in self-defence, they are condemned by the West. This is the real international Western physical justice and its hypocrisy against the victims.

Examples such as that of the situation with Palestine help us understand how the fundamental components of the control of justice are periodically modified to impact criminal justice and human rights by those in control of lies and the power of physical justice. Similar situations arose during the Second World War, during which the Jewish race was annihilated through lies and the control of physical justice. However, the brutal governments did not admit their mistakes. Therefore, when physical justice becomes far removed from moral justice, it is tantamount to a refusal to accept the peaceful essence of moral justice and thus leads to problems concerning the interpretation and application of justice.

> *One may even assert that the 30 years of religious war in Europe culminated in the Second World War against the Jews. This war was not only a political war but also – more significantly in this context – a religious war waged by a specific faction of Christians against minority religious groups, ending with the annihilation of millions of people in Europe. A source of shame for human history is that a group of "enlightened" European Christians exterminated entire groups within their society with blasé and egoistic selfishness. The barbarity of medical experimentation during this time period diminished the value of medical ethics and future development. Ironically, these obvious criminal conducts were not considered sin. Even today, murdering the entire population of Palestine by the Zionist political government is still not viewed as a sin, but rather as a way to achieve the theory of God.* Under the contemporary historical context of civilisation, the Zionist political regime engages in war crimes, crimes against humanity, and genocide against the inhabitants of occupied territories.[184]

[184] Farhad Malekian, *Exploitation of Christian Islamic International Criminal Justice* (New York, Nova Sciences Publishers, 2024), pp. 1-2; Farhad Malekian, *Concreting*

Consequently, the system of justice causes confusion in the understanding of the truth and its role. The system of international law or the moral force of the international community of nations cannot operate properly when this happens. It would be very unfair to assert that the brutal criminal conduct carried out against the Jews during the Second World War was legitimate. It is equally unfair and immoral to say that the occupation of Palestine by the Jews along with their murder and the seizure of their properties are acceptable.

Otherwise, we would be expressing a double standard of morality and change our direction with regard to our own economic, military, and political considerations with the intention of imposing unlawful physical justice. At the same time, we should definitely believe that the function of moral justice is to abolish all types of immorality or unequal immoral judgments. That is why we insist that the presence of moral justice in our constitutions must be compulsory. In this respect, we have done nothing except increase the number of victims. The wars waged by occupation forces across the globe should be condemned. In other words, we must condemn any form of physical justice, as well as all crimes, including genocide. Mediation is impossible to reach when it is being implemented by unjust powers.

3. Mixing Justice with Economic Gain

It is important to base our arguments regarding all matters of law and justice on the moral needs of our actions. Thus, within discussions concerning rules of law, rules of justice, and rules of the analysis of the essence of justice, the methods of settling differences of all kinds should not be neglected in order to understand the theory of understanding moral justice. The means of motivating, stimulating, and inspiring the methods of settling difference must not only be rational and neutral, they must also recognize the rights of victims in order to ensure that the principles of justice are being treated equally. We should not adopt humanitarian passions and prejudices that can affect and destroy the elements of formative justice. What suggests wisdom does not also suggest unwise actions. Although both include the term "wise," they are naturally different from one another. They have two different directions situated on different platforms of the understanding of human equal essence and rights.

Righteousness in International Criminal Justice (New York, Nova Sciences Publishers, 2024).

Based on this, we continue to insist that the future centres of the union of man must be based on moral justice if real peace is going to be seen within the civilisation of man and if we wish to reduce the human suffering that has arisen due to our infinite greed. Unfortunately, the industrial interests of man to produce massive weapons to use to reach their goals have resulted in the rise of attacks on nations and the occupation of their lands. Consequently, the notion of justice has shown itself to be an inconvenient philosophy when it comes to the real definition of its policy in conjunction with the principles of moral justice. We refer here to justice for all, or justice in accordance with reality, and not to the economic considerations that constitute the business of justice. This is because that is not the value of justice, nor what the principles of morality and righteousness require.

Justice must be completely separated from the notion of economic gain, whether or not it is present in the sphere of moral substance. The fact is that the principles of moral justice orient the rightful human understanding and the necessity of separating justice from economic interests. This implies that justice must not mix with the economic interests of conflicting parties. However, we must then ask: what is the true feature of justice in national, regional, and international conflicts? We should endeavour to make it clear that this juridical sphere of international justice is not limited to the wills of the strong parties and is instead rooted in the facts underlying the conflicts. Therefore, in the course of justice, we need to have goodwill for the truth while distancing ourselves from evil.

A clear example here is the presentation of the Palestinian case in different United Nations meetings. A considerable number of resolutions of the General Assembly and the Security Council recognize the right of Palestinians to their home land. Such assertions were even made in the Security Council around sixty years ago. Thus, when we speak about justice, we must respect the words of our resolutions, which imply the rights of nations who are deprived access to their homeland. Additionally, if the situation were reversed, we would seek the same rights for the Jews. Therefore, we are not using the principle of morality to distinguish between races or any ethnic group, but rather to identify what the reality of justice and truth is and what makes it impossible to achieve.

We ought to make judgements with full confidence while respecting certain essential principles of humanity. This is imperative when it comes to the vital principles of morality.[185] In other words, no coercive force should exist within our judgments, references to evidence, witnesses, or any other documents that could immorally influence the decrees of the courts, negotiations, meetings, and the General Assembly of the United Nations.[186] Although we are showing the path to rightful judgments and justice, we are simultaneously aware of the fact that achieving a righteous morality in justice is very difficult and not free from the intrigues of justice and the nature of the economic interests of physical justice.

3. Dismissing Any Conscientiousness

The moral restraint of physical justice also curbs the positive movement of moral justice and may bring the very unlawful courses of war during which crimes against humanity, war crimes, genocide, and the use of a large number of unlawful weapons occur. The intention of moral justice is thus to restrict and prevent powerful states from terrorizing the vocabulary of justice by various means. If justice cannot perform its duty, then it is just an empty expression. Thus, although many governments claim to be fighting for the settlement of justice and its interests, in reality they are hindering true justice. They ignore the fact that one can prevent bloodshed and promote moral justice with the right and equitable humour of humanity.

This is why it is often said that morality is the honey of international relations, and immorality is the poisonous weapon of destruction. We can see this with the actions of the United States, the United Kingdom, and many other Western countries.[187] The position of moral justice has been compromised by the evil academy of physical justice on many occasions, and as a result, economic advantages have shaped the sphere of justice. A thoroughly logical justice unfortunately cannot be enforced. This is one of the reasons why the philosophies of many writers have not been successful. The biggest problem

---

[185] Farhad Malekian, *Imperative Philosophy of International Criminal Justice: Visible Power – Invisible Essence* (New York: Nova Science Publishers, 2022).

[186] For an ethical understanding of judgments consult Robert Alexy, *'Effects of Defects—Action or Argument? Thoughts about Deryck Beyleveld and Roger Brownsword's Law as a Moral Judgment'* (Ratio Juris, 2006), pp. 169–79; Johan Zammito, *The Genesis of Kant's Critique of Judgment* (University of Chicago Press, 1992).

[187] Examine Andreas Schueller, The ICC, British War Crimes in Iraq and a Very British Tradition, https://opiniojuris.org/2020/12/11/the-icc-british-war-crimes-in-iraq-and-a-very-british-tradition/; see also https://www.icc-cpi.int/sites/default/files/itemsDocuments/201209-otp-final-report-iraq-uk-eng.pdf.

with justice is that it follows the madness of authorities and puts the lives of innocent people at serious risk. As previously stated, this is what happened during the Second World War when the Jews of Europe were targeted by European governments, both directly and indirectly.

This is also what is happening currently with the Palestinian population and their homeland as a result of the policies of a number of Western governments. Therefore, any efforts made at promoting peace have been hindered and cannot influence the settlement of justice in accordance with the principles of moral justice. There is therefore very little hope for success against the evil governments of our time, the crushing burden of which is based on the development of modern military armaments. As a result, when justice is controlled and decided upon by evil governments due in part to their significant investments in armament, then there cannot be any justice for the victims. It is not enough to set up the United Nations Assembly or speak about physical justice that lacks any morality or truth.

We need to understand that justice and righteousness are, and must be, imperative for any government that claims to promote democracy while continuing to produce weapons and trade arms.[188] Are such visible trades not tokens of the immorality of the policies of governments? Is the engagement of their governments and social media against victims not immoral? We should not lose sight of the fact that all of these moral justice violations have been carried out through the implementation of physical justice under the direction of powerful nations such as the United Kingdom, the United States, and France. International safety is thus guarded by the opposite circumstances of moral law, moral justice, and moral judgments. This means that the safety of international human rights law and international criminal justice is solely based on the vocabulary of lies, which in turn is based on who-knows-how and who-obeys-who. This is how we arrive at the very serious international criminal violations behind the doors of justice and express preference of our interests over the rights of others.

This phenomenon is known as physical justice, and hitherto no attempt has been made to address the problems of justice and its violations by those who control the main principles of justice. The platforms of justice should not be violated, and are nothing more than a reflection of the truth that supports the actual practice of justice. While this is a fact and should be respected, it is

---

[188] Farhad Malekian, *Imperative Philosophy of International Criminal Justice: Visible Power – Invisible Essence* (New York: Nova Science Publishers, 2022); Parish Matthew, *International criminal law – Justice or Mirage*? Transonflict (2013).

not, and the peculiarities and conditions that are necessary for understanding true justice are violated by political and legal authorities. Consequently, the essential principles governing the elimination of justice, have been implemented without any conscientiousness, and therefore, justice and its implementation have not been successful at any level. Indeed, these difficulties in the implementation of justice by authorities have created significant international problems, and justice has been treated with evil principles.

4. Selfishness Impelling Justice

One of the serious dangers of physical justice is that it permits violations to protect its own position and avoid being criticized by other legal systems that effectively control the system of international criminal justice. This means that a number of governments are forced to comply with the physical justice of the superpower governments and take a similar position to the international policies of those governments. If governments do not adopt such a policy, then their international political, economic, and military policies will be restricted by the big, powerful governments. A recent example of this is the ongoing war between Israel and Palestine and the very brutal military campaign being carried out by the Israeli government in Palestine. The conflict is essentially based on the unlawful, unjust, and immoral occupation of Palestine.[189] However, when it comes to the implementation of the rights of the oppressed, there is no alternative but to fight and protest, which means that the United Nations does nothing regarding the establishment of the rights of Palestinians. The fact is that not only is the physical justice of international criminal law paralyzed, but even the minimal expectations of physical justice are not being met.[190]

---

[189] Farhad Malekian, *Paralysing International Criminal Justice* (New York: Nova Science Publishers, 2021). N. Chomksy and Barsamian D., *Keeping the Rabble in Line*. Boston: Common Courage Press (1994); N. Chomsky, *Media Control: The Spectacular Achievements of Propaganda* (New York: Seven Stories Press, 2003).

[190] Examine Robert Cryer, 'The Doctrinal Foundations of International Criminalisation,' in M. Cherif Bassiouni, ed., *International Criminal Law*, Vol. 1, (2008), pp. 107-128. See also Robert Cryer, *Prosecuting International Crimes, Selectivity and the International Criminal Law Regime* (Cambridge University Press, Cambridge, 2005); Farhad Malekian, *Powertionism in International Criminal Justice* (New York: Nova Science Publishers, 2022); Georg Schwarzenberger, 'The Problem of an International Criminal Law,' 5 Current Legal Problems (1950) 265; Edward M. Wise, 'Prolegomenon to the Principles of International Criminal Law,' 16 New York University Law Review (1970) 562; Farhad

This implies the fact that the brutal physical justice of superpowers keeps the physical justice of other governments under control. This can be seen with the atrocities currently being carried out by the Israeli government against the Palestinian population. It is imperative that we recognize and condemn the systematic killing of populations and their children. This is why it is necessary to discuss the values of physical justice and its control in order to protect against unjustified attacks.[191] A number of governments around the world are contributing to the ongoing violations being committed against the Palestinians by encouraging violations against unarmed people. This is not only seen in the statements of governments that have control over NATO and its allies, but also in the statements of the Secretary General of the United Nations. As a result, there is a great anarchy in the system of international justice that does not follow any principles of moral justice nor a simple method of physical justice. Governments thus permit the killing of other nations in the world in accordance with their own interests.

We must again reference the events of the Second World War and the savage killing of *innocent Jews* and compare it to the murder of the Palestinian.[192] We are speaking about human beings and nothing more. It does not matter if it is Jews who are being killed under physical justice or

---

Malekian, *International Criminal Law: The Legal and Critical Analysis of International Crimes* (2 vols. 1991); Farhad Malekian, *Principles of Islamic International Criminal Law: A Comparative Search* (2011); Farhad Malekian, *The Monopolisation of International Criminal Law in the United Nations: A Jurisprudential Approach* (2nd ed., 1995); M. Cherif Bassiouni (ed.), *International Criminal Law* (5 vols., 1999); Farhad Malekian, 'International Criminal Responsibility,' in M. Cherif Bassiouni (ed.), International Criminal Law, (1999).

[191] Farhad Malekian, *Imperative Philosophy of International Criminal Justice: Visible Power – Invisible Essence* (New York: Nova Science Publishers, 2022).

[192] "The battle between religious authorities within and outside of nations continues, and the priority of religion or religious theory between various religions has become a source of great contention among Muslims, Christians, and Jews. This was even seen in old Egyptian culture, where religious authorities had strong political authority through the monopolisation of general population and encouraging trust of their man-made gods, regardless of their physical form. Worth mentioning here are the supporters of Christ or Mohammed who believed that the occupation of power was equal to that of the authority of the Security Council today. The fact that both religions were created to bridge the long distance needed to be travelled to locate love in the mind of man must not be forgotten – and the noble pursuit of not forgiving the crimes they had personally committed while condemning others for theirs. However, the power struggle and the real definition of law – of power and man – and the true identity of individual's personalities have continued to battle throughout time without coming to any particular conclusion." Farhad Malekian, *Exploitation of Christian Islamic International Criminal Justice* (New York: Nova Science Publishers, 2024), p.4.

Muslims.[193] However, it seems that the governments of the world today make a distinction between humans and animals, i.e., between Jews and Palestinians. Members of the first group are seen as humans, while members of the latter are seen as animals. This implies that the first group should not be harmed and has the right to occupy and plunder nations and commit violations, murder, and genocide. However, these actions are not permitted for the second group, and if the group engages in such actions, then they are designated as criminals, violators, and terrorists - meaning that we are permitted to kill them like animals and speak to them like dogs. It is not impossible that the situation of the Palestinians will become much worse based on the fact that physical justice has been in place for less than seventy-eight years under the chief order of the British government, and the United States has officially permitted the slaughter of the Palestinian population by providing Israel with an endless supply of weapons. The situation is unfair and inequitable.

Additionally, actions carried out by the Palestinians in an effort to reclaim their occupied country, are considered violations of international criminal justice and crimes against the Jews. We therefore neglect to acknowledge that the Israeli government has been physically and mentally harming the Palestinians with the support of most Western Governments, which in turn support Israel in order to avoid political or economic complications. As previously stated, Western governments have their own rules of humanity and interpret human rights to benefit the Israeli government and grant them the permission to kill the Palestinians. These nations act out of self-interest and designate their targets/opponents as terrorists. Essentially, a state that is

---

[193] Mashood A. Baderin, 'Effective Legal Representation in '*Shariah*' Courts as a Means of Addressing Human Rights Concerns in the Islamic Criminal Justice System of Muslim States.' 11 *Yearbook of Islamic and Middle Eastern Law* (2006), pp. 135-167; Mashood A. Baderin, *International Human Rights and Islamic Law* (New York, NY: Oxford University Press, 2005); Mashood A. Baderin, *International Law and Islamic Law* (Ashgate, 2008); A Mashood Baderin, 'A Comparative Analysis of the Right to a Fair Trial and due Process under International Human Rights Law and Saudi Arabian Domestic Law', 10 (3) *The International Journal of Human Rights* (2006); M. Cherif Bassiouni, 'Protection of Diplomats under Islamic Law', 74 *American Journal of International Law* (1980), pp. 609-655; M. Cherif Bassiouni, Islam: Concept, Law and Word *Habeas Corpus*, 2 *Rutgers Camden Law Journal* (1970); M. Cherif Bassiouni, Studies in Early Hadith Literature (Indianapolis, 1978); M. Cherif Bassiouni, 'Sources of Islamic Law and the Protection of Human Rights' in Bassiouni, the Islamic Criminal Justice System (1982); M. Cherif Bassiouni, *The Shariah and Islamic Criminal Justice in the Time of War and Peace* (Cambridge University Press, Cambridge, 2014); Mashood A. Baderin, 'Islamic Socio-Legal Norms and International Criminal Justice in Context: Advancing an 'Object and Purpose'cum 'Maqáṣid' Approach' in T. Gray, Islam and International Criminal Law and Justice (Torkel Opsahl Academic EPublisher, 2018).

motivated by less selfish impulses for economic, military, or political gains is likely to lose significantly more than those that commit aggressive and brutal physical justices against other states. It is not impossible for the big political powers to completely annihilate a nation and then claim they were implementing international criminal justice. This is what they did in Iraq, Afghanistan, Syria, and Vietnam in the name of international law. This has been done in a considerable number of countries and is known being done to the Palestinians in an attempt to force them to abandon their homeland.[194]

As previously discussed, there are very different attitudes toward physical justice and moral justice. This is particularly evident in the practices of the most powerful states in the world. The specific situation that has arisen in relation to the existence of Israel and Palestine is a clear example of the evidence concerning the differences between physical justice and moral justice. *Implementers of physical justice are always identified as victims and view those who demand the establishment of their rights as oppressors. This is one of the main reasons why moral justice has been condemned, even though it is meant to protect everyone. There is therefore no diminution of the causes of crimes committed under the authority of physical justice against the principles of moral justice. This is in so far as the rules of physical justice have influenced the minds of the masses. This is particularly evident with the crimes committed by criminal powertionist governments around the world, and those crimes are supported by most European governments and their populations.*

Such governments increase their own power through the criminal conduct carried out under the theory of physical justice. We must not put aside the fact that the systems of international criminal justice and international human rights are just different interpretations of the same thing. This implies the fact that both systems of human rights and international criminal justice function under the law of force or the law of physical justice of authoritarian governments. In other words, various classes of governments in Europe

---

[194] Examine Farhad Malekian, *Paralysing International Criminal Justice* (New York: Nova Science Publishers, 2021). Consult also other wars: Farhad Malekian, *Documents on the Principles of International Human Rights* (Norstedts Juridik AB, 2007); see *also* Werner Feld, *The Court of the European Communities: New Dimension in International Adjudication* (Springer, 1964); Amnesty International, *The International Criminal Court: Making the Right Choices-Part V* (1998); Richard J. Goldstone, *For Humanity: Reflections of a War Crimes Investigator* (Yale University Press, 2000); M. Cherif Bassiouni and Peter Manikas, *The Law of the International Criminal Tribunal for the Former Yugoslavia* (Transnational Publishers, 1996); John Carey and John R. Pritchard (eds.), *International Humanitarian Law: Origins, Challenges and Prospects* (Brill–Nijhoff, 2000); Thomas M. Franck, *Fairness in International Law and Institutions* (Oxford University Press, 1997).

officially promote the violent settlement of disputes and the occupation of Palestinian rights. Thus, there is no recognition of the wrongfulness of the acts of genocide and crimes against humanity committed by the brutal governments. As a result, attacking and killing sick people in hospitals is also permitted based on the will and interests of the physical justice. In addition, the Israeli Defence Forces (IDF) military soldiers can use the Palestinian population as a human shield, but they are permanently innocent. That means that the judicial arms of the occupation or the Israeli military courts have always judged its soldiers as innocent during decades in occupied territories. Despite this, Palestinians are both violators and aggressive. Our reference here is to the more than 300,000 cases that have been brought to the Military Courts of the Zionist criminal government. Justice is pursued by the Zionist government out of a selfish motive.

5. Vanity of the Philosophy of Morality

It is vain to speak in the language of moral justice here when the violation of the provisions of moral justice is directly and indirectly permitted by most European governments.[195] These states ignore the fact that they created the Zionist government in Israel in order to gain both political and economic benefits as well as to eliminate the oppressed population of Palestine. Thus, saying that the European governments have civilized other countries ignores the fact that they colonized countries across the globe. We are not opening the markets of morality with our political and military actions, rather we are opening a market of killing other nations by supporting the conducts of the

[195] Exmine the statements of Bertrand Russell and the Russell International War Tribunal held in Stockholm, Sweden, May 2-10, 1967 and Roskilde, Denmark from November 20 to December 1, 1967. The Tribunal was essentially created as a result of different meetings in London in 1966. J. Duffett, *Against the Crime of Silence* (New York, London, 1968). W. Michael Reisman, 'Legal Responses to Genocide and Other Massive Violations of Human Rights,' 59 *Law and Contemporary Problems* (1996), p. 75; William L. Hurlock, 'The International Court of Justice: Effectively Providing a Long Overdue Remedy for Ending State-Sponsored Genocide (Bosnia-Herzegovina v. Yugoslavia),' 12 *American University Journal of International Law and Policy* (1997), p. 299; Beth van Schaack, 'The Crime of Political Genocide: Repairing the Genocide Convention's Blind Spot,' 106 Yale Law Journal (1997), p. 2259; John D. van der Vyver, 'Prosecution and Punishment of the Crime of Genocide,' 25 *Fordham International Law Journal* (1999), p. 286; Mary Robinson, Genocide, War Crimes, Crimes Against Humanity, 25 *Fordham International Law Journal* (1999), p. 275; Matthew Lippman, 'Genocide,' in *International Criminal Law*, Vol. I (M. Cherif Bassiouni, ed., 2008) pp. 405-455.

Israeli government. This goes beyond the Palestinian population's housing situation. It implies the fact that moral justice does not exist at all as a result of states ignoring the murder of other states over the course of decades and the plight of their populations.

Thus, the only thing that matters is the dream of the military glory of the dirty, brutal policies of the United States, Britain, France, and their allies. It is all about self-interest and the prosperity of Europe and other countries in the world through the application of one-eyed justice at all times. Justice that is based on physical justice is therefore the most catastrophic form of justice that can be seen in the description of moral justice. As a result, any comparison between physical justice and moral justice is not only wrong, but also creates controversy in our philosophy of justice and its interpretations in the judgments of international criminal tribunals.[196] These controversies can particularly be seen in the description of justice, however political parties and their authorities also face them when they approach a political or criminal dilemma.[197] This means that they lose sight of justice and fairness in the interpretation of the terms of the law and allow their own personal justice to interfere.[198]

They may also change the real definition of justice, and still believe that they are right and giving the best definition of justice. The reason for this is simple: the right to interpret the rules and principles of justice is under their control, particularly behind the desk of the corrupt Security Council. Therefore, powertionist governments believe that they can determine justice based on individual cases. This implies that they continue to be unjust and violate all terms of moral justice, thereby devaluing it. We have stated that the causes of the difference between justice and injustice stem from inserting our own interpretations which in turn promote the principles of corrupt injustice, thereby increasing the number of victims.

A modern sovereign of the notion of justice and humanity is no longer based on the value of our own understandings, but rather on the leisure of the principles of justice and their approach to the truth. The idea comes from pursuing justice for all individuals without violating their rights. In other words, the justice system is regrettably under the control of the political parties. Therefore, violent acts have to end if the system of justice is to

---

[196] Consult G. Bigi, 'Joint Criminal Enterprise in the Jurisprudence of the International Criminal Tribunal for the former Yugoslavia and the Prosecution of Senior Political and Military Leaders: The Krajišnik Case' 14 *Max Planck United Nations Yearbook*, (2010), pp. 51-83.

[197] *Id.*

[198] *Id.*

promote fairness. The philosophy of justice, which permits killing as an honour for maintaining its principles and control of power, is no longer justice, but rather the evil presentation of power and malicious vanity for those who resort to such interpretations.

The causes of injustice in the interpretations of equality, morality, and human rights can no longer be beneficial for any party based on the fact that we create the possibility of such an interpretation of justice for other parties as well when they have the power under their control. There are some crises in the system of international criminal justice that are indeed very detrimental to the mechanism of justice and the application of its principles. This includes when the principles of national criminal justice present their own definitions of justice based on physical justice, which itself arises from the control of power. This way of thinking and acting in the final stage rescinds the moral philosophy of law, which should be powerful and compelling. Consequently, the system of international criminal justice can no longer approach its principles as they are prescribed in its provisions nor implement them as they should be.

This also indicates that the provisions of physical justice interfere in international criminal justice and the manifestation of moral justice. It also indicates that the notion of an ideal presentation of the principles of international human rights and fairness is impossible and every principle of international criminal justice must be sacrificed, and as a result, justice can never be seen. A clear example of this is the centuries-long criminal policies implemented by British governments, along with their barbarism against most nations of the world. Despite their crimes, the British have always been viewed as innocent. The powertionist governments control international justice and pretend to act in good faith, but they in fact promote injustice. They actually subvert the autonomous or self-ruling nature of the law and devastate the moral substance of the law. There is therefore no guarantee that if every government chose to act properly, that international law would be protected. If this were the case, then the traditional merit of the principle of categorical imperative would be respected at the international level, and morality would not perish.[199] However, this is not the reality. This is why the theory of morality is applied in vain.[200]

---

[199] Farhad Malekian, *Imperative Philosophy of International Criminal Justice: Visible Power – Invisible Essence* (New York: Nova Science Publishers, 2022).

[200] *Id.*

6. Misleading Mechanisms of Justice

The terrifying fact is that important rights are not being defended by the merit of physical justice, and consequently, the brutalities, barbarities, atrocities, and aggressive acts of governments persist. As a result, wars and genocides persist as well. Therefore, there are no wise governments or wise politicians that can bring hope to the tablecloth of justice. The disappearance of wisdom diminishes the development of fair justice and its mechanism of morality, which in turn leads to more wars. If we look beyond the mechanism of physical justice, we can no longer find the great principles of the family of moral justice, and instead enter the darkness of our unwise decisions and perpetuate the commission of crimes.[201]

The application of unjust physical justice against other nations and their resources is one of the main causes of war. Other causes relating to misinterpretations of the function of justice cause more harm to the body of justice and eliminate moral justice. One such example of this injustice is the Israeli government's commitment to forcing the Palestinians out of their territory.[202] This injustice not only harms Palestinians, but also the innocent Jews. No wise government occupies other countries and asserts the right to control them. Professor Richard Falk emphasises that

> International law is challenged by the character of the prolonged Israeli occupation of the West Bank and Gaza. The literal situation, it is true, has not been adequately anticipated in the treaty framework set forth in

---

[201] "One of the reasons for the conflicts is that a characteristic set of elements for assigning the fundamental rights, duties, and obligations arising from the institute of international criminal justice or international social cooperation which is acceptable to all states without any due regard to their size and strength is lacking. For example, the framework of the ICC, although promising, rests obviously on the military strength of the United States. In other words, it is up to the United States to accept or reject the implementation of certain rules concerning the application of criminality to the acts of certain individuals under the machinery of the ICC." Farhad Malekian, 'Emasculating the Philosophy of International Criminal Justice in the Iraqi Special Tribunal,' Cornell International Law Journal, 58/5 (2005), p. 678.

[202] Farhad Malekian, International Criminal Law: The Legal and Critical Analysis of International Crimes (2 vols. 1991), at 281, 285, 392; see also Amnesty International Annual Report 1974-75 (1975); Amnesty International, Report on Torture (1975); Amnesty International, Amnesty International Report, 88-89, 340-45 (1984); Richard A. Falk, World Order Conceptions and the Peace Process in the Middle East, in Building Peace in the Middle East 189-96 (Elise Boulding ed., 1994); Richard A. Falk & Burns H. Weston, The Relevance of International Law to Palestinian Rights in the West Bank and Gaza: In Legal Defense of the Intifada, 32 Harvard International law Journal (1991), pp. 129-157.

> the modern law of war, even though it can be persuasively assessed from a perspective that relies upon relevant international legal principles, doctrines, and rules... In such circumstances, there is no acceptable excuse for invoking a condition of legal indeterminacy or-worse--deferring to the *de facto* circumstances imposed by Israeli annexationist designs. As with the international campaign against apartheid, the moral clarity of the legal situation suggests the appropriateness of mobilizing as much international pressure as possible to end the circumstance of unlawful occupation and to encourage the proper fulfillment of Palestinian claims of self-determination, a process that is fully compatible with Israel's own legitimate rights of statehood and security. Ending Israel's occupation of the West Bank and Gaza, we stated at the outset, comports not only with the future peace and stability of the Middle East and the world but, as well, with the requirements of international law and justice. The reverse emphasis is likewise true. Ending Israel's occupation of the West Bank and Gaza comports not only with the requirements of international law and justice but, as we have seen in the on-going Persian Gulf crisis, with the future peace and stability of the Middle East and world.[203]

We should remember that the preservation and safeguarding of the balance of righteousness in international criminal justice is much more significant than maintaining the equilibrium of power to protect moral justice and fair physical justice. If this is not seen in the exercise of power and cultivation of fairness in the system of international criminal justice and its judgments, then justice presents the theory of colonisation of man by power politics, and the cost of justice is the victimisation of more nations and the implementation of unjust decisions. We can refer to this as the great misinterpretation of justice and serious violations of the principles of international human rights under the auspices of criminal courts. Consequently, it is highly improbable that justice will be implemented correctly, and instead more injustice is promoted within the international arena. The fact is that if the principles of fairness or the troops of justice are used contrary to their given purpose to serve or preserve moral justice, then it would be a utopian dream to protect the weak members of the United Nations. This implies that the decisions of the minority must be enforced by the vast

---

[203] Id, p. 156-157. Visit https://heinonline.org/HOL/Page?handle=hein.journals/hilj32&div=8&g_sent=1&casa_token=&collection=journals.

majority of the world's nations. This can be done in various ways, including by promoting brutal wars or by threatening organisations such as NATO.

We are referring here to both philosophy of law and its proper implementation as well as the theory of rights that has to be seen within the theory of physical justice. If such a theory does not promote proper channels for achieving justice and the role of hospitality for the victims, then we are manipulating the vocabulary of justice to fit our own demands and interests. This means that we have given the theory of monopolisation of justice full priority without regard for the rights of others or our duties to follow the rights of the subjects of justice. It also means that we treat the subjects of rights or justice as the enemies of our own injustice. The right to fairness and justice should therefore not be limited to those who control physical justice. In other words, all rights contain a significant substance that belongs to all mankind in virtue of universal rights, i.e., international human rights and, in certain cases, international criminal justice.

Moreover, the rights of human beings should not be in the possession of certain individuals or authorities who control national law or international law. The notion of justice therefore contains the proper rights of human beings and should not be permitted to be infinitely scattered through the monopolisation of physical justice. Thus, the notion of justice must, at all times, reconcile the existence of the rights of its subjects without any violation or disqualification of their rights for the advantage of others. In sum, all individuals, including those who have taken power of law and justice under their control, are responsible for maintaining the rights of others, regardless of their social or international standing. This is an established principle of the system of justice and the jurisdiction of the law - even if it is not respected.

The monopolisation of justice in the case of national or international justice takes advantage of the principles of justice for private reasons, and therefore the common needs are used to plunder power politics. In other words, when physical justice robs the subjects of the law, it goes against moral justice and the rights of individuals. This right to justice exists regardless of a person's cultural or ethnic background Thus, the systems of international human rights and international criminal justice must be evaluated with regard to the fact that every individual in our international society has the right to justice and to have their rights defended. That is, injustice present in the processes of justice invalidates the rights of others and the victims of unjust treatment and injustices lose the right to defend themselves.

The right to self-defence may therefore end in conflict or war and make more victims of unlawful practices such as occupation, which in turn generates the right to self-determination. This is why every provision of international human rights speaks about the correct treatment of its subjects and about subjects being equal in the eyes of national or international justice.[204] This is why the principles of corrupt physical justice are typically opposed to moral justice. The examples of the Jews during the Second World War and the current example of the Palestinians enduring the criminal conducts of Israeli Zionist military aggressive power both reflect this humiliation of mankind under the power of physical justice. We should try to prevent the litany of evils that can afflict the subjects of justice and human civilisation as a whole.

7. Restricting the Threat of Physical Justice

We should not put aside the fact that all men are equal, and this equality should not be violated at any time for any reason, even when one party is not allied with the super-military governments. Therefore, the basis of all legitimate authority among men is its natural equal existence and not the provisions of the physical justices that discriminate between men. Admittedly, the system of international human rights never permits any government to enslave the members of another nation, thereby forcing a nation to submit itself to the orders of another government.[205] Governments that resort to the use of force or occupation are considered criminal states. Criminals in such states use the power of the government to serve their own interests and therefore violate the rights of other nations.

We are forced to avoid arbitrary decisions concerning the rights of others and gradually take possession of their rights based on our own interests. Based on this, we should avoid violating international provisions by promoting illogical defences or absurd statements about the development of wars. The theory of justice must therefore not permit the murder of millions of individuals in the name of supporting humanity as doing so would reflect the use of the system of international human rights law to our own advantage. This is why resorting to unlawfully interpreting the system of international criminal

[204] See Roht-Arriaza Naomi, 'State Responsibility to Investigate and Prosecute Grave Human Rights Violations in International Law,' 78 *California Law Review* 451 (1990); Samuel Moyn, *Not Enough: Human Rights in an Unequal World*, (2018); T. Meron, 'On Hierarchy of International Human Rights' 80 *American Journal of International Law*, (1986), 1; Farhad Malekian, *Documents on the Principles of International Human Rights* (Stockholm: Norstedts Juridik AB, 2007); Ian Brownlie, Documents on Human Rights (2010).

[205] Examine generally *id*.

justice is not permitted. It is illegitimate and should be avoided at all times. In order to combat this, we must abandon unjust reasoning concerning the power of physical justice under the authority of the superpower nations and instead promote the principles of moral justice.

These are objective reasonings, and their missions are not designed for personal gains but for the securities of all nations, both large and small. To say that we have the right to issue commands to other nations is the same as saying that we have the right to monopolize their rights and enslave them, suggesting that they have no right to express their views on such significant economic, political, and cultural issues. These findings demonstrate the seriousness of violations of human rights principles that govern slavery abolition.[206] That is why the principle that men are born free should not be disregarded by physical justice. In other words, physical justice should not restrict the natural rights of man by promoting the resort to the use of force, guns, and occupation. Furthermore, before we codify the system of physical justice and empower it as the law of the land, we should be sure that its provisions do not grant unlimited power to the political authorities and permit the interference of personal interpretations.

The law should not contain provisions that could permit the violation of the rights of other nations. Our intention is not to give priority or respect to the law of any one nation, but rather to keep the principles of equal justice or moral justice achievable under any legal system. This is done to benefit the subjects of the law and ensure that they are granted equal, unconditional rights that apply to all groups and nations equally. *Promoting equal rights is actually a gift of moral justice and should be respected at all times. In order to foster*

[206] See also international conventions such provisions of Declaration on Social Progress and Development, 1969, Universal Declaration on the Eradication of Hunger and Malnutrition, 1974, Declaration on the Elimination of All Forms of Intolerance and of Discrimination Based on Religion or Belief, 1981, Declaration on the Human Rights of Individuals Who are not Nationals of the Country in which They Live, 1985, Vienna Declaration and Program of Action: World Conference on Human Rights, 1993, Draft United Nations Declaration on the Rights of Indigenous Peoples, 1994, Cairo Declaration of Human Rights in Islam, 1990, American Convention on Human Rights, 1969, African Charter on Human and Peoples' Rights, 1981, Arab Charter on Human Rights, 2004, European Convention for the Protection of Human Rights and Fundamental Freedoms of 1950 as amended by Protocol No. 11 of 1998, Charter of Fundamental Rights of the European Union, 2000, Convention on the Reduction of Statelessness, 1961, Supplementary Convention on the Abolition of Slavery, the Slave Trade, and Institutions and Practices Similar to Slavery, 1956, Declaration on the Protection of Women and Children in Emergency and Armed Conflict, 1974, International Covenant on Civil and Political Rights, 1966, International Convention on the Protection of the Rights of All Migrant Workers and Members of Their Families, 1990.

equal justice, all unequal invisible forces in the inner structure of the law must be hindered and any arbitrary decisions made by any government must be identified as violations of the basic rights of man. In other words, we must prevent the implementation of unjust laws and promote the reasonable imposition of equal rights.

Renewal of every nation's right to exist by resorting to unlawful interpretations of human rights and international criminal justice is equivalent to the renewal of a nation's right to exist as such. Therefore, such renunciations are incompatible with the natural rights of all men and violate the system of international criminal justice. *Physical justice should not take the natural rights of man under its control, as Chapter VII of the United Nations does under the system of monopolisation of the Security Council. Therefore, any decision made by the Security Council, whether in the form of a resolution or not, leads to the removal of basic rights for nations due to the promotion of the use of force and aggression.*

Thus, the physical justice that is found within the provisions of Chapter VII of the Charter of the United Nations is naturally against the principles of moral justice and is also inconsistent with peremptory rules of law. In addition, the veto right outlined in Chapter VII is against the entire structure of the United Nations. This is based on the fact that the organisation claims to promote equality among all individuals, groups, and nations, but then it identifies some as being more qualified than others and grants them power. No nation-state can go against this brutal rule of physical justice; if it does, it will be condemned by the proponents of monopolisation and may remain in political isolation. That is why the intention of moral justice is to prevent empty and contradictory principles, norms, and provisions that may be set up with the purpose of taking the power of justice under absolute control.

This in turn grants a nation with unlimited control and obligations through the hidden power of Chapter VII of the United Nations. We are referring to the fact that the United Nations' physical justice system is heavily reliant upon the conditions created by its permanent members. This indicates that the absence of the equivalence of proper norms for all states of the international legal community has already promoted a system of physical justice equivalent to physical military force marching and living in accordance with the provisions of Chapter VII. *Therefore, the system of physical justice within the Charter negates equality between its members itself. This in turn implies that the existence of equal rights among states does not apply to all members, and certain states are instead under the monopolized control of the super-powerful governments. In short, the rights of all nations belong to the Security Council permanent members.*

8. Motives of Untruthful Justice

The monopolisation of the rights of other nations, whether in the form of physical justice in Chapter VII of the Charter or in the form of national physical justice, is certainly visible. This can be seen in the monopolized provisions of the Chapter and all immoral resolutions that have been passed by the Security Council to date. Examples of such resolutions include the resolutions on Apartheid presented in the General Assembly, which were all blocked by certain members of the organisation, including the United States, the United Kingdom, France, and Israel. The policy of imposing unequal physical justice promoted by those governments has remained unchanged until now. Certain governments have power over laws and force other governments to comply with their basic decisions according to various means and reasonings. We must remember that equal justice cannot arise from the monopolisation of the central issues of law and systematic violations of international criminal justice.[207] Therefore, where there are no constant norms of equality in the basic philosophy of law, everything concerning the notion of equal justice falls under the authority of the gun.

Furthermore, the principle of equality conforms with the established rules of international human rights, thereby implying that it must be respected.[208] The right to achieve the moral substance of justice is therefore natural and not a matter of choice. Due to this, no nation has the right to massacre, conquer, or occupy another nation's territory. Therefore, moral justice accordingly offers fair justice and prevents any government from killing the citizens of another nation with the goal of preventing them from achieving their rights. It is clear that there is a vicious cycle of physical justice that constantly confronts the established universal rights of man. A conversation regarding the legitimate or illegitimate right in the case of clear evidence of unequal physical justice, such as the provisions of Chapter VII, is consequently null and void.

---

[207] *Id.*

[208] Michael J. Perry, A Global Political Morality: Human Rights, Democracy, and Constitutionalism (Cambridge University Press, 2017); Farhad Malekian, *Tour de force of Moral Virtue in International Criminal Justice* (New York: Nova Science Publishers, 2022), p. 103. Consult also Farhad Malekian, *The Mirage of International Criminal Law, Kant Metaphysics of Mens Rea* (Cambridge Scholars Publishing, 2018).

Therefore, the terms "physical justice" and "moral justice" contradict each other due to their different intentions toward the value of man and its substance. The idea of physical justice is accordingly bound by the principles of moral justice at all times - if the public rights of all mankind want to survive.

Objectively, the standard of morals constitutes a practical discipline that has more skill than law and that demands unconditional obedience to the principles of truthfulness per which all men ought to act. This implies that when we have admitted the authority of the law and its provisions, we have also created the idea of duty. The duty of man to fulfil the obligations of the law generates the theory of obligations that must be respected. However, if we do not bind ourselves to these obligations because of our range of broad authorities, we use our position over the given obligations of the law and demand the empowerment of the force of physical justice above moral justice. Hence, there is no room for quarrels between the provisions of the given system since its policies are under the control of the politics of the law. Consequently, the practical science of moral justice becomes purely theoretical.

Therefore, such a theory does not require legal force to be imposed, and the physical force of authority takes priority over the universal understanding of moral force and its righteousness. As a result, the universal doctrine of expediency and the notion of morality become the tools of power and their interpretations. Consequently, we may directly or indirectly deny that the notion of universal moral justice is correct or state that it does not exist at all. *The present situation regarding conflicts and the occupation of the power of physical justice by the criminal government of Israel and its citizens is clear evidence of this monopolized power of jurisdiction over universal moral justice. A very simple question is what caused Israel's citizens to ignore the seventy-eight years of brutality committed by their government against the Palestinian population by all means? The next question is how can they demand the release of hostages taken by the Palestinian armed forces but not the release of millions of Palestinians who are imprisoned in their homeland and by the Zionist government? This reflects that there is no theory of wisdom in the extreme application of physical justice, and such justice is no longer justice, but instead reflects the permission to commit international crimes such as genocide and crimes against humanity.*[209]

[209] Professor Falk reasoning concerning Palestine occupation is very relevant here. He says that "Traditionally, the law of war has sought to delineate the legal limits of belligerent conduct by balancing the customary principle of military necessity, on the one hand, against the customary principles of humanity and chivalry, on the other. In our modern era of

While we wish to increase the rights of all people with the principles of universal moral justice and prevent the violations thereof, the condition of physical justice cannot stand alongside the principles of moral justice, except to neutralize the righteous nature of moral justice. As a result, there is significant conflict between the politics and policies of physical justice on one side and moral justice on the other. This means that both notions of justice can be completely against one another, and the possibility of them harmonizing naturally decreases. The question then arises: how can the supporters of physical justice overcome the good principles of moral justice? Any compromise between the two ideologies is not only impossible, but also redundant to the honesty of justice. These theories represent the evolution of the theory of unlawful justice and frequently contradict the basic definition of equality for men. The murder of Palestinians is a clear indication of the difference between the theoretical maxim of morality and the physical maxim of morality. This means that every possible objection to the evil nature of physical justice is met with more evil politics.[210]

---

mechanized warfare, the principle of chivalry, "a somewhat romantic inheritance from the Medieval Ages" that denounces and forbids resort to "dishonourable (treacherous) means, dishonorable expedients, and dishonorable conduct during armed conflict," is said to have diminished in its distinctiveness relative to the principle of humanity. And in the tension ever present between the remaining two principles, manifested in the customary principles of discrimination and proportionality, the line of compromise, again because the conduct of war has become more and more impersonal, has "tended to be located closer to the polar terminus of necessity than that of humanity." Nevertheless, except insofar as it imposes a duty of obedience on the part of the inhabitants of a militarily occupied territory vis-a-vis the commands of the occupying authorities, the law of war insists absolutely upon the principle of humanity over that of military necessity in the administration of a belligerent occupation, emphasizing the principles of discrimination and proportionality. While "the administration of the occupant is in no wise to be compared with ordinary administration, for it is distinctly and precisely military administration," the protection and humane treatment of the inhabitants of a militarily occupied territory remain fundamental to the international law of belligerent occupation, 66 and a long list of the rights guaranteed such inhabitants is carefully spelled out principally in Hague IV and Geneva IV, and in the 1977 Protocol Additional I to the 1949 Geneva Conventions as well." Richard A. Falk & Burns H. Weston, The Relevance of International Law to Palestinian Rights in the West Bank and Gaza: In Legal Defense of the Intifada, 32 Harvard International law Journal (1991), pp. 129-157, pp. 144-145.

[209] *Id*, p. 156-157. Visit https://heinonline.org/HOL/Page?handle=hein.journals/hilj32&div=8 &g_sent=1&casa_token=&collection=journals.

[210] The United States governments are involved in sabotage and conspiracies in various areas around the globe. See Daniel Kovalik, Plot to Overthrow Venezuela: How the U. S. Is Orchestrating a Coup for Oil (Hot Books, 2019).

Chapter 7

Iniquitousness Within Corrupted Physical Justice

1. Hypothetical Rights to Justice

Moral justice does not equate to the superiority of one person over another nor does it represent the presentation of morality by one's own will. Moral justice aims to ensure that justice does not fail to take all necessary measures against injustices. Moral justice creates opportunities to strengthen its power of righteousness based on a proper understanding of human rights frameworks connected with international law and international criminal justice.[211] It also refers to the cosmopolitan essence of recognising each other's rights and not ignoring the basic rights of a nation - as we see are currently befalling in the territories of occupied Palestine. This situation reflects a battle of physical justice versus moral justice in terms of the law, cultural norms, and ethical substance. This indicates that we resort to impracticable or unattainable physical justice organized and imposed by the ideals of military guns and military superiors. In other words, injustice aims to undermine the fairness of justice, rights, and established resolutions of the United Nations. Furthermore, physical justice crushes moral justice and brings new rules of its own with it. However, these rules have been organised and negotiated by the physical force of guns and not by the norms of international jurisprudence.

This is precisely what the Zionist government does to innocent, unarmed civilians. Additionally, a considerable number of Western governments violate the empirical principles of human rights, criminal justice, and the humanitarian nature of moral justice as well.[212] This naturally taints the principles of maxims concerning appropriate moral justice and cause panic and a significant loss of life among civilians. Consequently, within such physical justice, we cannot hope to find an assured underpinning of morality upon which we can build up a system of international human rights for all men

---

[211] Farhad Malekian, *Concreting Righteousness in International Criminal Justice* (New York, Nova Sciences Publishers, 2024), p. 121, 171, and 193.

[212] Consult Susan O'Connor, 'Up in Arms: A Humanitarian Analysis of the Arms Trade Treaty and Its New Zealand Application,' 11 *New Zealand Yearbook of International Law* (2013), pp. 73–105; John Carey and John R. Pritchard (eds.), *International Humanitarian Law: Origins, Challenges and Prospects* (2000).

in the world. This means that we cannot believe that no defence or resistance forces will be established against unfair and immoral acts of physical justice in response to occupations or killings. Physical justice is against the established universal rights of man by nature.

In this situation, we face the fact that the principles of moral justice do not yield to the brutalities performed by the force of physical justice, and as a result, serious conflicts arise. In other words, arguments for physical justice become aggressive, violate all notions of morality, and hinder any chance of survival for the theories of moral justice. Consequently, a series of demands for fake rights by physical justice make it impossible to predict with certainty the results of moral theories and their principles for the establishment of the rights of the oppressed through the immoral acts of oppressors. As the conflict develops concerning the establishment of the perishable rights of those victims of physical justice, the complicated situation leads to the victims being murdered and to justice ultimately going to war.

All this stems from the very unlawful theory of physical justice, which does not submit itself to the establishment and respect of the rights of other nations and forces them into a position of *nobodiness*. However, the oppressed may hope that things will turn out well and that physical justice will be terminated by the big powers or the Security Council. However, that is just a utopian dream. Therefore, the victims' rights in the theory of moral justice require fighting against injustices, in order to remain on the path of achieving equality. This means that no rules of wisdom exist within physical justice, and its only goal is to kill and destroy without limit. A clear example of this is the situation faced by the Palestinians under the Israeli occupation.[213]

---

[213] PCHR, "Weekly report on Israeli human rights violations in the Occupied Palestinian Territory," No. 49/2008 (4-17 December), available online at: http://www.pchrgaza.org/files/W_report/English/2008/18-12-2008.htm; Al-Jazeera, "Israeli missile kills Gaza man," 18 December 2008, available online at: http://english.aljazeera.net/news/middleeast/2008/12/2008121721428340460.html: PCHR, "Weekly report on Israeli human rights violations in the Occupied Palestinian Territory," No. 50/2008 (18–23 December 2008), available online at: http://www.pchrgaza.org/files/W_report/English/2008/24-12-2008.htm; Reuters, "Hamas declares end to ceasefire with Israel in Gaza," 18 December 2008, available online at: http://www.reuters.com/article/topNews/idUSLI75623220081218; PCHR, "Weekly report on Israeli human rights violations in the Occupied Palestinian Territory," No. 51/2008 (24–31 December 2008), available online at: http://www.pchrgaza.org/files/W_report/English/2008/pdf/weekly%20report%2051.pdf; Mr. Fadi Qawasme, testimony at the public hearing in Geneva, 3 July 2009, and PCHR, "Weekly report on Israeli human rights violations in the Occupied Palestinian Territory," No. 26/2006 (29 June-5 July 2006), available online at: http://www.pchrgaza.org/files/W_report/English/2006/06-07-2006.htm; JTA, "Kassams hit Israel after terrorist killed," 16 December 2008, available online at:

The problem with physical justice is that instead of adopting the principles of international human rights law and international criminal justice as guidelines, thereby promoting equivalent justice and the power of moral justice and human rights norms as imperative frameworks for the creation of acceptable justice, it does the opposite. This means that the authorities in power only seek to achieve their goals and intend to sacrifice the rights of other nations. A clear example of this is the Israeli regime, which did not exist seventy-seven years ago, but which is today working to eliminate the Palestinian state with the power of physical justice. This is the character of the Zionist criminal government, which claims to work for humanity. The fact is that:

> The population of Palestine is suffering due to the misinterpretation of Rabbinic Zionist political ideology's religious influence on the inhabitants of the occupied land. The idea was initially supported by British imperialists and continues under the umbrella of the US government. The fact of the matter is that the Jewish theory of religion has also been divided into different political branches, as has the Islamic theory, and these divisions in the theological theories harm their invisible unity. In fact, there are many Jewish individuals who are honest and are against the illegal occupation and the commission of genocide, terror, and savagery through the *international crimes of blackboard-barbarism.*[214]

Consequently, everything concerning moral justice, human rights, and the principle of self-determination is ignored by the immoral and criminal philosophy of the aggressive Zionist government. This means that the principles of morality become incapable of providing for and defending the rights of victims. Evil gives priority to any principle of morality. This has been the nature of the Zionist government since it came to power and occupied Palestine with the assistance of the powerful criminal governments in the United Nations.[215] Insofar as principles of human rights conform to ideas of right and the prevention of injustice, the theory of the Zionist government does

---

http://jta.org/news/articleprint/2008/12/16/1001575/kassams-hit-israel-after-terrorist-killed?TB_iframe=true&width=750&height=500;

[214] Farhad Malekian, *Exploitation of Christian Islamic International Criminal Justice* (New York: Nova Science Publishers, 2024), pp. 36-37.

[215] Consult J. I. Ross, *Controlling State Crime* (2nd Edition, New Brunswick, NJ: Transaction Press, 2000).

the opposite and brags about its knowledge of the hypothetical history of its own civilisation in Palestine.[216] The question then is: What can come from all these lies and claims?[217] The only path that remains for the Zionist criminal government is to use the power of guns in order to convince others to adopt the rules of their own corrupt morality.[218]

2. Fabricating a Moral Christmas

A practical man benefits from the theory of wisdom and its moral principles. The principle of morality also follows the principle of enlightenment, although we admit that the notion of enlightenment is itself subject to discussion. Nevertheless, it outlines how one can reach a sufficient understanding of the fact that forcing evil norms or imposing one's own interests onto someone else is against the judicious norm of law. Instead, there must exist equally applicable norms. However, since the juridical notion of physical justice has largely disappeared, the verdict of evil physical justice goes against the hope for justice and the equality of arms. The authorities of physical justice often pretend that they know what is truly right and wrong based on their observation of human nature, regardless of the fact that the basic rights have already been established and should not be interpreted differently. However, they do. The authorities of brutal physical justice, e.g., in Israel, will never be willing to do what is required in order to bring about peace and equality in accordance with UN principles and restore the rights of the victims. We should not forget the fact that it is imperative for all authorities to respect the rights of all individuals under the provisions of all legal constitutions.

The distributive unity of the wills of moral attitudes and its norms or principles are all necessary for attaining a peaceful iteration of justice and prevent war crimes, crimes against humanity, torture, genocide, apartheid, and

[216] "Where Islamic, Christian, or Zionist practices go against the basic principles of unity, they violate the entire system of humanity as a whole. The aforementioned example of this is Israel. The control of the world through the power of economics creates massive difficulties in establishing peace and justice for the population of the world. However, the Israeli government is not alone in its political, economic, and criminal policies; the American government runs all its basic policies through the force of its military power. It means both states violate the virtues of essence in theological modes as well as the imperative rules of international criminal justice that are to be respected and not infringed upon in pure international relations." *Id.*, p. 38.

[217] *Id.*

[218] *Id.*

the humiliation of the rights of children. We must understand that the form of physical justice exercised in certain occupied countries in the Middle East, or those that were exercised in territories under colonial rule, is the most inhuman form of humiliation justice. The collective or universal unity that exists in the essence of moral justice is not only essential for the existence of man, but also for the understanding of the body of law. The solution to this difficult and brutal policy of physical justice must be solved and realized in the shadow of the rights of all individuals, groups, and nations.

The notion of diversity among nations or groups must come to a solution that produces a common, united will that will not give priority to any one nation over the others. The provisions of international human rights have failed to do this and are therefore decorative and ineffective in practice. This is why the principles of universal moral justice struggle for and demand the enforcement of practical respect for human beings and their personalities. Hence, *this practical realisation prepares us to encounter a considerable number of deviations in our actual experience of the enforcement of physical and moral justice. Since we cannot take the moral charisma and disposition of its will into account, we simply confuse it with the elements of physical justice. This becomes particularly dangerous when our multitude of expectations and interests prioritize the rights of all individuals and their right to exist in peace.*

Hence, understanding moral justice is imperative in all circumstances - and this does not need to be proven. Any authority who has the power of law and its control in their hands will not let the population of the country dictate laws and say what they can or cannot do. This is particularly true concerning the physical justice of international law and not the moral justice of the same law. It has actually been proven that dictatorship is always the consequence of physical justice, not moral justice. This is particularly evident concerning certain international organisations under the control of the states that created international organisations such as the UN to serve their own interests. As previously stated, the UN is controlled by certain powerful governments and certain militarily strong nations. This means that certain states and their alliances will not submit to the judgment of any government or International Criminal Court in The Hague. This also includes the resolutions adopted by the General Assembly or the Security Council of the UN. Most strong governments enjoy controlling external law, i.e., international law, international criminal law, and international criminal justice.[219]

The problem with physical justice is that it goes beyond national and international law, which means that one continent may feel superior to another. This is especially true in the case of the European continent, which feels like it dominates other continents and is arrogant as a result. This is why the physical justice of Western governments has always been seen as a priority for understanding morality. They call their own policies the best egalitarian systems. Given this interpretation, moral justice has been monopolized by a considerable number of European governments. That is why a large amount of the African population has been seen as slaves. These slaves have also been forced to follow the sexual moral attitudes of Western countries and have been exploited for different reasons, including sexual pleasure.

3. The Dangers of Political-Legal Morality

If there is freedom to achieve our legal rights, if there is a clear understanding of our moral law, and our system of international human rights is effective and respects the fundamental rights of man, then we are forced to ensure that the system of moral justice takes priority over physical justice and is enforceable under all circumstances. That is, in fact, the real intention of human rights justice, or it at least should be. This means that the physical justice of the system of human rights ought to enjoy the moral circumstances of justice and be enforced in accordance with moral standards. The question may then arise: which one is really the notion of moral standard? Is the moral standard of justice different from the physical standard of justice? If so, how in what way?

Upon initial assessment, the fairness of physical justice eligibility is based on an actual or potential event related to physical justice, which in turn serves as the basis for a suspected question. As a result, not all forms of justice can be considered legitimate, fair forms of justice. This is because whenever we speak about physical justice, we are also speaking about its fairness and the scope of its morality—which is also why we speak about moral justice when we are speaking about physical justice. Additionally, this is also why we discuss the outcome of court proceedings once they have concluded, including when case law is involved. If case law is not itself good, then we are not

[219] Farhad Malekian, Powertionism in International Criminal Justice (New York: Nova Science Publishers, 2022).

speaking about good justice, but rather only about justice or justice that has been misunderstood by the judges of the court. This is also why we are so cautious and attentive to the reasons that have been presented during the procedures of the court.

All these matters depend on through which perspective we are looking at them with and the search for the definition of justice and its implementation. The meagreness of moral justice may therefore be more minimized with the terrorizing habit of physical justice. Of course, we are always speaking about the monopolisation of justice, which means a big monopolisation, a small monopolisation, or complete ignorance of justice. This arises regardless of how strong the international legal discipline is, and what measure of reparations have been foreseen in its basic instruction. All these instructions fall into place when the arms of the monopolized power are strong and guided by the power of certain governments - namely those that are driving the whole world into one corner to implement physical justice against the structure of moral justice. The power of physical justice is gained through politics, which involves utilizing the physical necessities predicted by dictatorial or tyrannical leaders of a regime. The idea of rightness is completely empty when faced with the practical face of an unwise man.[220]

If, on the other hand, we understand that the idea of rights is necessary and therefore must be conjoined with moral inspectors of rights rather than politics and be raised to the position of full moral practice for all men, then physical justice cannot properly be enforced and may ultimately fall into its own tyrannical traps. As a result of this, the possibility of reconciling unjustified norms or orders will surely decrease. Otherwise, immorality would continue to develop as it has been and victims will always remain victims. This is the present situation faced by the Palestinian population and their rights, which are being taken away by the big politically-powerful governments to serve their own interests.[221] The Palestinians are perishing, not

---

[220] See Jose E. Alvarez, Judging the Security Council, 90 AM. J. INT'L L. 1 (1996); Thomas M. Franc, The "Power of Appreciation": Who Is the Ultimate Guardian of UN Legality?, 86 Am. J. INT'L L. 519 (1992); Keith Harper, Does the United Nations Security Council Have the Competence to Act as Court and Legislature?, 27 N.Y.U. J. INT'L L. & POL. 103 (1994). Schachter correctly indicates that "it had [become] evident to international lawyers as it had to others that States that made and applied law were not governed by morality or 'natural reason'; they acted for reasons of power and interest. It followed that law could only be ascertained and determined through the actual methods used by the States to give effect to their 'political wills'. Oscar Schachter, International Law in Theory and Practice (1991), p.36.

[221] *Id.*

because of the existence of moral justice, but because of its non-existence, which is going to be a source of shame for human civilisation.[222]

Therefore, the most aggressive form of physical justice is imposed by the strong terrorist governments that plan to exterminate the existence of the Palestinian population. We cannot imagine a moral politician or egalitarian being involved in this situation. That is to say, one who understands the harsh and authoritarian elements of physical justice can also understand that a political moralist who wants rights to be established and protected and who also wants rights to not follow the evil ethical terror of the powertionist governments does not exist, and morality means nothing more than the dangerous physical morality of those who are fighting against an unarmed nation.

4. Despotic Rules of Barbarity

It is always possible that we could develop the idea of moral justice in the arena of international human rights law and present more principles, provisions, and rules. This means that the notion of morality can be regulated into physical justice, but if such a notion of morality is respected, it raises the question of who is in power and who wants morality to be in power. Thus, we are trying to prevent a despotic notion of morality. In the name of implementing human rights law and its valuable provisions, we terminated the essence of morality in the rules and promoted the atrocities of physical justice in the name of moral justice. This causes tension with the rules of moral wisdom and brings certain elements of justice into force, including by adopting measures without sufficient deliberation. This is because the principles of human rights, which are supposed to be based on moral justice, have been overestimated by the legal power of authoritarian powers.

As a result of this, physical justice goes in the wrong direction, and not only turns against the principles of international human rights, law but also against the universal natural rights that must be respected at all times.[223] However, the powertionist governments and their policies do not have any respect for natural law, and such a concept is indeed meaningless. Despite this

---

[222] *Id.*

[223] Consult also Francesca P Albanese, Lex Takkenberg, Palestinian Refugees in International Law (2nd Edition, 2020); Study the report of Francesca Albanese file:///C:/Users/uub-b24-1502/Downloads/a-hrc-55-73-auv%20(1).pdf.

being understood by the authorities, they do not make any moral improvements and instead increase their barbarity in an attempt to achieve their impossible goals. This means that they violate moral law to the point that the barbarity of physical justice continues to grow and ultimately becomes impossible to prevent.[224]

This is because when the basic principles of morality are smashed into pieces, the framework of humanity no longer exists, and barbaric conduct becomes the leading tool of physical justice against moral justice. Consequently, justifying this barbarity of physical justice no longer functions, and those practices bring the antagonistic idea of rights into reality. On the pretext that such moral principles are not good, physical justice becomes dominant. However, physical justice cannot present a good version of equality and promote the necessary respect of rights, particularly for victims.

No politician bases their actions on morality and the principles of international human rights law and international criminal justice. Therefore, if certain defects exist in the implementation of moral justice in opposition to physical justice, it is because of the shameful politicians who believe in imposing physical justice. These politicians also believe that physical justice is nothing more than the use of force, power, weapons, and lies in the pursuit of their own interests. This is why we say that physical justice is often the definition of tyranny, autocracy, totalitarianism, and despotic monocratic decisions. Consequently, in order to apply physical justice, one needs to sacrifice moral justice and then harm people under the system of international law in the name of implementing and achieving their own rights.

This is what is currently happening under the power of the physical force of the Israeli government, which calls their actions "physical justice" - and it is one of the most horrible forms of physical justice in the world. Contrary to the politics of powertionist governments, we speak about the Zionist dictatorship, Zionism as presenting Nazism, Zionism as the manifestation of terrorist movements, and Zionism as the true face of barbarism. Here, we are speaking about the international criminal law constitution, which has long since been destroyed by those who have the power of physical power under their control and express it as a practical feature of moral justice.[225] *Therefore,*

---

[224] *Id.*

[225] G. Schwarzenberger, 'The Problem of an International Criminal Law,' 5 *Current Legal Problems* (1950); G. Schwarzenberger, *International Jus Cogens?,* 43 *Tax. L. Rev* (1965), p. 476; D. Shelton, 'Normative Hierarchy of International Law' 80 *American Journal of International Law* (1986), 1; see also Egon Schwelb, *Crimes Against Humanity, British Yearbook of International Law* (1946) 178.

it would undeniably be absurd to request that every political argument be measured and followed by the necessary conditions of moral justice based on the fact that physical justice originates from a basis of inhumanity.[226]

At the same time, a dictatorial ruler may be required to respect moral justice to a certain extent. However, such a notion is completely absent from the practice of the Israeli government, which has instead been replaced by Nazi barbarity and the IDF using human beings as human shields. This means that the best possible constitution of international human rights law as expressed by its creators faces the most despotic rule of physical justice. In accordance with these constitutions and agreements, the existing philosophy of moral justice loses its values and becomes the domain of the strongest physical justice. This has been a recurring problem whenever physical justice takes on the character of evil savagery and becomes the final word of justice.

5. The Vices of Physical Judgments

The unfortunate fact is that injustice always comes wearing the cloth of justice since it is saved and can be renamed to justice, fairness, equality, and, most commonly, the implementation of a very high level of international human rights law. This indicates that authorities of physical justice will follow their usual method of protecting everything from injustice. This is the claim of justice. This means that with the simple term of "protection," physical justice prevents any justice movements and succeeds in murdering moral justice. Physical justice also then creates despotic compulsory laws that are enforced by those who are in power and have control over government decisions. This is precisely the situation that can be seen with the immoral and unfair practices of the Israeli Zionist government.

There is consequently no trace of moral reason in the practice of relevant government. Instead, the Israeli government claims to be fighting against injustice and terrorist movements by forcing and validating certain legal dictatorial obligations on the rights of the victims. It is in accordance with these measures of injustice that physical justice survives and succeeds in massacring civilians, and particularly children. Thus, in certain situations, physical justice does not bring equality or freedom through its words and actions and instead brings suffering and anguish. Therefore, leaving out any trace of reason or ignoring any wise decision based on the substance of human

226 *Id.*

rights norms is impossible and any claim to it is superficial. Therefore, by looking at the problems of physical justice and moral justice, we find that the reasons presented by the theories of physical justice are empirical nonsense and promote the violation of the rights of others.

Even though the reasoning of moral justice and physical justice may have different understandings of the reality of the situation, the fact is that moral justice is based on basic reason and not any order. However, physical justice acts contrary to the theory of moral justice in order to serve its own interests and not substantive humanitarian reasons.[227] This means that its theories generally contradict rights. Although these theories are indeed introduced as justice, they are against the principles of moral justice in practice. This indicates that a physical justice system can govern and defend itself on moral lines as long as people are unable to understand its reasoning. It therefore controls not only the most significant elements of international human rights and international criminal justice, but also gradually becomes capable of convincing people that it has a high level of morality as well as a moral understanding of the given situation.

In this way, the physical justice system defeats moral justice and then conquers and controls the idea of the authority of a given law. Physical justice is based on the moral power of the law and therefore dresses in clothes containing the principles of morality and all its reasoning. As a result, authorities become capable of self-legislation, self-strategizing, self-decision, and also the power to kill millions. This is known as the power of brutality, the power of control, and the power of genocidal crimes. The final stage of this is called *blackboard-barbarism*, which is founded on the theory of the primacy of the Israeli-Zionist criminal government. Due to this, Zionism insists that the Palestinian population must be slaughtered like cattle in order to have moral justice in the world and achieve the equality of arms.

Zionists believe that the Palestinians should be violently removed from their homes, thereby resulting in the complete destruction of their civilisation. Physical justice wants to see the effects of its physical decisions not only in writing, but in practice. The spirit of physical justice has thus even caused the

---

[227] Examine Antonio Cassese, (ed.), *The New Humanitarian Law of Armed Conflict* (Naples: Editoriale Scientifica, 1979); Karima Bennoune, 'As-Salamu 'Alykum? Humanitarian Law in Islamic Jurisprudence,' 15 *Michigan Journal of International Law*, (1994), pp. 605-643; Kesolofetse Lefenya, 'Use of Explosive Weapons in Densely Populated Areas: Implications for International Humanitarian Law,' *African Yearbook on International Humanitarian Law* (2014), pp. 68–86; Thomas G. Weiss, *Military-Civilian Interactions: Humanitarian Crises and the Responsibility to Protect* (2nd ed., Rowman & Littlefield Publishers Inc, Lanham (MD), 2005).

brutal murder of Palestinian children. This is how physical justice works, plans, and implements its decisions with the presence of both *mens rea* and *actus reus*. This is what occurred during the wars in Iraq, Syria, Lebanon, Afghanistan, Vietnam, Cambodia, and in many other parts of the world as a result of physical reasoning.

Although such physical justice should no longer be permitted based on the adoption of a considerable number of conventions within the body of international human rights law, it regrettably still has power and authority, thereby implying that it is also influential and commanding. All of this indicates the use of military forces or stratagems to see the end of the evil victory of physical justice over moral justice. In the end, all of these immoral physical justice movements affect the external relations between various individuals, groups, and nations and bring antagonism, serious arguments, immeasurable fights, and ultimately culminate in wars. However, the most dangerous form of this is when a war is waged by a government against unarmed civilians who have been colonized by physical justice. Moreover, the most brutal form is when a government occupies a land based on its unjustifiable physical justice arguments and commits a Holocaust against the entire population of the occupied land.

Therefore, we engage in a form of conflict against those who have the right to resist and who are, in all situations and within our arguments, actually the victims. This means that we cannot take the rights of moral justice or the rights of the victims away by carrying out immoral acts and decisions. At the same time, the strongest condemnation of aggressive acts comes from the consequences of our actions and not our own personal judgments. Hence, when such estimation of actions is completed and proven, the one whose physical justice caused the injustices is responsible for any crimes committed. This is particularly significant as it concerns international crimes.

6. Mistreatment of the Framework of Justice

It is true that these physical justices are not justice and instead have natural and physical political consequences.[228] Moreover, there is no need to prove

[228] Farhad Malekian, *Allegations by Political Laundering* (Cambridge Scholars Publishing, 2019); Farhad Malekian, 'Emasculating the Philosophy of International Criminal Justice in the Iraqi Special Tribunal,' Cornell International Law Journal, 58/5 (2005), pp. 675-725; Farhad Malekian, 'Comparative Substantive International Criminal Justice,' in Ronald C.

that physical justice is wrong because the result of any action ultimately demonstrates its nature.[229] Those who commit serious war crimes, crimes against humanity, genocide, torture, aggression, or other crimes, never feel shame during the judgment of any political government or any international court. The reason for this is simply that they have already demonstrated their will and interests in the course of implementing their power.[230] As far as this injustice goes, it is not the revelation of these injustices that makes sense, but rather the very high value of wisdom in the face of moral justice.

The guiding principles of a government may come from its constitution, but how they are interpreted and who has the power to control them is the most essential argument. Moral justice obviously does not have any notion of wrongful physical justice in its content, while physical justice should have the rightful principles of moral justice as its basic content. If a government has a policy of injustice, that policy may embarrass the rulers. However, this is dependent on their personal understanding. As a result, such governments can blame others as a consequence of the unsuccessful use of physical justice. This is the true face of physical justice under certain circumstances.

With all these twists and junctions concerning the immoral doctrine of physical justice and attempting to identify what is right, what is wrong, and what is justice, the major, unsolvable problem is the use of law and morality over those who are completely without morality. Therefore, the theory of the expediency of wisdom, which wishes to replace peace and prevent any notion of injustice and victims, morphs into a state of war, savagery, and the extermination of millions. This is what the system of international justice and the reality of universal morality are facing at all times. Therefore, any ideas about rights and morality are killed at their inception, and any further arguments concerning the establishment of justice perish as well. This means that the powertionist governments that control all forms of justice do not care what the opposite party or the victim present.[231]

This policy is obviously not new and is even more present in the theory of the systems of international law and international criminal justice, which are the real tools used by powerful governments to dictate their views outside of their territories. Consequently, the politics of the manipulation of law,

---

Slye (ed.), *The Nuremberg Principles in Non-western Societies: A Reflection on their Universality, Legitimacy and Application* (2017), pp. 10-44.

[229] *Id.*

[230] *Id.*

[231] Farhad Malekian, *Powertionism in International Criminal Justice* (New York: Nova Science Publishers, 2022).

justice, morality, and peace result in powertionist governments refusing to acknowledge the rights of the victims. The authorities of these governments attribute all the appropriate honour and justice to their own righteous judgment. Even though they are aware of the fact that they are killing rights, morality, and justice behind closed doors, they still make up excuses for their criminal actions. In this way, they avoid implementing the proper wise definition of justice in practice and continue to exert their authoritarian power over moral justice, and as a result, permanently harm the victims' dignity, integrity, and *somebodiness*.[232]

This situation is not dependent upon the intelligence of the victims, simply because the authority enforcing practical justice is the source and is the one monopolizing the unifying principle of those who control the justice of the law. That is why having the skill or quality of being wise and planning to reach the essence of moral justice does not help and justice refers to the quality of the mistreatment of its principles by those who decorate its words and world. Consequently, we must end these arguments concerning which philosophy of justice is better than the other, i.e., physical or moral justice. Our argumentation will therefore demonstrate its characteristic sophistry, since the theory of justice is not about who presents a better argument, but rather about who can correctly and extensively kill the theory of the seed of justice.

The theory of justice reveals the hidden character of physical justice. The false character of justice advocates its criminal actions through various means. A clear example of this can be seen with the conduct of the criminal American company, Blackwater, which killed victims of all ages in Iraq while claiming to promote the rights of physical justice under the criminal orders of American powertionist governments. According to the statements of relevant governments, it was right and just to kill anyone who was against American or NATO activities.[233] This is how the theory of physical justice and the systems of international human rights and international criminal justice are interpreted and supported by those who are responsible for true equality, justice, and peace according to the United Nations Charter.[234] Therefore, the

---

[232] Farhad Malekian, *International Criminal Law, the Law of Somebodiness, the Law of Nobodiness* (New York: Nova Science Publishers, 2021).

[233] Farhad Malekian, 'Emasculating the Philosophy of International Criminal Justice in the Iraqi Special Tribunal,' *Cornell International Law Journal*, 58/5 (2005).

[234] Examine Chapter one and seven of the Charter of the United Nations Statute. Article 1 of the Charter emphasises "The Purposes of the United Nations are: 1. To maintain international peace and security, and to that end: to take effective collective measures for the prevention and removal of threats to the peace, and for the suppression of acts of aggression or other breaches of the peace, and to bring about by peaceful means, and in conformity with the

ultimate principle from which their procedures for a permanent peace stem from shows that all the evil criminal conduct on the surface of international relations is generated by the antagonist[235]theories of physical justice.

The idea is that the morals of political powertionist governments start where moral politicians end, thereby subordinating values to own personal interests. This signifies prioritizing the task at hand. Powertionist governments undermine the intention of bringing law and politics into harmony with morality. As a result, we face brutalities, atrocities, and the complete mistreatment of the basic philosophy of justice. Therefore, it is impossible to make the practical philosophy of justice consistent with itself and deal with the problems stemming from the nonexistence of practical moral justice. The arguments presented by physical justice erase the logical reasoning of moral philosophy as the object of free choice of justice principles based on the values of moral understanding and the rejection of physical justice. Thus, any discussions about moral justice appear invalid and nonsensical in the minds of brutal criminal governments.[236] Thus, the end of justice implies the unconditional necessity of the control of justice by the authorities in power.

7. Marching Against Moral Codes

Solving the problem of moral justice when it confronts physical justice is indeed impossible. This is because these systems of justice are constantly in conflict with each other. The theory of moral justice seeks to correct the system of physical justice, and since this is not acceptable with the political expediency of physical justice, the theories conflict, leading to fights that are so devastating to moral justice that the whole idea of moral justice is always

---

principles of justice and international law, adjustment or settlement of international disputes or situations which might lead to a breach of the peace; 2. To develop friendly relations among nations based on respect for the principle of equal rights and self-determination of peoples, and to take other appropriate measures to strengthen universal peace; 3. To achieve international cooperation in solving international problems of an economic, social, cultural, or humanitarian character, and in promoting and encouraging respect for human rights and for fundamental freedoms for all without distinction as to race, sex, language, or religion; and 4. To be a center for harmonizing the actions of nations in the attainment of these common ends."

235 See generally J. I. Ross, *Controlling State Crime* (2nd Edition, New Brunswick, NJ: Transaction Press, 2000); J. I. Ross, *Varieties of State Crime and its Control* (Monsey, NY: Criminal Justice Press, 2000).

236 Farhad Malekian, *Powertionism in International Criminal Justice* (New York: Nova Science Publishers, 2022).

on fire with the evil mentality of the authorities of physical justice. Therefore, extensive knowledge of moral justice is needed to bring recognition to it within the international community. The reason for this is that physical justice has not only occupied the basic sources of other nations, but it also controls the idea of morality.

A clear example of this is that the United States, which is the basic reason for the genocide of the Palestinian population, is actually benefitting from the starvation of the population of Gaza and yet has built a temporary pier to help the victims. This is how physical justice acts. It provides the Israeli military arms with the most advanced weapons to exterminate the population of Gaza and then simultaneously hijack the opinion of the world. The example above demonstrates how the absurdity of the system of physical justice humiliates the essence of morality and eliminates the legal and moral essence of the *somebodiness* of the victims.[237] It is therefore required that one first examines the practices of physical justice in all analyses of the principles of justice. Additionally, in order to succeed concerning the outcome of all investigations and examinations of the brutal habits of physical justice, we must find a way to abandon all these aggressive behaviours.

As far as the idea of perpetual peace and justice is concerned, it is uncertain as to whether or not we can reach their practical reality and not just their theoretical one. The fact is that obedience to the rules and theories of physical justice will never be seen as long as the rights of the victims are being violated. This is particularly evident concerning the ongoing commission of international crimes in Gaza.[238] There are a large number of further examples

---

[237] Farhad Malekian, *International Criminal Law, the Law of Somebodiness, the Law of Nobodiness* (New York: Nova Science Publishers, 2021).

[238] Examine Farhad Malekian, Paralysing International Criminal Justice (New York: Nova Science Publishers, 2021), pp. 220-221. Examine also See also JTA, "Kassams hit Israel after terrorist killed," 16 December 2008, available online at: http://jta.org/news/articleprint/2008/12/16/1001575/kassams-hit-israel-after-terrorist-killed?TB_iframe=true &width=750&height=500; PCHR, "Weekly report on Israeli human rights violations in the Occupied Palestinian Territory," No. 49/2008 (4-17 December), available at: http://www.pchrgaza.org/files/W_report/English/2008/18-12-2008.htm; Al-Jazeera, "Israeli missile kills Gaza man," 18 December 2008, available online at: http://english.aljazeera.net/news/middleeast/2008/12/2008121721428340460.html: PCHR, "Weekly report on Israeli human rights violations in the Occupied Palestinian Territory," No. 50/2008 (18–23 December 2008), available at: http://www.pchrgaza.org/files/W_report/English/2008/24-12-2008.htm; Reuters, "Hamas declares end to ceasefire with Israel in Gaza," 18 December 2008, available online at: http://www.reuters.com/article/topNews/idUSLI 75623220081218; PCHR, "Weekly report on Israeli human rights violations in the Occupied Palestinian Territory," No. 51/2008 (24–31 December 2008), available online at: http://www.pchrgaza.org/files/W_report/English/2008/pdf/weekly%20report%2051.pdf; Mr. Fadi Qawasme, testimony at the public hearing in Geneva, 3 July 2009, and PCHR,

that prove that barbarity within the practice of physical justice has no limit. Even more uncertain is the system of international criminal justice, which is actually the presentation of international physical justice used by powertionist governments to hide their own criminality and accuse other nations of their own crimes.

It is evident that those who commit crimes always appear in the clothing of the victims. It is also quite obvious to everyone that the victims are often in the eyes, thoughts, and decisions of the criminal powertionist governments - those who force the powertionist governments to go to war.[239] At the end of the day, sufferers are criminals, and criminals are the real sufferers. This leads us to the conclusion that while physical justice emphasizes fairness, discretion cautions us against making false statements, presenting evidence via the use of force, and promoting gunfire with the propaganda of the superpower states. In fact, political moralists, who are carriers of physical justice, enter into a war with violence or cunning but still claim the contrary and believe that the war started because of the will of the victims - who are seen as criminals by those in leading the law. That is why the theory of accusation put on the victims is really annoying.

Generally speaking, the idea of right, which alone could bring peace and respect for all time and increase the value of the notion of moral justice, is used as a secondary subject rather than the real definition of the notion of right. Thus, both subjects of justice, i.e., physical and moral justice, are equally wrong. Physical justice is the wrongful delineation of its own rules, while moral justice is the result of the power of the former. At the same time, the transgression of the rules of international law has been aggressive. This indicates a unilateral destruction of the system of justice and that permission has been given to the powertionist governments to wage war in accordance with Chapter VII of the Charter. This indicates that any international crime committed under the politico-legal interests of the powertionist governments, including genocide, is permitted and does not violate moral or physical justice. However,

> The Convention on Genocide has listed a number of recognitions of various crimes. The convention came into existence because of massive

---

"Weekly report on Israeli human rights violations in the Occupied Palestinian Territory," No. 26/2006 (29 June-5 July 2006), available online at: http://www.pchrgaza.org/files/W_report/English/2006/06-07-2006.htm.

[239] Farhad Malekian, *Powertionism in International Criminal Justice* (New York: Nova Science Publishers, 2022).

> brutality against religious identities, i.e., the Jews. The problem with otherness became so great that it grew all over Europe, and many nations helped to erase the existence of the Jews from European society. This was one of the most wretched examples of inhumane conduct against a group. The ethical or moral facts do not confirm brutalities because of religious or other identities. Brutal acts are brutal and cannot be anything else. These statements hold true regardless of the controversies which have always existed between various races in the world. Another clear example of this is the political Zionism of he government of Israel against Palestinians in their own land. These conducts are certainly condemned under the body of contemporary international criminal justice.[240]

After all, this is the most incorrect form of the system of physical justice, i.e., one which serves the violators of justice more than its guardian. This form of the monopolisation of justice ensures that war will continue to be waged throughout history. The issue is that there is no one has heeded the warning concerning the notion of unjust physical justice. Justice is the private mechanism of power politics, and that is the most essential reason why the victims of injustice continue to increase, and the provision that orders the course of universal morality under the system of international human rights faces barriers made of guns and walls of immorality. This not only endangers the system of international criminal justice, but it is also harmful to the entire system of human unity, which is guided by affection and care.

Overall, the moral code and attitude of mankind cannot be extinguished, and humanitarian reasons for moral justice are fitted to the conscious understanding of the philosophies of right and wrong based on the substance of that principle of justice. This is what the world is witnessing today in response to the savage commission of genocide against the Palestinian population. This means that when physical justice increases its brutal savagery, as seen with the Zionist Israeli criminal government, the principle of moral justice grows stronger to advance wisdom and prove the cultural and inherited rights of the victims. However, at the same time, it is true the perpetrators of genocide are becoming increasingly guilty of committing grave international crimes.[241]

---

[240] Farhad Malekian, Exploitation of Christian Islamic International Criminal Justice (New York, Nova Sciences Publishers, 2024), pp. 138-139.

[241] Farhad Malekian, *Paralysing International Criminal Justice* (New York: Nova Science Publishers, 2021); Francesca P Albanese, Lex Takkenberg, Palestinian Refugees in International Law (2nd Edition, 2020); Study the report of Francesca Albanese file:///C:/Users/uub-b24-1502/Downloads/a-hrc-55-73-auv%20(1).pdf.

Chapter 8

Conclusion

It is neither practical nor logical to bring the spirit of law under the control of arms. However, this has been done repeatedly by those who believe that their views and interpretations are beyond the system of justice. As a result, the system of justice yields itself to the power of military guns, and in the end, not only are international crimes committed, but these crimes also give rise to the establishment of hierarchy and authoritarianism. Accordingly, justice establishes a permanent struggle between universal moral justice and the authorities that impose physical justice. However, we should highlight that, in theory, there is no disagreement between morals and politics as long as the necessary reasonableness of justice is not being violated. In practice, this is impossible, and therefore the essence of moral justice conflicts with the unlawful and immoral requirements of practical physical justice. This disagreement between both justices exists today, and will continue to persist, because of the dishonesty of physical justice in its essence and the lack of moral justice. A clear example of this is the Charter of the United Nations, which contradicts moral integrity in Chapter VII, which sanctions the inequality of arms and completely disregards the principle of morality.

Certainly, we cannot separate law from its origin and believe that the law should not be in line with the principles of natural morality. In fact, this is an imperative principle. Additionally, all political authorities must kneel before the principle of morality, which introduces rights, justice, and the equality of arms. If we can understand this, then the respect for perpetual morality should be recognized as a duty of all governments. In other words, the notion of morality seeks the kingdom of pure practical reason. Consequently, there is no need to comment further on the level and degree to which a common conception of moral justice should look. Moral justice is the presentation of fairness and the natural duty of all individuals, groups, and organisations. As previously stated, from the standpoint of the assurance of the rights of all human beings, in particular the reestablishment of the rights of victims, physical justice is obligated to respect the main moral understanding of the law and should not force the imposition of any individual or governmental decision that violates the basic principles of justice and contradicts their intentions. It is now equally obvious that we ought to trust the equal rules of morality and not impose rules of moral understanding of the law through the aggressive force of dictatorial authorities, as has been seen in occupied Gaza.

The trust and confidence in the system of moral justice being respected by the authorities of physical justice is one of the significant principles that should be applied to ensure the appropriate settlement of disputes. This indicates a significant extension of the opportunity and assessment of common valuable schemes of collaboration between the definitions of physical and moral justice.[242] As a result, it is clearly rational for those who impose physical justice to gain humanity rather than to waste the principles of humanity during armed conflicts or genocides in other nations. This is not to talk about barbarity, but rather to agree to the principles of fairness, justice, equality, and the respect for the dignity of all men. The intention is to ensure that the promised principles of humanity are entered into various international conventions such that they can easily be implemented and remain free from political and malicious intrigues. At the same time, speaking about physical justice and enforcing it with weapons does not decrease differences, rather the basic impetuses for conflicts drastically increase. Obviously, without this mutual and multilateral understanding of the problem of physical justice against the principle of equal moral justice, nothing can be accomplished, and the problems of war, atrocities, and brutalities remain the leading evil excuses for the application of authentic justice. It is the reciprocal recognition and common awareness of immorality that bring respect to those who are the instruments of the monopolisation of power politics.

In other words, if the right to a reasonable morality of judgment is in fact instrumental, then we can acknowledge that we are ignoring the legal systems of justice and the values of their existence. This means that our judgments rely on the claim of authority alone, which is not recommended, particularly when physical justice is in full possession of autocratic power. Of course, legal systems assert that those with the authority to work with the legal system and enforce its rules have the right to express their opinions in all situations. This

---

[242] Examine L. M. Baum, 'Pursuing Justice in a Climate of Moral Outrage: An Evaluation of the Rights of the Accused in the Rome Statute of the International Criminal Court,' 19 *Wisconsin International Law* (2001), p. 197; Michael C. Davis, Wolfgang Dietrich, Bettina Schoolman and Dieter Sepp., *International Intervention in the Post-Cold War World: Moral Responsibility and Power Politics* (New York: M.E. Sharpe, Inc., 2003); M. J. Detmold, *The Unity of Law and Morality: A Refutation of Legal Positivism* (Canada: Law Book Co. of Australasia, 1984); Lon Luvios Fuller, *The Morality of Law* (Virginia: Yale Law University, 2nd ed., 1969); Alasdair MacIntyre, *After Virtue: A Study in Moral Theory* (Notre Dame: University of Notre Dame Press, 1982).

is how they make sense of the modern monopolisation of jurisprudence. In fact, this paradox of positivism and physical justice challenges the existence of natural law. As a result, physical justice power is difficult to fight against because of its significant influence on morally justified principles. Normally, the politicians who legislate the systems of international law and criminal justice are members of governments that execute the rules of international law whenever they see fit. Governments ignore or respect the decisions of judges based on what best suits their international legal policies. They actually have the formal right to do so, but they also have the right to claim that the physical judgments are more than authentic.

This is precisely what the powertionist governments are doing to the Palestinian population.[243] Unfortunately, different orientations of physical justice established an understanding of the practical interpretation of the law rather than an assertion of the power of moral justice by powerful governments. Therefore, physical justice asserts that it is permitted to occupy moral authority for itself. Physical justice orders claim both that their bodies have the right to make normative positivist decisions, and that those normative decisions are actually based on moral justice. Of course, this is how fascist, dictatorial, autocratic, tyrannical, oppressive, totalitarian, and authoritarian systems of physical justice express the principles of their justice and present them as morals in the name of democracy, or the "war of civilisation against barbarism." Physical justice claims that its rules are just. That is to say, physical justice seeks to lead the understanding of the law and stabilize the power of its intentions. Additionally, by purporting to promote the moral and norms of modern civilisation, it may instead permit the massacre of the population of an occupied country.

Notably, this claim of physical justice is normally very successful due to the strength of the ties with other countries. Thus, when the moral reasons have been used as tools to lead and adopt the particular regulations of physical justice, they become persuasive strategies for the roles of decisions, procedures, and judgments. Therefore, any claim that the rules of physical justice are substantively right may weaken the position of moral justice and thereby cause deep conflicts between physical and moral justice. This is particularly evident in the case of contemporary proxy wars created by the leading authorities of NATO. In its strongest form, physical justice claims that its power is derived from the provisions of the Charter of the United Nations,

---

[243] Farhad Malekian, *Powertionism in International Criminal Justice* (New York: Nova Science Publishers, 2022).

which indicates that it perfectly reproduces the immutable principles of true justice authorized by the treaty making power. This also indicates that it represents the best available legal and political compromises that can be reached in international politics. Thus, this explanation legitimises the criminal actions or criminal decisions of the alliances of the United States. If UN law was morally and legally correct, then it would be legally correct to obey such a law. However, the law is actually based on the principles of unequal treaties, and an unequal treaty is principally wrong, null, and void. Therefore, any law that claims to possess legitimate moral authority but in fact does not, is essentially unjust and imposes unjust or tyrannical dictatorial decisions.

We should not forget the fact that law cannot be well-defined without referring to moral justice, and that moral justice constitutes the basis for the presentation of all accurate judgments. This means that there must be a level of connection between physical justice and moral justice, and when physical justice does not respect the elements of morality, it also violates the merit and values of its own roots.[244] This is regardless of the fact that legal positivism denies that there is a necessary connection between morality, law, and justice. This objection can be made as long as it does not harm the necessary elements of independent judgments. This is because justice means freedom in the heart of judgments, and no alternative interests exist within the structure of justice. That is why physical justice contradicts this simple ethical philosophy of justice. We are referring here to moral and political philosophy, both of which are integrated into the structure of physical and moral justice.

The conflict of physical justice against moral justice becomes more brutal and aggressive when inequalities in the background conditions of judgments, or in our case, the prevention of the application of moral resolutions, are prevented and undermine the fairness of international human rights provisions and international criminal justice. This is why we continually draft and redraft conventions in order not to lose the key moral and philosophical elements that

---

[244] Examine Pardo Pilar Villanueva Sainz, 'Is International Criminal Law a Living Discipline?,' 3:4 The International Journal of Human Rights (1999), pp. 92-100; Farhad Malekian, *Tour de force of Moral Virtue in International Criminal Justice* (New York: Nova Science Publishers, 2022); Farhad Malekian, *Imperative Philosophy of International Criminal Justice: Visible Power – Invisible Essence* (New York: Nova Science Publishers, 2022); Farhad Malekian, *Powertionism in International Criminal Justice* (New York: Nova Science Publishers, 2022); M. Cherif Bassiouni, 'A Comprehensive Strategic Approach on International Cooperation for the Prevention, Control and Suppression of International and Transnational Criminality, Including the Establishment of an International Criminal Court,' 15 Nova Law Review 353 (1991).

indicate why we have laws in order to achieve justice. Therefore, unlawful physical force must be prevented and lies must be condemned in order to prevent the victims from suffering. The intention is to ensure that the legal and moral characterisation of individuals is safeguarded. Virtuous moral wisdom requires the development and promotion of habits in order to save the lives of individuals. The absence of this habit brings wars, genocide, and acts far worse than the Holocaust.[245]

All discussions and arguments in this book therefore concern how to solve the quandary of the system of justice, or at least how to reduce conflicts and suffering as much as possible. *The only way to be free from the quandary of international human rights arguments and the systematic quandary of the provisions of international criminal law and justice is to abolish the illegal, unfair, monopolised, and immoral power of the Security Council. Therefore, the work of the Council must be terminated and its resolutions must be repealed. All decisions must be discussed and negotiated under the legal authority of the General Assembly and voted according to the rule of consensus.* This is the only way to prevent powertionist governments from acting as the authoritative power of the United Nations and its decision-makers. It is imperative to prosecute and punish those who violate international human rights laws, and to prevent their impunity.[246]

---

[245] For instance see *Report of the Independent Inquiry into the actions of the United Nations during the 1994 genocide in Rwanda*, UN Doc S/1999/1257, (1999) [Rwanda Report].

[246] Study the report of Francesca Albanese file:///C:/Users/uub-b24-1502/Downloads/a-hrc-55-73-auv%20(1).pdf; Farhad Malekian, *Powertionism in International Criminal Justice* (New York: Nova Science Publishers, 2022); https://www.ohchr.org/en/press-releases/2024/03/states-must-adhere-obligations-under-genocide-convention-prevent-further. Consult also Francesca P Albanese, Lex Takkenberg, Palestinian Refugees in International Law (2nd Edition, 2020).

Appendix

Public Affairs Section - United States Embassy - Vienna, Austria FACT SHEET: United States Policy on the International Criminal Court[1]

U. S. A. Decision

On May 6, 2002, the U. S. formally notified the United Nations that the U. S. does not intend to become a party to the Rome Statute.

Background

In 1998, a UN diplomatic conference in Rome composed of representatives from 160 countries adopted a treaty, known as the "Rome Statute," to create an International Criminal Court.

The United States signed the treaty on December 31, 2001. However, at that time, then President Clinton stated the treaty was fundamentally flawed and that he would not forward the treaty to the Senate for advice and consent to ratification. He also recommended that his successor not forward the treaty to the Senate.

The Rome Statute provides that the treaty will enter into force on the first day of the month after the 60th day following the date on which the 60th country submits its instrument of ratification to the UN.

On April 11, 2002, the total number of ratified countries surpassed 60.

The treaty entered into force on July 1, 2002.

---

[1] https://web.archive.org/web/20031129170524/http://www.usembassy.at/en/download/pdf/icc_pa.pdf.

Significant Problems with the ICC Treaty

Jurisdiction

The ICC purports to have jurisdiction over certain crimes committed in the territory of a state party, including crimes committed by nationals of a country that is not party to the treaty. Thus the court would have jurisdiction for crimes alleged against U. S. citizens, including U. S. service members, in the territory of a party to the treaty (Article 12), despite the fact that the U. S. declined to be a party.

New Crimes

A state party to the treaty can avoid prosecution of certain crimes, thereby exempting its nationals from the ICC's jurisdiction for these crimes. A non-party cannot elect such exemptions in the case of amendments (Article 121). The U. S. finds this to be unacceptable.

Aggression

The crime of "aggression" is included within the court's jurisdiction, but has not been defined. The parties to the treaty will amend it to define this crime and specify the conditions under which the Court has jurisdiction over this crime (Article 5). Only parties to the treaty can be exempted from the jurisdiction of the Court for the crime of aggression per Article 121. In addition, many states advocate conditions for the exercise of jurisdiction by the ICC that could bring the court into conflict with the UN Security Council and the UN Charter.

Prosecutor

The prosecutor can proceed with an investigation on his or her own initiative with the agreement of two judges of a three-judge panel (Article 15). This could lead to politically motivated prosecution, to which the U. S. strongly objects.

Accountability

The prosecutor is not responsible to an elected body or to the UN Security Council, and the Court lacks judicial review. The structure of the Court fails to account for sufficient checks and balances, which the U. S. considers fundamental to the pursuit of justice.

Reservations
In a serious departure from accepted practice, the treaty does not permit states to take reservations (Article 120).

Lack of Review
The ICC is required to defer to the national prosecution unless the court finds that the state is unwilling or unable to carry out the investigation or prosecution (Article 17). However, by leaving the decision over the "willingness" of a state ultimately to the ICC, the treaty would allow the ICC to review and possibly reject a sovereign state's decision not to prosecute or a sovereign state's court decision not to convict in specific cases.

Alternative Mechanisms

The U. S. continues to be a forceful advocate for accountability for perpetrators of war crimes, genocide, and crimes against humanity.

The U. S. is confident that there are more suitable alternatives to the ICC in the field of International Justice.

Alternative mechanisms include:

Domestic Accountability: Encourage states to create credible justice institutions in their own state rather than abdicating responsibility to an international body.

Where domestic legal institutions are lacking, but domestic will is present, the international community must be prepared to assist in creating the capacity for the sovereign state to address the violations. This includes political, financial, legal, and logistical support.

Where domestic will is non-existent, the international community can intervene through the UN Security Council, consistent with the UN Charter. Ad hoc international mechanisms may be created under the auspices of the UN Security Council, as was done to establish the international tribunals for the former Yugoslavia and Rwanda. Additionally, hybrid courts consisting of international participants and the affected state's participants can be authorized, such as in the case of Sierra Leone.

Summary

The U. S. is emphatically committed to international accountability for war crimes, genocide and crimes against humanity.

The United States strongly opposes the ICC treaty because it is seriously flawed.

The United States is currently and will continue to work together with other nations to avoid any disruptions that might be caused by the treaty.

Other mechanisms either already exist or may be established to ensure international accountability for war crimes, genocide, and crimes against humanity. The most fundamental mechanism is domestic state accountability. In the absence of state accountability, the international community must act or assist the state, or in the most dire of circumstances, the UN Security Council may be required to establish situation-specific mechanisms to ensure justice.

This is consistent with the UN Charter, which has been accepted by virtually all nations.

Bibliography[*]

Albanese F. P., Lex Takkenberg, Palestinian Refugees in International Law (2nd Edition, 2020).

Alexy R., *'Effects of Defects - Action or Argument? Thoughts about Deryck Beyleveld and Roger Brownsword's Law as a Moral Judgment'* (Ratio Juris, 2006), pp. 169–79.

Alexy R., 'The Dual Nature of Law, *Ratio Juris'* (2010), pp. 167–82.

Alexy R., 'The Reasonableness of Law' in *Reasonableness and Law* Ed. Giorgio Bongiovanni, Giovanni Sartor, and Chiara Valentini (Dordrecht: Springer, 2009), pp. 5–15.

Alexy R., Discourse Theory and Fundamental Rights' in *Arguing Fundamental Rights* Ed. Agustín José Menéndez and Erik Oddvar Eriksen (Dordrecht: Springer, 2006), pp. 15–29.

Alexy R., *On the Concept and the Nature of Law* (Ratio Juris, 2008), pp. 21: 281–99.

Allison H., *Kant's Theory of Freedom* (Cambridge University Press, 1990).

Amato A. D., 'It's a Bird, It's a Plane, It's *Jus cogens*' 6 *Connecticut Journal of International Law*, (1990).

Ambion B. C., Organisation of a Court of International Criminal Jurisdiction, 29 *Philippine Law Journal* 345 (1954).

Andreopoulos G. J., (ed.), *Genocide: Conceptual and Historical Dimensions* (Philadelphia, 1994).

Annacker C., 'The Legal Régime of erga omnes Obligations in International Law' 46 *Austrian Journal of Public International Law*, (1994), pp. 131–66.

Aquila R. E., *Matter in Mind: A Study of Kant's Transcendental Deduction* (Indiana University Press, 1989).

Arts K., Vesselin Popovski. (eds.), *International Criminal Accountability and the Rights of Children* (Heidelberg: Springer, 2006), pp. 37–52 and 53–65.

Austin J., *The Province of Jurisprudence Determined and the Uses of the Study of Jurisprudence* (1954).

Baderin M. A., *International Human Rights and Islamic Law* (New York, NY: Oxford University Press, 2005).

Baderin M., A., 'A Comparative Analysis of the Right to a Fair Trial and due Process under International Human Rights Law and Saudi Arabian Domestic Law,' 10 (3) *The International Journal of Human Rights*, (2006).

Bantekas I., Susan Nash, *International Criminal Law*, (2007).

---

[*] Mention here neither includes nor excludes in the text. It neither confirms nor rejects the work.

Barron A., (Legal) Reason and its "Others": Recent DevelopmentinLegal Theory, in *Introduction to Jurisprudence and Legal Theory: Commentary and Materials* (Schiff Penner, and Nobles, eds., 2002), 1038-63.

Bartlett E., *'What's Happening in Syria? The Media 'Kills the Truth,' 'Terrorism' is Described as 'Moderate Opposition.'* (Global Research, February 05, 2017).

Bartlett E., *How We Were Mislead about Syria.*

Bartlett E., *Is Eva Bartlett Credible?* https://www.quora.com/Is-Eva-Bartlett-credible (Accessed: 14th 2016).

Bassiouni C., 'International Crimes: Jus cogens and Obligatio Erga Omnes' 59 *Law and Contemporary Problems*, (1996).

Bassiouni M. Cherif and Benjamin B. Ferencz, The Crime Against Peace and Aggression: From Its Origins to the ICC, in *International Criminal Law,* vol. I, (M. Cherif Bassiouni, ed. 2008), pp. 207-242.

Bassiouni M. Cherif, (ed.), *International Criminal Law* (US: Ocean Publication, 3 vols., 1999).

Bassiouni M. Cherif, (ed.), *International Terrorism and Political Crimes* (1975).

Bassiouni M. Cherif, 'A Comprehensive Strategic Approach on International Cooperation for the Prevention, Control and Suppression of International and Transnational Criminality, Including the Establishment of an International Criminal Cour,' 15 *Nova Law Review*, 353, (1991).

Bassiouni M. Cherif, 'The Discipline of International Criminal Law,' in M. cherif Bassiouni (ed.), *International Criminal Law*, Vol. 1, (2008), pp. 5-40.

Bassiouni M. Cherif, 'The Subjects of International Criminal Law: Ratione Personae' in M. Bassiouni Cherif (ed.), *International Criminal Law*, Vol. 1, (2008), pp. 41-70.

Bassiouni M. Cherif, Benjamin B. Ferencz, *The Crime Against Peace and Aggression: From Its Origins to the ICC, in International Criminal Law*, vol. I, (M. Cherif Bassiouni, ed. 2008).

Bassiouni M. Cherif, *Crimes Against Humanity in International law*, (1999).

Bassiouni M. Cherif, *Criminal Justice in the Time of War and Peace* (Cambridge University Press, Cambridge, 2014).

Bassiouni M. Cherif, *Introduction to International Criminal Law*, (2005).

Bassiouni M. Cherif, The Discipline of International Criminal Law, in *International Criminal Law,* Vol. I (M. Cherif Bassiouni, ed., 2008).

Bassiouni M. Cherif, *The Shariah and Islamic Criminal Justice in the Time of War and Peace* (Cambridge University Press, Cambridge, 2014).

Baum L. M., 'Pursuing Justice in a Climate of Moral Outrage: An Evaluation of the Rights of the Accused in the Rome Statute of the International Criminal Court,' 19 *Wisconsin International Law Journal* (2001).

Beccaria C., *On Crimes and Punishments*, (1764).

Bellamy A., *Responsibility to Protect: the Global Effort to End Mass Atrocities* (Polity Press, Cambridge, 2009).

Bellamy R. (ed.), *C Beccaria, On Crimes and Punishments*. (1995).

Benneh E. Y., 'Sovereignty Immunity and International Crimes,' 22 *Ghana Law Journal*, (2002–2004), 112.

Bennett J., *Kant's Analytic* (Cambridge University Press, 1966).

Bennett J., *Kant's Dialectic* (Cambridge University Press, 1974).

Bennoune K., 'As-Salamu 'Alykum? Humanitarian Law in Islamic Jurisprudence,' 15 *Michigan Journal of International Law*, (1994), pp. 605-643.

Berman S. (ed.), *The Oxford Handbook of Legal Pluralism* (Oxford University Press, 2019).

Berman S., *Global Legal Pluralism: A Jurisprudence of Law Beyond Borders Global* (2012).

Bermann G. A. Roger J. Goebel, William J. Davey, Eleanor M. Fox et al., *Cases and Materials on European Community Law* (1993).

Bernstein R. J. *Radical Evil: A Philosophical Interrogation* (New York: Blackwell Publisher, 2002).

Bianchi A., 'Human Rights and the Magic of Jus cogens,' 19 *European Journal of International Law*, (2008), pp. 491-508.

Bigi G., 'Joint Criminal Enterprise in the Jurisprudence of the International Criminal Tribunal for the former Yugoslavia and the Prosecution of Senior Political and Military Leaders: The Krajišnik Case' 14 Guyer Paul, *The Cambridge Companion to Kant,* (1992).

Bigi G. 'Joint Criminal Enterprise in the Jurisprudence of the International Criminal Tribunal for the former Yugoslavia and the Prosecution of Senior Political and Military Leaders: The Krajišnik Case' 14 *Max Planck United Nations Yearbook*, (2010), pp. 51-83.

Bird G., *Kant's Theory of Knowledge*, (Humanities Press, 1962).

Bix B., 'Natural Law: The Modern Tradition' in Jules Coleman and Schott Shapiro (eds.), *The Oxford Handbook of Jurisprudence and Philosophy of Law*, (2002).

Bloxham Donald, *Genocide on Trial: War Crimes Trials and the Formation of Holocaust History and Memory* (2001).

Boas G., *International Criminal Justice: Legitimacy and Coherenc*e, (2012).

Boas G., William A. Schabas (eds.), *International Criminal Law Developments in the Case Law of the ICTY* (2005).

Boot M., *Genocide, Crimes against Humanity, War Crimes*: *Nullum Crimen Sine Lege and the Subjective Matter of Jurisdiction of the International Criminal Cour*t, (2002).

Brilmayer L., *American Hegemony: Political Morality in a One Superpower World* (1994).

Broomhall B., *International Justice and the International Criminal Court: Between Sovereignty and the Rule of Law* (2003).

Browning C., *The Path to Genocide: Essays on Launching the Final Solution*, (2002).

Browning D. (eds.), *Universalism vs. Relativism: Making Moral Judgements in a Changing, Pluralistic, and Threatening World* (Rowman and Littlefield Publishers, United Kingdom, 2006).

Brownlie I., *International Law and the Use of Force by States* (Oxford: Oxford University Press, 1996).

Brownlie I., *Principles of Public International Law* (Oxford: Clarendon Press, 5th ed., 1998).

Brunnée J., 'The Prohibition on Torture: Driving *Jus cogens* Home?' 104 *Proceedings of the Annual Meeting of the American Society of International Law*, (2010).

Buchanan A., 'Toward a Drone Accountability Regime,' 29 (1) *Ethics and International Affairs*, (2015), pp. 15–70.

Burke-White W. W, 'Implementing a Policy of Positive Complementarity in the Rome System of Justice,' 19 *Criminal Law Forum*, (2008), 59-89.

Burns P. 'An International Criminal Tribunal: The Difficult Union of Principle and Politics,' 5 *Criminal Law Forum*, (1994).

Byers M. 'Conceptualising the Relationship Between *Jus cogens* and *Erga Omnes Rules*' 66 *Nordic Journal of International Law*, (1997).

Caenegem R. C., Van, *European Law in the Past and the Future: Unity and Diversity over Two Millennia* (Cambridge: Cambridge University Press, 2001).

Cançado T., A. '*Jus cogens* in Contemporary International Law,' *UN Audiovisual Library*, (http://www.un.org/law/avl).

Carvin S., 'Getting Drones Wrong,' 19 (2) *International Journal of Human Rights*, (2015), pp. 127–141.

Cassese A. and Albin Eser (eds.), *The Rome Statute of the International Criminal Court: A Commentary* (2002).

Cassese A. and Paola Gaeta, *Cassese's International Criminal Law* (3rd, 2013).

Cassese A., (ed.), *The New Humanitarian Law of Armed Conflict* (Naples: Editoriale Scientifica, 1979).

Cassese A., 'First Annual Report of the ICTY,' *Yearbook of International Law Commission*, (1994).

Cassese A., 'For an Enhanced Role of Jus cogens' in Cassese, A (ed.), *Realizing Utopia*, (2012).

Cassese A., Albin Eser, Giorgio Gaja and Robert E. Conor, *Justice at Nuremberg* (1980).

Cassese A., *International Criminal Law* (Oxford: Oxford University Press, 2nd, ed., 2008).

Cassese A., On the Current Trends Towards Criminal Prosecution and Punishment of Breaches of International Humanitarian Law, 9 *European Journal of Internaitonal Law* 2 (1998).

Chinkin C., '*Jus Cogens*, Article 103 of the UN Charter and Other Hierarchical Techniques of Conflict Solution,' 17 *Finnish Yearbook of International Law* (2008), pp. 63-90.

Chomksy N. and Barsamian D., *Keeping the Rabble in Line*. Boston: Common Courage Press (1994).

Chomsky N., *Media Control: The Spectacular Achievements of Propaganda.* New York: Seven Stories Press (2004).

Chossudovsky M., *War and Globalisation: The Truth Behind September 11* (Global Outlook, 2002).

Christian P., Scherrer, *Iraq: Genocide by Sanctions* (2011).

Clark M., *Nietzsche on Truth and Philosophy* (1991).

Clark R. S., 'The Crime of Apartheid,' in M. Cherif Bassiouni (ed.), *International Criminal Law*, vol. I (1986), pp. 299-323.

Clark R., *War Crimes – A Report on United States War Crimes against Iraq* (Maisonneuve Press, 1992).

Claus K., 'Aggression and the Use of Force in International Law,' *Proceedings of the 108th Annual Meeting of the American Society of International Law,* No. 108, 2014, pp. 325–346.

Cohen M., 'Moral Aspects of the Criminal Law,' 49 *Yale Law Journal* (1949), pp. 987-1026.

Crawford J., Olleson S., 'The Continuing Debate on a UN Convention on State Responsibility,' 54 *ICLQ*, (2005), 959–71.

Cryer R., 'The Doctrinal Foundations of International Criminalisation,' in M. cherif Bassiouni, ed., *International Criminal Law*, Vol. 1, (2008), pp. 107-128.

Cryer R., *Prosecuting International Crimes, Selectivity and the International Criminal Law Regime* (Cambridge University Press, Cambridge, 2005).

D'Amato A., 'It's a Bird, It's a Plane, It's *Jus cogens'* (1990) 6 *Connecticut Journal of International Law.*

D'Amato A., 'The Moral Dilemma of Positivism,' 20 *Valparaiso University Law Review*, (1985-86), 43-53.

D'Amato A., 'The Moral Dilemma of Positivism,' 20 *Valparaiso University Law Review* (1985-86), 43-53.

Danilenko G., 'International Jus cogens: Issues of Law-Making,' 2 *European Journal of International Law* (1991).

Dautricourt J. The Concept of International Criminal Court Jurisdiction-Definition and Limitations of the Subject, in *A Treatise on International Criminal Law* 636 (M. C. Bassiouni & V. P. Nanda eds., 1973).

Davis M. C., Dietrich Wolfgang, Bettina Schoolman and Sepp Dieter, *International Intervention in the Post-Cold War World: Moral Responsibility and Power Politics* (M. E. Sharpe, Inc., 2003).

de Hoog A. J. J., 'The Relationship between *Jus cogens*, *Obligations Erga Omnes* and International Crimes: Peremptory Norms in Perspective,' 42 *Österreichische Zeitschrift für öffentliches Recht und Völkerrecht* (1991).

de Hoogh A., *Obligations Erga Omnes and International Crimes: A Theoretical Inquiry into the Implementation and Enforcement of the International Responsibility of States* (Kluwer The Hague, 1996).

de Wet E., 'The Prohibition of Torture as an International Norm of *Jus cogens* and its Implementation for National and Customary Law,' 15 (1) *European Journal of International Law* (2014), Vol. 15, No. 1, 97-121.

de Wet, E., '*Jus Cogens* and Obligations Erga Omnes' in de Wet, E and Vidmar (eds.), J *Hierarchy in International Law: The Place of Human Rights*, (2012).

Delmas-Marty M., 'The Contribution of Comparative Law to a Pluralist Conception of International Criminal Law,' 1 *Journal of International Criminal Justice*, (2003), pp. 13-25.

DeSon J. S., 'Automating the Right Stuff? The Hidden Ramifications of Ensuring Autonomous Aerial Weapon Systems Comply with International Humanitarian Law,' 72 *Air Force Law Review*, (2015), pp. 85–122.

Detmold M. J., *The Unity of Law and Morality: A Refutation of Legal Positivism* (Canada: Law Book Co. of Australasia, 1984).

Dhanapala J., *Under-Secretary-General for Disarmament Affairs United Nations, International Law, Security, and Weapons of Mass Destruction*, (New York, 9 May 2002).

Dhokalia. 'Problems Relating to *Jus Cogens,*' in S. Agrawala (ed.), *Essays on the Law of Treaties*, (1972).
Dickson J., *Evaluation and Legal Theory*, (2001).
Don P., Jim Hoffman, *Waking Up from Our Nightmare, the 9/11/01 Crimes in New York City* (New York: I/R Press, 2004).
Douzinas C., Peter Goodrich and Yifat Hachamovitch, *Politics, Post modernity and Critical Legal Studies* (1994).
Drost P. N., *The Crime of State: Genocide* (Original from Indiana University, 1959).
Dryer D. P, *Kant's Solution for Verification in Metaphysics* (Allen and Unwin, 1966).
Duffett J., *Against the Crime of Silence* (New York, London, 1968).
Dugard J., 'Lifting the Guise of Occupation and Recourse to Action before the ICJ and ICC,' *Palestine Yearbook of International Law,* Vol. 17, 2013–14, pp. 9–27.
Duncan A. R. C., *Practical Reason and Morality* (Nelson, 1957).
Dupuy P., 'Some Reflections on Contemporary International Law and the Appeal to Universal Values: a Response to Marti Koskenniemi' 16 *European Journal of International Law,* (2005).
Duţu M., *Vespasian V. Pella*. (1897-1952) Founder of International Criminal law, Promoter of the Unification of the Criminal Law, *Architect of the International Criminal Justice* (Universul Juridic, Bucharest, 2012).
Eric D., *Principes de Droit des Conflits Armés*, (2nd, ed. 1999).
Ewald F., 'Unger's Philosophy: A Critical Legal Study,' 5 *Yale Law Journal* 665(1988).
Ewing A. C., *A Short Commentary on Kant's 'Critique of Pure Reason'* (Methuen, 1978).
Falk R. A. & Burns H. Weston, The Relevance of International Law to Palestinian Rights in the West Bank and Gaza: In Legal Defense of the Intifada, 32 Harvard International law Journal (1991), pp. 129-157.
Falk R., 'The Accountability of Leaders: A Challenge to Civil Government and Society' in Jeremy Brecher, Jill Cutler, Smith Brendan, *In the Name of Democracy: American War Crimes in Iraq and Beyond* (American Empire Project), (New York: Metropolitan Books, Henry Holt and Company, 2005).
Falk R., *Slouching Toward a Palestinian Holocaust,* www.transnational.org/Area.../Falk Palestine Genocide.html, 20 October 2010.
Falk R., *The Vietnam War and International Law (*Princeton University Press, 1968).
Farmer J., *The Ground Truth: The Story Behind America's Defense on 9/11* (New York: Riverhead Books, 2009).
Feimpong J. K. & S. Azadon Tiewel, 'Can Apartheid Successfully Defy the International Legal System?' 5 *The Black Law Journal* (1977), pp. 287-311.
Fein B., *'Hillary Clinton's 5 lies about Syria, Terror Threat,'* The Washington Times (25 October, 2016).
Feld W., *The Court of the European Communities: New Dimension in International Adjudication* (1964).
Ferencz B. B. 'Ending Impunity for the Crime of Aggression,' 41 *Case W. Res. J*, (2009), pp. 281-290.
Ferencz B., 'An International Criminal Code and Court: Why They Stand and Where They're Going,' 30 *Columbia Journal of Transnational Law*, (1992), 375.
Ferencz B., *International Criminal Court* (2 vols. 1980).

Findlay E. por Mark J, I*nternational and Comparative Criminal Justice: A Critical Introduction* (Routledge, London, 2013).
Finnis J. (ed.), *Natural Law*, (1991).
Finnis J., *Aquinas: Moral, Political and Legal Theory* (1998).
Fischer-Lescano A., Teubner G., 'Regime Collision: The Vain Search for Legal Unity in the Fragmentation of Global Law,' 25 *Michigan Journal of International Law*, (2004), pp. 999-104.
Fitzpatrick P. (ed.), *Dangerous Supplements: Resistance and Renewal in Jurisprudence* (1991).
Focarelli C., 'Promotional Jus cogens: A Critical Appraisal of *Jus Cogens*' Legal Effects' 77 *Nordic Journal of International Law*, (2008), 429.
Fouladvand S., *Complementarity and Cultural Sensitivity: Decision-making by the International Criminal Court (ICC) Prosecutor in Relation to the Situations in the Darfur Region of the Sudan and the Democratic Republic of Congo* (DRC), (2012).
Franck T. M., *Fairness in International Law and Institutions* (1997).
Fuller L. L., *The Morality of Law* (Virginia: Yale Law University, 2nd, ed., 1969).
Fuller S., "Playing Without a Full Deck: Scientific Realism and the Cognitive Limits of Legal Theory," 97 *Yale Law Journal* 549 (1988).
Gebrehana T., Duty to negotiate: An Element of International law (1978).
Gebrehana T., T Arbitration - An Element of International Law (1984).
George J. Andreopoulos, (ed.), *Genocide: Conceptual and Historical Dimensions* (Philadelphia, 1994).
George R. P. (ed.), *The Autonomy Of Law: Essays On Legal Positivism*, (1995).
George R. P., *Natural Law Theory: Contemporary Essays*, (1994).
Gerhard O. W. Mueller & Edward M. Wise (eds), *International Criminal Law* (1965).
Glennon M. J., 'De l'Absurdité du Droit Impératif (Jus cogens)'/*On the Absurdity of Imperative Law (Jus cogens)* 110 *Revue Générale de Droit International Public*, (2006), 529.
Goldstone R. J., For Humanity: Reflections of a War Crimes Investigator (2000).
Gómez R., *A., El Ius Cogens Internacional* (Estudio Histórico Crítico), (1982).
Goodrich P., *Languages of Law* (1990).
Gracia-Amador, 'The Crime of Apartheid: Responsibility and Reparations,' *Review of Contemporary Law* (1981), pp. 31-38.
Gray C., *International Law and the Use of Force*, (2000).
Grayeff F., *Kant's Theoretical Philosophy* (Barnes & Noble, 1970).
Green P. J. and Ward, T., State crime, Human rights, and the Limits of Criminology, 27 *Social Justice* (2000), pp. 101–120.
Greenawalt A. K. A., 'The Pluralism of International Criminal Law,' 86 *Indiana Law Journal*, (2011), 1063-1130.
Grover S., *Prosecuting International Crimes and Human Rights Abuses Committed Against Children – Leading International Court Cases*, (2010), pp. 169–279.
Haas J. De, *History of Palestine - The Last Two Thousand Years* (USA: Macmillan, 1934).
Hannikainen L., *Peremptory Norms (jus cogens) in International Law: Historical Development, Criteria, Present Status* (1988).
Haque A. A., *Law and Morality at War* (2017).

Harees L., *The Mirage of Dignity on the Highways of Human 'Progress': the Bystanders Perspective*, (2012).

Harle V., *Ideas of Social Order in the Ancient World* (1998).

Harris J. W., Legal Philosophies, 2 edition (1997).

Harris W., *Tyranny on Trial* (Dallas: Southern Methodist University Press, 1999).

Hart H. L. A., *The Concept of Law,* 2nd ed., (P. A. Bulloch and J. Raz, eds., 1994).

Hartnack J., *Kant's Theory of Knowledge* (Harcourt, Brace and World, 1967).

Heller K. Jon, 'The Shadow Side of Complementarity: The Effect of Article 17 of the Rome Statute on National Due Process,' 17 *Criminal Law Forum* (2006), available at file:///C:/Users/admin/AppData/Local/Temp/SSRN-id907404.pdf.

Heller K. Jon, *The Nuremberg Military Tribunals and the Origins of International Criminal Law* (2010).

Hickey J. E., *Challenges to Security Council Monopoly Power over the Use of Force in Enforcement Actions: The Case of Regional Organisations*, 10 Ius Gentium 75 (2004).

Hitchens C., *The Trial of Henry Kissinger* (London: Verso Books, 2001).

Hoffe O., *Immanuel Kant* (State University of New York Press, 1994).

Hoover J. *Moral Practices: Assigning Responsibility in the International Criminal Court*, 76 *Law and Contemporary Problems* (2014), pp. 263-86.

Hughes G., Validity and the Basic Norm, 59 *California Law Review* 695 (1971).

Huntington C., 'Plato's Theory of Law,' 56 *Harvard Law Review*, (1942), pp. 559-587.

Hurd H., Challenging Authority, 100 *Yale Law Journal* 1611 (1991). https://www.gordogan.com.hr/gordogan/wp-content/uploads/2011/10/2001-Hitchens-The-Trial-of-Henry-Kissinger.pdf.

Hurlock W. L., "The International Court of Justice: Effectively Providing a Long Overdue Remedy for Ending State-Sponsored Genocide (Bosnia-Herzegovina v. Yugoslavia)," 12 *American University Journal of International Law and Policy* (1997).

Husabø E. J., Ingvild Bruce, *Fighting Terrorism through Multilevel Criminal Legislation: Security Council Resolution 1373, the EU Framework Decision on Combating Terrorism and their Implementation in Nordic, Dutch and German Criminal Law* (Martinus Nijhoff Publishers, 2009).

Huskey K. with Aleigh Acerni, Justice at Guantanamo: One Woman's Odyssey and Her Crusade for Human Rights (2009).

Ineke B. 'Towards a Strong System of Supervision: The Human Rights Committee's Role in Reforming the Reporting Procedure under Article 40 of the Covenant on Civil and Political Rights,' *Human Rights Quarterly*, 17. 4, (1995), pp. 766-793.

Jacovides A., *Treaties Conflicting with Peremptory Norms of International Law and the Zurich-London 'Agreements,'* (1966).

James P., Jonathan Friedman, Globalisation and Violence, Vol. 3: *Globalizing War and Intervention* (London: Sage Publications, 2006).

Janis M. W., 'The Nature of *Jus* Cogens' 3 *Connecticut Journal of International Law*, (1988), 59.

Jevons W. S., *The Theory of Political Economy* (London: Macmillan and Co., 1871).

John C. and John R. Pritchard (eds.), *International Humanitarian Law: Origins, Challenges and Prospects* (2000).

Jørgensen, *The Responsibility of States for International Crimes* (OUP Oxford 2000).

Jori M. (ed.), *Legal Positivism* (1992).

Jori M. (ed.), *Legal Positivism,* (1992).

Kairys D.(ed.), *The Politics of Law: A Progressive Critique* (1982).

Kant I., *Answering the Question: What is Enlightenment?* (1784).

Kant I., *Critique of Judgment* (1790).

Kant I., *Critique of Pure Reason* (1781).

Kant I., *Groundwork of the Metaphysic of Morals* (1785).

Kant I., *Metaphysical Foundations of Natural Science* (1786).

Kant I., *Opus Postumum* (1995).

Kant I., *Perpetual Peace, and Other Essays on Politics, History, and Morals* (1784).

Kant I., *Perpetual Peace: A Philosophical Sketch* (1795).

Kant I., *Practical Philosophy* (editor: Mary J. Gregor, 1999).

Kant I., *Prolegomena to Any Future Metaphysics* (1783).

Kant I., *Religion within the Bounds of Bare Reason* (1793).

Kant I., *The Critique of Practical Reason* (1788).

Kant I., *The Metaphysics of Morals* (1797).

Kant I., *The Only Possible Argument in Support of a Demonstration of the Existence of God* (1763).

Kant I., *The Science of Right* (1790).

Kawasaki K., 'A brief Note on the Legal Effects of *Jus Cogens* in International Law,' 34 *Hitotsubashi Journal of Law and Politics* (2006), pp. 27-43.

Kelman M., *A Guide to Critical Legal Studies* (1987).

Kelsen H., 'Will the Judgement of the Nürenberg Trial Constitute a Precedent in International Law,' 1 *International Law Quarterly* (1947), 153.

Kelsen H., 'Will the Judgement of the Nürenberg Trial Constitute a Precedent in International Law,' 1 *International Law Quarterly* (1947), 153.

Kelsen H., *What is Justice? Justice, Law and Politics in the Mirror of Science* (1957).

Kelsen H., *What is Justice? Justice, Law and Politics in the Mirror of Science* (1957);

Kemal S., *Kant's Aesthetic Theory: An Introduction* (St. Martin's Press, 1992).

Khadduri M., *Major Middle Eastern Problems in International Law*, (1972).

Kitcher P., *Kant's Transcendental Psychology* (Oxford University Press, 1990).

Klein D., F., 'A Theory for the Application of the Customary International Law of Human Rights by Domestic Courts,' 13 (2) *Yale Journal of International Law* (1988), pp. 332-365.

Kolb R. 'Jus cogens, Intangibilité, Intransgressibilité, Dérogation 'Positive' et 'Négative' 109 *Revue Générale de Droit International Public* (2005), 305.

Koskenniemi M. 'Solidarity Measures: State Responsibility as a New International Order?' 72 *BYIL*, (2001), pp. 337–56.

Koskenniemi M., "The Politics of International Law," *European Journal of International Law* (2011).

Kos-Rabcewicz-Zubrowski L., The Creation of an International Criminal Court, in *International Terrorism and Political Crimes* 519 (M. Cherif Bassiouni ed., 1975).

Kramer R. C., Michalowski, R. and Kauzlarich, D., 'The origins and development of the concept and theory of state-corporate crime,' 48 *Crime and Delinquency* (2002), pp. 263–282.

Kress C., 'Aggression and the Use of Force in International Law,' *Proceedings of the 108th Annual Meeting of the American Society of International Law* (2014), pp. 325–346.

Kuper L., *International Action against Genocide* (Minority Rights Group Report No. 53, London, 1982).

Kuper L., *The Prevention of Genocide* (New Haven and London, 1985).

Lefenya K., 'Use of Explosive Weapons in Densely Populated Areas: Implications for International Humanitarian Law,' *African Yearbook on International Humanitarian Law* (2014), pp. 68–86.

Leonetti. 'Interprétation des traités et règles impératives du droit international général (jus cogens),' 24 *ÖZÖR*, (1973).

Linderfalk U., 'The Creation of Jus cogens – Making Sense of Article 53 of the Vienna Convention,' *Max-Planck-Institut für ausländisches öffentliches Recht und Völkerrecht* (2011), pp. 259-278.

Lippman M., 'Genocide,' in *International Criminal Law*, Vol. I (M. Cherif Bassiouni, ed., 2008) pp. 405-455.

Luper-Foy S., 'Introduction: Global Distributive Justice' in Steven Luper-Foy (ed.), *Problems of International Justice* (London: Westview Press, 1988), pp. 1-24.

Lyons D., 'Moral Aspects of Legal Theory,' in Kenneth Himma and Brian Bix (eds) *Law and Morality* (2005).

MacGregor 'State Immunity and *Jus cogens,*' 55 *International & Comparative Law Quarterly* (2006), 437.

MacGregor D., 'September 11 as 'Machiavellian State Terrorism,' in Paul Zarembka, *The Hidden History of 9-11-2001* (New York: Seven Stories Press, 2008).

MacIntyre A., *A Short History of Ethics: a History of Moral Philosophy from the Homeric Age to the Twentieth Century* (1965).

MacIntyre A., *After Virtue: A Study in Moral Theory* (University of Notre Dame Press, 1982).

Madsen W., Jean-Charles, Guillaume Dasquie. *Forbidden Truth: U.S.-Taliban Secret Oil Diplomacy,* Saudi Arabia and the Failed Search for bin Laden, (2002).

Malekian, F. and Kerstin Nordlöf, 'International Legal Status of Children' in Jay S. Albanese (ed.), *The Encyclopaedia of Criminology & Criminal Justice* (United States: Wiley-Blackwell (5 volumes, 2013), vol. III, pp. 1173-1178.

Malekian, F., 'Armenian Genocide and the Questions of Responsibility of the Turkish Government,' *House of Commons Conference on the Armenian Genocide, Armenian Solidarity, British-Armenian All-Party Parliamentary Group, No Security Publication* (2007), pp. 31-9.

Malekian, F., *Barrels of Justifications Violating International Criminal Responsibility* (New York: Nova Science Publishers, 2025).

Malekian, F., 'Comparative Substantive International Criminal Justice,' in Ronald Slye (ed.), *The Nuremberg Principles in Non-western Societies: A Reflection on their Universality, Legitimacy and Application* (2017), pp. 10-44.

Malekian, F., 'Conundrums of *Jus Cogens:* In Case Law' (Part II), No. 13 *Вісник Південного регіонального центру Національної академії правових наук України,* (No. 13 *Journal of the South regional Center of National Academy of Legal Sciences of Ukraine)* (2017), pp. 12-21.

Malekian, F., 'Conundrums of *Jus Cogens*: in International Criminal Law' (Part I), *Вісник Південного регіонального центру Національної академії правових наук України (No.12 Journal of the South regional Center of National Academy of Legal Sciences of Ukraine)* (2017), pp. 8-16.

Malekian, F., 'Emasculating the Philosophy of International Criminal Justice in the Iraqi Special Tribunal,' *Cornell International Law Journal*, 58/5 (2005), pp. 675-725.

Malekian, F., Hypocrisy in International Criminal Justice (New York: Nova Science Publishers, 2025).

Malekian, F., International Crime of Blackboard-Barbarism ((New York: Nova Science Publishers, 2025).

Malekian, F., '*International Criminal Responsibility,'* in *International Criminal Law* (M. Cherif Bassiouni, 2[ed], ed., 1999).

Malekian, F., 'International Criminal Responsibility: International Criminal Responsibility of Individuals' in M. Cherif Bassiouni, *International Criminal Law,* Vol. *Crimes* (2[ed], ed., New York: Transnational Publishers, 1999).

Malekian, F., *'Islamic Law Justice Systems' in* Jay S. Albanese, *The Encyclopaedia of Criminology and Criminal Justice* (United States: Wiley-Blackwell (5 volumes, 2013), vol. III, pp. 1220-1225.

Malekian, F., 'Judging International Criminal Justice in the Occupied Territories,' 12 *International Criminal Law Review* (2012), pp. 627-869.

Malekian, F., 'Mutilating the Philosophy of Justice in the Time of Armed Conflicts,' *Contemporary Journal of International Criminal Law* (2007).

Malekian, F., 'The Canon of Love against the Use of Force in Islamic and Public International Law: Part II: The Anatomy of Love Against Violations,' 15 *International Criminal Law Review*, 2015), pp. 861-895.

Malekian, F., 'The Canon of Love against the Use of Force in Islamic and Public International Law: Part I: The Chamber of Love within Legal Discipline,' 15 *International Criminal Law Review*, 2015), pp. 591-628.

Malekian, F., 'The Child as an Autonomous Subject of Justice' in Farhad Malekian, Kerstin Nordlöf, *Sovereignty of Children in Law* (Cambridge: Cambridge Scholars Publishing, 2012), pp. 2-55.

Malekian, F., 'The Functions of International Criminal Law and the Problem of Positivism and Neutralism Philosophy,' *Contemporary Journal of International Criminal Law* (2007).

Malekian, F., 'The Heaven of Justice with Love,' *The Journal of the Henry Martyn Institute* (2017), pp. 5-29.

Malekian, F., 'The Homogeneity of International Criminal Court with Islamic Jurisprudence,' 9 (4) *International Criminal Law Review* (2009), pp.595-621.

Malekian, F., 'The Laws Governing Crimes against Women Constituting *Obligatio Erga Omnes*' in David Wingeate Pike, *Crimes Against Women* (2011).

Malekian, F., 'The Miserable Wedding of Naturalism into Positivism,' 2 *ID EST Journal* (2009).

Malekian, F., *Allegations by Political Laundering* (Cambridge Scholars Publishing, 2019).

Malekian, F., and Kerstin Nordlöf, *Confessing the International Rights of Children: The Basic documents with Analysis (*Cambridge: Cambridge Scholars Publishing, 2012).

Malekian, F., *Classical Morality in International Peremptory Criminal Law* (Newcastle: Cambridge Scholars Publishing, 2018).

Malekian, F., *Classical Morality in International Peremptory Criminal Law* (Newcastle: Cambridge Scholars Publishing, 2021).

Malekian, F., *Concreting Righteousness in International Criminal Justice* (New York: Nova Publishers, 2024).

Malekian, F., *Condemning the Use of Force in the Gulf Crisis* (Almqvist & Wiksell International, 1st ed., 1992).

Malekian, F., *Conscience of Judges in International Criminal Law, the Heart of Judgements* (New York: Nova Science Publishers, 2021).

Malekian, F., *Conscience of Lawyers in International Criminal Law, the Burden of Doppelgängers* (New York: Nova Science Publishers, 2021).

Malekian, F., *Conscience of Prosecutors in International Criminal Law, the Heart of the Matter* (New York: Nova Science Publishers, 2021).

Malekian, F., *Conundrums of Paternalism in International Criminal Justice* (New York: Nova Science Publishers, 2024).

Malekian, F., *Corpus Juris of Islamic International Criminal Justice* (Newcastle: Cambridge Scholars Publishing, 2017).

Malekian, F., *Documents on the Principles of International Human Rights* (Stockholm: Norstedts Juridik AB,2007).

Malekian, F., *Exploitation of Christian Islamic International Criminal Justice* (New York: Nova Science Publishers, 2024).

Malekian, F., *Gravity of Wisdom in International Criminal Law* (New York: Nova Science Publishers, 2021).

Malekian, F., I*mperative Philosophy of International Criminal Justice: Visible Power – Invisible Essence* (Nova Sciences Publishers, 2022).

Malekian, F., *International Criminal Law of Children* (New York: Nova Science Publishers, 2021).

Malekian, F., *International Criminal Law, the Law of Somebodiness, the Law of Nobodiness* (New York: Nova Science Publishers, 2021).

Malekian, F., *International Criminal Law: The Legal and Critical Analysis of International Crimes* (2 vols. 1991).

Malekian, F., *International Criminal Responsibility of States: A Study on the Evolution of International Responsibility of States with particular Emphasis on the Concept of Crime and Criminal Responsibility* (Stockholm, 1985).

Malekian, F., *International Criminal Vacations: Tears of Justice* (New York: Nova Science Publishers, 2024).

Malekian, F., *Judgments of Love in Criminal Justice* (Switzerland: Springer: 2017, 2018).

Malekian, F., *Jurisprudence of International Criminal Justice* (Introduction by Professor Benjamin B. Ferencz, the former Prosecutor of the Nuremberg Tribunal (Cambridge: Cambridge Scholars Publishing, 2014).

Malekian, F., Kerstin Nordlöf, *Prohibition of Sexual Exploitation of Children Constituting Obligation Erga Omnes* (Cambridge: Cambridge Scholars Publishing, 2013).

Malekian, F., Kerstin Nordlöf, *The Sovereignty of Children in Law* (Cambridge: Cambridge Scholars Publishing, 2012).

Malekian, F., *Orchestrating Diversity in International Criminal Justice* (New York: Nova Science Publishers, 2021).

Malekian, F., *Paralysing International Criminal Justice* (New York: Nova Science Publishers, 2021).

Malekian, F., *Powertionism in International Criminal Justice* (Nova Sciences Publishers, 2022).

Malekian, F., *Principles of Islamic International Criminal Law: A Comparative Search* (Netherlands: Brill & Nijhoff, 2011).

Malekian, F., *Prohibition Governing Child Soldiers Constituting an Integral Part of Jus Cogens and Obligatio Erga Omnes*, XVII *World Congress of the International Association of Youth and Family Judges and Magistrates*, Belfast, Northern Ireland, 27 August – 2 September (2006).

Malekian, F., *System of International Law: Formation, Treaties, Responsibility* (Uppsala, 1987).

Malekian, F., *The Concept of Islamic International Criminal Law, A Comparative Study* (Netherlands: Brill, 1994).

Malekian, F., *The Mirage of International Criminal Law*: Kant Metaphysics of *Mens Rea* (Cambridge: Cambridge Scholars Publishing, 2018).

Malekian, F., *The Monopolisation of International Criminal Law in the United Nations , A Jurisprudential Approach* (Stockholm: Almqvist Wiksell International, 1st ed., 1993).

Malekian, F., *The Monopolisation of International Criminal Law in the United Nations , A Jurisprudential Approach* (Stockholm: Almqvist Wiksell International, 2nd ed., 1995).

Malekian, F., *Tour de force of Moral Virtue in International Criminal Justice* (Nova, Science Publishers, 2022).

Malekian, F., *Trading Virginity of International Criminal Justice* (New York: Nova Science Publishers, 2020).

Malekian, F., Utipolitianist International Crimiminal Court ((New York: Nova Science Publishers, 2025).

Manacorda S., 'Cesare Beccaria e la pena dell'ergastolo' *Jus* (2015), pp. 165–182.

May L., 'Habeas Corpus as *Jus cogens* in International Law' 4 (3) *Criminal Law and Philosophy* (2010), 249–265.

May L., *Aggression and Crimes Against Peace* (New York: Cambridge University Press, 2008).

May L., *Crimes against Humanity: A Normative Account* (New York: Cambridge University Press 2004).

May L., *War Crimes and Just War* (New York: Cambridge University Press, 2007).

Mendus S., 'The Importance of Love in Rawls's Theory of Justice' 29 (1) *British Journal of Political Science* (1999), pp. 57-75.

Meron T., 'On Hierarchy of International Human Rights' 80 *American Journal of International Law*, (1986), 1.

Meron T., *The Humanisation of International Law* (Netherlands: The Hague Academy, 2006).

Meyssan T., *11 September 2001: L'effroyable Imposture*, (2002).

Mokhtar A., '*Nullum Crimen, Nulla Poena, Sine Lege*: Aspects and Prospects,' 26 *Statute Law Review*, pp. 41-55.

Morten B., Emiliano J. Buis, *Philosophical Foundations of International Criminal Law* (2018).

Mosaddeq A., N. (2006), "Terrorism and Statecraft: Al-Qaeda and Western Covert Operations after the Cold War," Zarembka, P. (Ed.) *The Hidden History of 9-11-2001*. (*Research in Political Economy, Vol. 23*), Emerald Group Publishing Limited, Bingley, pp. 149-188. https://doi.org/10.1016/S0161-7230(06)23005-0.

Moyn S., *Not Enough: Human Rights in an Unequal World*, (2018).

Muchnik P., *Kant's Theory of Evil: An Essay on the Dangers of Self-love and the Aperiodicity of History* (Lexington Books, 2010).

Mueller G. O. W., 'International Criminal Law: Civitas Maxima,' 15 *Case Western Reserve Journal of International Law* (1985).

Mullins Christopher W., Kauzlaric David, Rothe Dawn, "The International Criminal Court and the Control of State Crime: Prospects and Problems," 12(3) *Critical Criminology* (2004), pp. 285-308.

Naiman A. *'9/11: The Simple Facts — Why the Official Story can't Possibly be True,'* (US: Soft Skull Press, 2011).

Nieto C., Chris Brandt, Howard Zinn (Foreword), Masters of War: Latin America and U.S. Aggression From the Cuban Revolution Through the Clinton Years (2003).

Nietzsche F. W., *The Will to Power,* https://en.wikisource.org/wiki/The_Will_to_Power.

Nietzsche F., *The Genealogy of Morals: A Polemic* (translated J. M. Kennedy, Vol. 8th, 1913).

Nozary F., *Unequal Treaties in International Law* (Stockholm, 1971).

O'Connor Susan, 'Up in Arms: A Humanitarian Analysis of the Arms Trade Treaty and Its New Zealand Application,' 11 *New Zealand Yearbook of International Law* (2013), pp. 73–105.

O'Neill O., *Constructions of Reason: Explorations of Kant's Practical Philosophy* (Cambridge University Press, 1989).

Ogunfolu A., Oludayo Fagbemi, 'I Have a Drone: The Implications of American Drone Policy for Africa and International Humanitarian Law,' 23 (1) *Revue Africaine de Droit International et Comparé* (2015), pp. 106–128.

Olivecrona K. 'The Imperative Element in Law,' *Rutgers Law Review* (1964).

Olson Peter M., 'The Lawfulness of Russian Use of Force in Crimea,' 53 (1) *Revue de Droit Militaire et de Droit de la Guerre* (2014), pp. 17–40.

Orakhelashvili A., 'The Impact of Peremptory Norms on the Interpretation and Application of United Nations Security Council Resolutions' 16 (1), *The European Journal of International Law* (2005), pp. 59-88.

Orakhelashvili A., *Peremptory Norms in International Law* (2006).

Osiel M. J., Why Prosecute? Critics of Punishment for Mass Atrocity, 22 *Human Rights Quarterly* 118 (2000).

Osiel M., *The End of Reciprocity* (Cambridge University Press, 2009).

Otterman M., *American Torture: From the Cold War to Abu Ghraib and Beyond* (Pluto Press, 2007).

Pardo P. V. S., 'Is International Criminal Law a living discipline?,' 3:4 *The International Journal of Human Rights* (1999), pp. 92-100.

Paris Declaration, International Conference on Sanctions Against South Africa (And Special Declaration on Namibia), 27 May1981, Published by the United Nations Center Against Apartheid.

Parish M., *International criminal law – Justice or Mirage? Transonflict* (2013).

Paton H. J., Kant's Metaphysic of Experience (Humanities Press, 1961).

Patrides C. A., Joseph Anthony Wittreich. *The Apocalypse in English Renaissance Thought and Literature: Patterns, Antecedents, and Repercussions* (Manchester University Press, 1984).

Patterson D.(ed.), *Postmodernism and Law* (1994).

Paulus A., 'Jus cogens in a Time of Hegemony and Fragmentation,' 74 *Nordic Journal of International Law* (2005), pp. 297-334.

Paust J. 'The Reality of Jus cogens,' 7 *Connecticut Journal of International Law* (1991), 83.

Pellet A., 'Comments in Response to Christine Chinking and in Defense of Jus cogens as the Best Bastion against the Excesses of Fragmentation,' 83 *Finnish Yearbook of International Law* (2006).

Pellet A., 'Vive le crime! Remarques sur les degrés de l'illicité en droit international' in United Nations/International Law Commission (ed.), I*nternational Law on the Eve of the Twenty-first Century: Views from the International Law Commission* (United Nations New York 1997), pp. 287–315.

Penrose M. M.'Lest We Fail: The Importance of Enforcement in International Criminal Law An Essay on the Nature and Immutability of Truth,' 15 (2) *American University International Law Review* (1999), pp. 321-394.

Perelman C., *The Idea of Justice and the Problem of Argument* (1963).

Peterson J., 'Unpacking Show Trials: Situating the Trial of Saddam Hussein,' 48 *Harvard International Law Journal* (2007).

Postema G. J., *Bentham and the Common Law Tradition* (1986).

Potter R. B., *War and Moral Discourse* (Richmond, Va., John Knox Press, 1969).

Power J., *Conundrums of Humanity: The Quest for Global Justice* (2007).

Protector J. H.., *Islam and International Relations* (New York, 1965).

Ragazzi M., *The Concept of International Obligations erga omnes* (Clarendon Press Oxford 1997).

Rahmdel M., 'Money Laundering in Iranian Law: Present and Future,' *Journal of Money Laundering Control* (2002).

Rahmdel M., 'The *Ne Bis In Idem* Rule in Iranian Criminal Law,' *Journal of Financial Crime* (2004).

Rahmdel M., The Role of the Courts in the Reform of Iranian Criminal Law Policy,' *Criminal Law Forum*, (2006).

Rawls J., *A Theory of Justice* (1999).

Raz J., 'Why the State?' in N. Roughan and A. Halpin (eds) In *Pursuit of a Pluralist Jurisprudence* (CUP 2017).

Raz J., *Ethics in the Public Domain: Essays in the Morality of Law and Politics* (Oxford: Oxford University Press, 1994).

Raz J., *The Morality of Freedom* (1986).

Reddy E. S., 'India and the Struggle Against Apartheid,' 26 *Indian Journal of International Law* (1986), pp. 551-567.
Reddy E. S., *Apartheid: The United Nations and the International Community* (1986).
Rehman J. *International Human Rights Law* (London and New York: Longman Pub Group, 2nd ed., 2010).
Reisman W. M., 'Legal Responses to Genocide and Other Massive Violations of Human Rights,' 59 *Law and Contemporary Problems* (1996), 75.
Reiss H. S., *Kant: Political Writings*, (2003).
Report of the Independent Inquiry into the actions of the United Nations during the 1994 genocide in Rwanda, UN Doc S/1999/1257, (1999) [Rwanda Report].
Rinceanu J., 'Criminal Liability of Legal Persons in Romania' in Riccardo Borsari, *Responsabilita` da reato deli enti* (Padova: Padova University Press, 2016). pp. 407–418.
Rinceanu J., 'The principle of legality (Nullum crimen sine lege) in Romania' in U. Sieber, S. Forster, & K. Jarvers (Eds.), *National Criminal Law in a Comparative Legal Context*, vol. 2 (1): Max-Planck-Institute für Ausländisches und Internationals Strafrecht, (2011), pp. 89-101.
Robertson G., *Crimes Against Humanity – The Struggle for Global Justice* (Penguin Books, 3rd ed., 2006).
Robinson M., "Genocide, War Crimes, Crimes Against Humanity," *25 Fordham International Law Journal* (1999), p. 275.
Roht-Arriaza N., State Responsibility to Investigate and Prosecute Grave Human Rights Violations in International Law, 78 *California Law Review* 451 (1990).
Roméo Dallaire's, *Shake Hands with the Devil: The Failure of Humanity in Rwanda* (Carroll & Graf, New York, 2003).
Rorty R., *Philosophy and the Mirror of Nature* (1990).
Rosen A. D. Kant's Theory of Justice (Ithaca, London: Cornel University Press, 1996).
Rosenstock R. 'An International Criminal Responsibility of States?,' in United Nations/International Law Commission (ed.), *International Law on the Eve of the Twenty-First Century: Views from the International Law Commission* (United Nations New York, 1997), pp. 265–85.
Ross J. I., *Controlling State Crime* (2nd Edition, New Brunswick, NJ: Transaction Press, 2000).
Ross J. I., *Varieties of State Crime and its Control* (Monsey, NY: Criminal Justice Press, 2000).
Schabas W. A., 'The Banality of International Justice,' 11 *Journal of International Criminal Justice* (2013), pp. 545–551.
Schabas W. A., *An Introduction to the International Criminal Court* (Cambridge University Press, 2011).
Schabas W. A., *Genocide in International Law: The Crimes of Crimes* (Cambridge University Press, 2000 and 2009).
Schabas W. A., Justice, 'Democracy and Impunity in Post Genocide Rwanda: Searching for Solutions to Impossible Problems,' 7 *Criminal Law Forum* (1996).
Schabas W. A., Justice, Democracy and Impunity in Post Genocide Rwanda: Searching for Solutions to Impossible Problems, 7 *Criminal Law Forum* (1996).

Schabas W. A., Sentencing by International Tribunals: For a Human Rights Approach, 7:2. *Duke Journal of Comparative & International Law* (1997), pp. 461-518.

Schabas W. A., *The Abolition of the Death Penalty in International Law*, (2002 and 2005).

Schachter O., *International Law in Theory and Practice* (1991).

Schwarzenberger G. 'The Problem of an International Criminal Law,' 5 *Current Legal Problems* (1950).

Schwarzenberger G., *International Jus Cogens?* 43 *Tax. L. Rev* (1965), p. 476.

Schwelb E., *Crimes against Humanity, British Yearbook of International Law* (1946) 178.

Seltzer G., 'The Rule of the South Africa Criminal Code in Implementing Apartheid,' 8 *Georgia Journal of International and Comparative Law* (1978), pp. 176-194.

Sevrine K., 'State Immunity and the Promise of *Jus Cogens*,' *Northwestern Journal of International Human Rights* (2011), Vol. 9, No. 2, pp. 149-183.

Shaffer T. L., 'The Legal Ethics of Radical Individualism,' 65 *Texas Law Review* (1997).

Shelton D., 'Normative Hierarchy of International Law,' 80 *American Journal of International Law* (1986), 1.

Simmonds N., *Law as a Moral Idea* (2008).

Sliedregt E. van., *Pluralism in International Criminal Law*, 25 Leiden Journal of International Law (2012), 847.

Smith N. K., '*Commentary to Kant's 'Critique of Pure Reason'* (Humanities Press, 1962).

Smith T. S., *Lecture Delivered over the Remains of Jeremy Bentham*, Esq., in the Webb-Street School of Anatomy & Medicine, on the 9th June, 1832 (London: Effingham Wilson, 1832).

Sowilet A., *The Problem of the Creation of a Permanent International Criminal Court* (1951).

Spiermann 'Humanitarian Intervention as a Necessity and the Threat or Use of *Jus Cogens*' 71 *Nordic Journal of International Law*, (2002), 523.

Spooner L., *Natural Law; or the Science of Justice: A Treatise on Natural Law, Natural Justice, Natural Rights, Natural Liberty, and Natural Society; showing that all Legislation whatsoever is an Absurdity, a Usurpation, and a Crime.* Part First. [1882], available at http://oll.libertyfund.org/titles/spooner-natural-law-or-the-science-of-justice-1882 (Accessed: on 18 December 2017).

Stern R., *Understanding Moral Obligation: Kant, Hegel, Kierkegaard* (Cambridge, Cambridge University Press, 2012).

Stone J. and Robert Woetzel, *Toward a Feasible International Criminal Court* (1970).

Sugarman D. ed., *Legality, Ideology and the State* (1985).

Sugarman D., (ed.), *Legality, Ideology and the State* (1983).

Svaček O., 'The Human Rights Dimension of the ICC's Complementarity Regime,' *Czech Yearbook of Public and Private International Law,* 2015, Vol. 6, pp. 273-288.

Tunnell K., *Political Crime in Contemporary America* (New York: Garland, 1993).

Unger R., The Critical Legal Studies Movement, *96 Harvard Law Review 561* (1983).

van Schaack B., "The Crime of Political Genocide: Repairing the Genocide Convention's Blind Spot," 106 *Yale Law Journal* (1997).

Van Schaack B., Ronald C. Slye, *International Criminal Law: Intersections and Contradictions* (2020).

Van Schaack B., Ronald C. Slye, *International Criminal Law: The Essentials* (2008).

Van Schaack B., Ronald Sly. (ed.), *International Criminal Law and Its Enforcement* (University Casebook Series, 2nd).

Vanhullebusch M. 'The Arab League and Military Operations: Prospects and Challenges in Syria,' 22 (2) *International Peacekeeping* (2015), pp. 151–168.

Vasilijevic V. A., Crimes against Peace: Between the Past and the Future, 43 *Jugoslovenska Revija Za Medunarodno Pravo* 425 (1996).

Verdross A., 'Forbidden Treaties in International Law: Comments on Professor Garner's Report on 'The Law of Treaties,'' 31 *American Journal of International Law*, (1937), 571.

Verdross A., 'Jus Dispositivum and *Jus Cogens* in International Law' 60 *American Journal of International Law* (1966), 55.

Vespesian P. V., 'Plan for World Criminal Code,' 17 *Revue Internationale de Droit Penal* (1946).

Vespesian P. V., 'Towards an International Criminal Court,' 44 *American Journal of International Law* (1950), 57.

Vespesian P. V., *La criminalité collective des états et le droit pénal de l'avenir, Bucarest : Imprimerie de l'état* (1925).

Vespesian P. V., *La Guerre-Crime et les Criminels de Guerre/War-Crime and War Criminals* (Paris, 1946).

Vespesian P. V., Plan d'un Code Répressif Mondial, 6 *Rewe International de Droit Pénal* 1948, (1955).

Vespesian P. V., *Revue Internationale de Droit Penal* (1928).

Virally M., 'Réflexions sur le Jus cogens' 12 *Annuaire Français de Droit International* (1966), 5.

Vischer K. R., *Martin Luther King Jr. and the Morality of Legal Practice: Lessons in Love and Justice* (2014).

Vyver J. D. van der, 'Prosecution and Punishment of the Crime of Genocide,' 25 *Fordham International Law Journal* (1999).

Waldock H., 'General Course on Public International Law,' 106 *Recueil Des Course* (1962), pp. 39-103.

Ward I., *An Introduction to Critical Legal Theory* (1998).

Weatherhall T., *Jus cogens International Law and Social Contract* (2015).

Weil P., 'Towards Relative Normativity in International Law,' 77 *American Journal of International Law* (1983).

Weisburd M., 'The Emptiness of the Concept of *Jus Cogens*, As Illustrated by the War in Bosnia-Herzegovina,' 17 *Michigan Journal of International Law* (1995-1996), pp. 1-51.

Weiss, T. G., *Military-Civilian Interactions: Humanitarian Crises and the Responsibility to Protect* (2nd ed., Rowman & Littlefield Publishers Inc., Lanham (MD), 2005).

Weller M., *Iraq and the Use of Force in International Law* (Oxford: Oxford University Press, 2010).

Wet D., 'The Prohibition of Torture as an International Norm of *Jus Cogens* and Its Implications for National and Customary Law,' 15 *European Journal of International Law* (2004).

Wright Q., Proposal for an International Criminal Court, 46 *American Journal of International Law* 60 (1952).

Whiteman M. M., '*Jus Cogens* in International Law: With a Projected List,' 7 *Georgia Journal of International and Comparative Law* (1977), p. 609.

Wilkes F. Klein & Daniel, United Nations Draft Statute for an International Criminal Court: An American Evaluation, in *International Criminal Law 526* (Gerhard O. W. Mueller & Edward M. Wise eds., 1965).

Schabas W. A., *Genocide in International Law, the Crime of Crimes* (2000).

Wippman D., Atrocities, Deterrence, and the Limits of International Justice, 23 *Forham International Law Journal* 473 (1999).

Czaplinski W., 'Concepts of *Jus Cogens* and Obligations Erga Omnes in International Law in the Light of Recent Developments,' 23 *Polish Yearbook of International Law* (1997–1998).

Wood A., *Kant's Ethical Thought* (Cambridge University Press, 1999).

Wright Q., 'The Scope of International Criminal Law: A Conceptual Framework,' 15 *Virginia Journal of International Law*, (1975).

Zaman R., 'Playing the Ace? *Jus Cogens* Crimes and Functional Immunity in National Courts,' 17 *Australian International Law Journal*, (2010), 53.

Zarembka P., *The Hidden History of 9-11-2001* (New York: Seven Stories Press, 2008).

Index

A

B

G

H

I

R

S

T

U